Nationalist Ideologies and the Production of National Cultures

Richard G. Fox, Editor

American Ethnological Society Monograph Series, Number 2
James L. Watson, Series Editor

Copyright © 1990 by the American Anthropological Association
   All rights reserved
   Printed in the United States of America
   Production Editor: Kathleen Cosimano
   ISBN: 0-913167-35-5

Library of Congress Cataloging-in-Publication Data
Nationalist ideologies and the production of national cultures / Richard G.
   Fox, editor.
      p. cm. – (American Ethnological Society monograph series; no. 2)
      Includes bibliographical references.
      ISBN 0-913167-35-5
      1. Nationalism. 2. Culture. 3. Ethnicity – Political aspects. 4. Ethnic
   groups – Political activity. I. Fox, Richard Gabriel, 1939 – . II. Series.
   JC311.N367   1989
   320.5' 4 – dc20   89-39216
                                                                                      CIP

**Copies of this title and other titles from the American Anthropological
Association may be ordered from:**
American Anthropological Association
2200 Wilson Boulevard, Suite 600
Arlington, VA 22201
Telephone: 703.528.1902
Fax: 703.528.3546

http://www.aaanet.org/publications/Books-and-Monographs.cfm

Contents

1   Introduction
     Richard G. Fox   1

2   An Innocent Abroad: How Mulla Daoud Was Lost and Found in Lebanon, or the Politics of Ethnic Theater in a Nation at War
     Judith L. Goldstein   15

3   Context and Consciousness: Local Conditions for the Production of Historical and National Thought among Hutu Refugees in Tanzania
     Liisa Malkki   32

4   Hindu Nationalism in the Making, or the Rise of the Hindian
     Richard G. Fox   63

5   The Production and Defense of "the Romanian Nation," 1900 to World War II
     Katherine Verdery   81

6   Nationalism, Traditionalism, and the Problem of Cultural Inauthenticity
     Brackette F. Williams   112

7   The Politics of Heritage in Contemporary Israel
     Virginia R. Dominguez   130

8   Failed Nationalist Movements in 19th-Century Guatemala: A Parable for the Third World
     Carol A. Smith   148

To my father, Joseph Fox

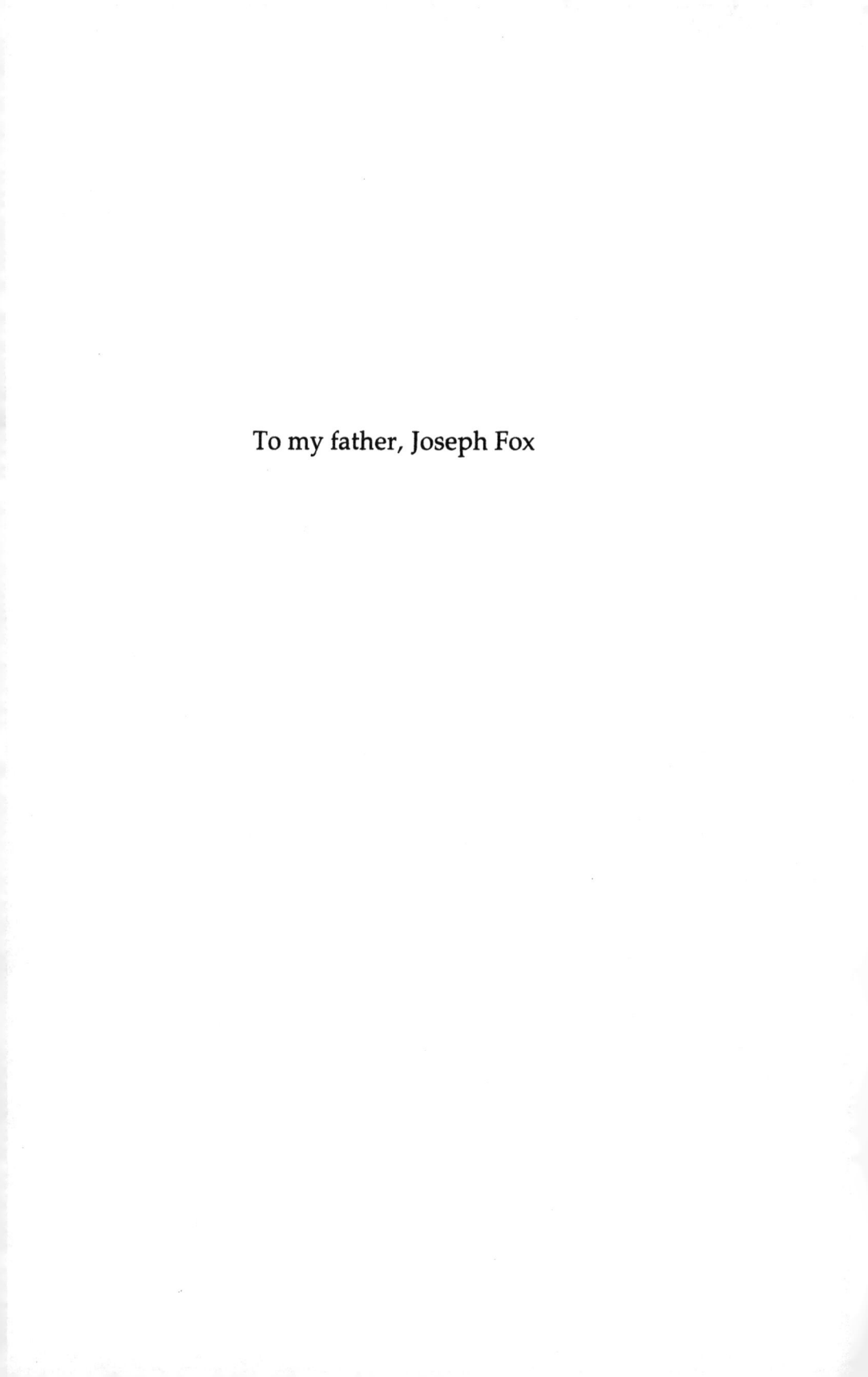

1
Introduction

Richard G. Fox
Duke University

Two generations of anthropologists ago, Ruth Benedict, Geoffrey Gorer, Margaret Mead, the psychiatrist Abram Kardiner, and others had considerable interest in national culture, or "national character," as they called it. Studying national character, they hoped, would permit anthropology to successfully bring complex societies within its purview—without sacrificing the pivotal interest in cultural forms that American anthropology had developed in the study of primitive societies. That endeavor, still worthy and not yet fully accomplished, informs the papers comprising this book.[1]

In these papers, however, national culture refers to something very different from what Mead, Gorer, and their colleagues had in mind. I start with their conception to highlight the difference. For these predecessors, and especially for Kardiner (1945), a national culture was constituted by a national character. By "national character," these anthropologists referred to a set of defining cultural traits that they took to be basic and typical of the population of a nation. There was, in Benedict's (1946) portrayal, a Japanese commitment to the concept of honor, to the worship of the emperor, or to other cultural configurations. Other studies, of Great Russians or Frenchmen for example, took national character to consist of a psychological constellation. It was a set of characteristic and identifying personality traits that constituted individual behaviors (see Gorer and Rickman 1949). These anthropologists also considered the reproduction of such national character or national culture. For them, a society's characteristic child-rearing techniques reproduced national cultural forms, including basic personality constellations. Parents and kinsmen therefore were the primary producers.

After World War II, the nation-building and modernization literature, mainly from sociology and political science, presented national culture differently. Lost was the concern in national character studies for the cultural traits and psychological syndromes that made each national culture distinctive. Gained was a sense that national culture developed over time, although the modernization approach only allowed a single-stranded evolution from "traditional" to "modern." This literature generally took economic and political infrastructure, rather than child-rearing techniques, as generative. It also shifted the locus of a national culture from a society to a state. Although modernization studies differed from the national character approach in several ways, they held an identical view of national culture in one respect—a view that we hope to transcend. A national culture was still a "thing." A state either had evolved a modern national culture fully or it had not, and, also like a thing, once properly constructed a national culture would not lose its shape or character. Various factors constructed it properly: urbanization, industrialization, education, internalization of modern values, and so forth (cf. Black 1966). Other factors, "overurbanization," traditionalism, and "involution" (Geertz 1963), for example, were considered dangerous to proper national culture in modernization studies. They were equivalent to overswaddling or inattentive parenting.

Anthropology today has thrown out both the bathwater and the baby of the old national character studies. We have also grown wary of the equally "hard" view of culture found in the modernization literature. These changes indicate how much the concept of culture has changed in recent years and is still changing today. The papers in this monograph represent this changing view of culture and hope to further it.

"National culture" in this volume does not have the hard, fully formed, or configured quality attributed to it by the anthropology of two generations ago. Neither does it have the erector-set character often presupposed in modernization studies: national culture does not consist of rigid institutional and cognitive pieces properly fitted together into a stable and immobile structure. For us, national culture is malleable and mobile. It is the outcome of a constant process of cultural production. A national culture is constantly being molded as individuals and groups confront their social worlds and try to (re)form them. Out of such confrontations emerge nationalist ideologies from which, in turn, a national culture gets produced.

Nationalist Ideologies

I use the phrase "nationalist ideologies" to refer to sets of cultural meanings that are labeled "nationalisms," "subnational identities,"

Introduction

and "ethnic nationalisms" in other approaches. "Nationalist ideologies" refer to the production of conceptions of peoplehood. Sometimes, the peoplehood conceived by a particular nationalist ideology requires an independent state or autonomous territory for its realization. The current efforts by militant Sikhs to create a separate state of Khalistan out of northern India is one such concept of peoplehood. Such nationalist ideologies often get labeled as "nationalisms" or "ethnic nationalisms." Other times, the peoplehood conceived by a nationalist ideology is believed to be realizable within a pluralistic state or outside an exclusive territory. Many Native American and Native Canadian populations, for instance, desire more responsive policies toward them from the existing American and Canadian states. These nationalist ideologies commonly get termed "racial identities," "ethnicities," or "subnationalisms." The variety of terms now in use obscures what we take to be better understood as a single phenomenon: the production of ideologies of peoplehood, that is, ideologies of common ("national") culture.

Distinguishing between nationalisms, ethnicity, and racial identities has always been difficult because the categories are too loose—or so we anthropologists commonly say. We readily admit that our scholarly terms are fuzzy and that they greatly overlap. Our easy admission of guilt in this respect hides a greater failure, however. The important "fuzziness" comes not from scholarship but from social life: from how people conceive of themselves or are conceived of by others, and how people live out and live with these conceptions. By too readily admitting the fuzziness of our scholarly categories, anthropologists cover up the fuzziness or malleability of everyday life. We thus preserve a false rigidity to our conception of culture and artificially fortify our belief that cultural productions can be classified as either racial, or ethnic, or nationalist. The reality, however, is that they are at any moment quite rubbery and that, over time, they can assimilate each other. An ethnic identity may easily become an ethnic nationalism; a nationalism that has failed to achieve an independent state may continue as an ethnic identity. Scottish and Welsh identities have moved back and forth over this range several times in the last century. We also overlook the social confrontations that produce the fuzziness of real life. For example, a conception of Jewishness as an ethnic (cultural) identity once did battle against assertions that Jews comprised a race. Nowadays, ideologies of Jewish ethnicity often confront claims that Jews (everywhere) form a nation.

Our term, "nationalist ideology," does away with the fuzziness of the categorical terms, "nationalisms," "racial identities," "ethnicities." We wish to emphasize what the social beliefs and practices labeled as ethnicity, racial identity, and nationalism share: they are all cultural productions of public identity. This single, encompassing term directs us to look at the different ways in which people conceive of themselves or are conceived of by others, rather than the different ways we might classify these conceptions. It leads us to see the processes by which these conceptions develop, alter, and intergrade in real life, rather than to ignore such processes in the interests of preserving our classificatory scheme and our erector-set conception of culture.

We do not reject the older approaches to national culture outright, however. We take elements from each in order to craft a new understanding. From national character studies we take an interest in the cultural particulars that make each national culture distinct, although we do not assume them to be primordial and unchanging. From the modernization approach, we adopt a concern for the making of national culture, although we reject its conceptions of an invariant evolutionary sequence or a necessary social progress.

National Culture

In this volume, we emphasize the relationship between a nationalist ideology as a set of cultural meanings and a national culture. That relationship is contingent and processual: the creation of nationalist ideologies anticipates a larger project, the forming or reforming of a national culture. A national culture starts out as a nationalist ideology, that is, a consciousness or perception of what the nation is or should be, which then may gain public meaning and be put into action. Usually there are several coexisting and even contradictory perceptions, which constitute competitive nationalist ideologies. A national culture emerges from the confrontation over what the nation should and will be among nationalist ideologies. Struggles among nationalist ideologies—contests over ideas as well as conflicts between people—may propel one nationalist ideology into dominance and leave others by the wayside. A national culture is always "temporary" because, whether antique or recent, its character and puissance are matters of historical practice; they are plastic constructions, not cultural givens.

These papers investigate and analyze the production of national culture and the contingencies surrounding it in various times and places and at various points of development. Katherine Verdery documents, for the time period up to World War II, the very active and long-standing competition over the definition of the nation in Romania. I show the same sort of confrontation between Hindu nationalist ideology and a national culture defined by secular democracy in India today. Sometimes, for example, as when they are contrivances of the state, one nationalist ideology may start out with an authority that the others lack. Virginia Dominguez describes the imprimatur the state of Israel gave and gives Zionism. Similarly, Brackette Williams shows the salience in Guyana of a nationalist ideology that, ironically, developed out of British colonial domination and ethnic stereotyping; British domination established the constraints within which Guyanese today struggle to produce a national culture. Other times, nationalist ideologies appear in the unusual circumstances of immigration or exile, as Judith Goldstein finds happening today among Iranian immigrants to Israel and Liisa Malkki discovers among Hutu refugees in Tanzania. Still other times, there may be powerful forces at work that suffocate an encompassing nationalist ideology, a condition that Carol Smith finds in Guatemala, where racial separatism rules: the failure of a 19th-century nationalist ideology, followed by dependent capitalist development, set conditions that made it imperative for the Guatemalan white elite to create two nations, one white and the other Indian, where there might have been only one. These are some of the contingencies that may affect the general process by which nationalist ideologies are created, and that may influence efforts to produce national culture.

The contentious issues constituting separate nationalist ideologies are many and varied: the boundaries of the nation(s), it may be said, are not coincident with the state (as, for example, in Guyana, Romania and Guatemala); the reigning national culture may be disowned for an alternative nationalist ideology (militant Hindus, Iranian immigrants and Hutu refugees do so); the national culture may be shot through with inconsistencies that give purchase to alternative or even contradictory identities (as in Israel or Romania). Even when one nationalist ideology becomes dominant and a national culture is produced, internal contradictions and new nationalist ideologies produced "from the bottom up" make a national culture rubbery, perhaps nearly molten under some circumstances—and certainly not possessing the "iron strength of the cultural walls" that Margaret Mead (1953 [1930]:163) wrote about.

Past anthropological accounts of nationalism studied in effect what we label "nationalist ideologies," but often with insufficient concern for the historical processes and personages by which these ideologies appeared and failed or succeeded. They often portrayed the production of nationalisms, subnational identities, ethnic identities, or ethnic nationalisms—all of which we include as nationalist ideologies—in a mechanical way, or they treated certain identities as primordial, or more fundamental and unchanging than others. We reject both positions. The "cultural pluralism" approach, for example, asserted that multiple ethnic and tribal identities in many states of the Caribbean and Africa prevented a national culture. It treated these identities as primordial rather than produced by circumstances and intentions. The alternative "plural society" orientation was closer to our thinking because it insisted that the colonial history and postcolonial institutions of these societies were primary in maintaining ethnic and tribal distinctions. Even this literature, however, assumed an overly neat fit between subnational identity and particular institutional complexes (for an overview, see van den Berghe 1973).

Much the same could be said for the succeeding ethnic nationalism literature, whether inspired by Weberian or neo-Marxist approaches. In this literature, subnational identities served the interests of intergroup competition or class exploitation in an exceedingly mechanical fashion. Fredrik Barth (1969), for example, assumed that such identities reflected social boundaries so mechanically that he regarded the cultural content as epiphenomenal—the cultural "diacritica," as he termed the distinguishing cultural forms, were completely at the disposal of social boundary maintenance. He therefore had to explain individual allegiances and identities in terms of an ethnocentric "market" or "maximizing" model—a model that strips cultural identities of their constituting effect on individuals. Abner Cohen (1969) favored a similar mechanical fit and maximizing model when explaining changes in ethnic awareness and sectarian allegiances among the Hausa. According to Cohen, Hausa identities mirrored attempts to protect a trade monopoly against competitors. In a neo-Marxist treatment of resurgent Celtic identities in the United Kingdom, Michael Hechter (1975) maintained that they reflected the superexploitation resulting from an ethnic division of labor, an "internal colonialism." The fact that these identities were under active constitution, that the proponents of Welshness, for example, were still in dubious battle over what it should be, that the upsurge of Celtic nationalism came almost a century after the internal colonialism Hechter proposed—these contingencies and proceedings did not alter the mechanical model (see Fox et al. 1981; Ragin 1979).

Missing from this work is precisely what this monograph argues for: the position that nationalisms (including so-called subnationalisms and ethnic nationalisms), responsive though they may be to material conditions, are nevertheless contingent and the outcome of processes in history, which cannot simply be taken for granted (cf. Fox 1985:163–164). Furthermore, the cultural materials, Barth's diacritica, with which they work—and fight—have a compelling effect on what happens. They constitute strong emotional commitments by individuals and enable "nonrational" cultural practices that maximization or exploitation models do not easily comprehend. Davydd Greenwood's (1976) study of Basque ethnic nationalism showed the deep cultural allegiance that individuals give to such cultural markers of identity, even when they have only recently been produced.

As individuals and groups reflect on, or imagine, nationalisms, or what we call nationalist ideologies, not only may new boundaries and social bonds be produced or old ones become solidified; new cultural meanings and deeply felt identities may also be cast. Nationalisms therefore depend, in Benedict Anderson's (1983) phrase, on an "imagined community," but we wish to place a somewhat different emphasis on his expression. For Anderson, the imagined community of the nation is a mass fiction; it is never clear who, if anyone, imagines particular communities, or if there is any difference in the resulting fictional community depending on who imagines it and how they do so. As Bruce Kapferer (1988:4) has recently argued—against Anderson as well as against much of the literature on nationalism—we need not conceive of nationalisms as a universal form. Kapferer sees the possibilities of diverse nationalisms arising from different cultural traditions, and he contrasts the case of a nationalism based on a historically grounded egalitarian code in Australia with one resting on a deeply embedded sense of hierarchy in Sri Lanka. These different nationalisms do not arise from the cultural traditions mechanically; they come about as people use them, although Kapferer takes the long-term dominance of one cultural tradition over a society much more for granted than we do.

The papers in this book also dispute a universal nationalism, but they do not accept the idea that the diversity of nationalisms arises only from deeply rooted and long-dominant cultural traditions. This is again to singularize when we want to pluralize, to speak of outcomes predetermined by super-hardened cultural tradition when we need to show individual projects and group confrontations in the creation of national culture. Michael Hertzfeld's (1982) treatment of the scholarly and political confrontations underlying images of Greek national culture is close to our approach. In 19th- and early 20th-century Greece, Romanists promulgated one image of the nation's august antiquity while Hellenicists publicized an equally elect but quite different cultural history. Hertzfeld's emphasis on the agonistic field in which these nationalisms were produced is salutary; we would only wish to add greater concern for the material interests and structural conditions that enter into such intellectual confrontations.

Each of the papers in this monograph investigates the relationship between nationalist ideology and national culture as contingent in two senses. The outcomes are predetermined neither by a universal form that nationalism must take nor by a weighty and hardened cultural tradition.

The first five papers in this book look at the production of national culture at an early point of development. They deal with the production of nationalist ideologies themselves; they therefore look at potential national cultures "from the bottom up." These papers show that such nationalist ideologies can develop even when there is an existing national culture that is supposedly dominant. Goldstein describes the creation of an ethnic theater among Iranian immigrants in Israel that at first dramatized the experiences of Iranians as commentaries on the immigrant condition. Since the war in Lebanon, however, the ethnic theater is no longer content to build ethnic or subnational identity. It has started to attack the very definition of Israel as a nation, using the experiences of Iranian immigrants as lessons about the society in general. Malkki also narrates the early stages of national consciousness, as it has developed under the peculiar conditions of exile among Hutu refugees in Tanzania. Not the theater, as in Goldstein's case, but the exile camp becomes the stage for this developing nationalist ideology. The refugees dispute the reigning national culture of the Tanzania they have abandoned by showing that purported age-old tradition is really only sometime history. Verdery chronicles the controversies over Romanian national identity, whether it was Latin, "Oriental," or autochthonous, and the consequences of this disputation for building the state and country. In this case, the controversy itself legitimates a national culture. By World War II, because of all the disputation over the Romanian nation, there was agreement that a Romanian Nation existed. The confrontation now largely concerned how best to conserve and strengthen it. I describe a street-level confrontation in India, as Hindu nationalists battle a state committed to secular democracy and as they try to forcibly assimilate (or eliminate) Muslims, Sikhs and other minorities into a redefined Hindu national identity. Beginning in the 1920s as a relatively weak movement, this alternative vision has steadily grown more powerful. By the 1980s it has become so puissant that even the ruling party must readapt its message of secular democracy to it.

The last three papers in this volume begin with national culture and show the difficulties and controversies that surround its construction or reproduction. They thus take a "top down" perspective and look at what happens after one nationalist ideology has become dominant, although not completely so. Dominguez shows, in the case of

Israel, that even when a national culture has been fairly successfully affirmed, it remains prey to internal contradictions, which may give rise to contestation. She points to the unresolved incorporation of both Zionism and Judaism into Israeli national culture. Combined but not resolved, Zionism and Judaism as nationalist ideologies provide purchase for contests between Sephardim and Ashkenazim concerning the nature of that national culture. Williams indicates the difficulties of constructing national culture in ethnically divided Guyana by detailing one particular failure, the inability to develop a common, and therefore national, ritual performance. The celebration of the ostensibly Shi'ite Muslim festival of Moharram in Guyana involved all ethnic groups at first. As it became "nationalized" in Guyana, however, Moharram accrued many new aspects, some of which, like gambling and drinking, offended Guyanese Muslims. Muslims were able to put a stop to what was in effect a celebration of Guyanese national identity because, given the compartmentalized ethnic "traditions" sponsored by colonialism, Muslims were still thought to have rights over this part of Guyanese national culture. Smith's paper on Guatemala perhaps represents the extreme case for national culture. Given the historical conditions under which Guatemala's white elite has reproduced, no national culture has developed or can develop, Smith maintains. The production of a national culture midway in the 19th century was overturned, and subsequently, as Guatemala developed an export economy, the white elite found that an ethnic division of labor, which segregated the population labeled Indian from the rest of the "nation," was in its best interests.

Not content to address nationalist ideologies as disembodied cultural productions, these papers also focus on the producers of nationalisms and builders of national culture, that is, both the agencies (forces) and agents (persons) that generate or maintain them. By this means, we document the factors that make for distinctive nationalist ideologies and, by extension, differing national cultures. The papers note the systematic relations within the world system or those between regions, classes and ethnic groups (the processes) that prove generative in combination with particular historical moments (the contingencies). Smith speaks of the requirements of Guatemala's dependent capitalism but also the country's white elite late in the 19th century. As background to recent contests over Israel's national culture, Dominguez notes Oriental Jews' increasing dissatisfaction with their treatment in Israel as they became the majority in the last generation. Goldstein documents the specific case of the immigrant Iranian Jews, whose production of a strong ethnic or subnational identity prepared the way for them to contest over the nature of Israel itself. Verdery shows the multifaceted competition—among state leaders, historians, sociologists, and others—for guardianship over the Romanian nation as it underwent ideological and political-economic construction between the world wars. I relate the production of Hindu nationalist ideology to the increasing defensiveness of a lower-middle class, as recent changes in India's agrarian economy and state policy empower other classes. This lower-middle class became dominant in the peculiar "intermediate regime" that arose in India after colonialism ended. Malkki shows that Hutu exile as it is actualized in a Tanzanian refugee compound provides the agency and agents for the production of a new nationalist ideology.

Culture

Our approach to national cultures is part of an ongoing review of the concept of culture, which I now wish to examine briefly. Culture, we are coming to think, is not a heavy weight of tradition, a set of configurations, a basic personality constellation that coerces and compels individuals. Culture is a set of understandings and a consciousness under active construction by which individuals interpret the world around them. Or, in a more behavioral view, it is a tool kit or set of scenarios that individuals use to implement or to stage their daily life. In either case, cultural production is not the result of a "once and for all" socialization process but, rather, a continual activity, coincident with ongoing social life itself. Similarly we have drained off much of the necessity and teleology of the nation-building literature. National culture is not an inevitable output of infrastructural investment. It is a contingent product, of history, of struggle. It is also not an invariant condition: it is not something a state either has or does not have. One can have it only partially or have it and then lose it. Furthermore, national cultural integration is a fluid process rooted in power, not a fixed condition of social health. Issues such as the separation of church and state, like ethnic nationalism, which supposedly any truly modernized state with a strong national culture would have solved long ago, can come up for grabs again, as the recent history of so many countries, our own included, indicates.

This emerging view of culture informs all the papers in this volume—even though the authors come at this question from rather different viewpoints, which are more varied than the simplistic labels, interpretive anthropology and political economy, by which I will nevertheless categorize them. Interpretive anthropologists and political economists are coming ever closer, a conjunction this monograph

Introduction

hopes both to illustrate and to further. I think there are two unstated theoretical orientations, of recent growth in anthropology, that underlie this conjunction. They are important points of reference for each of these papers—a conceptual backdrop, even though not necessarily directly acknowledged.

From the interpretive side, there has lately been much greater concern with the way in which culture gets practiced. An anthropology of cultural practice, which Ortner (1984) heralded as the orientation of the 1980s, means we look at the way people live with their cultural beliefs and how these beliefs are "envehicled" (to use Geertz's term) in daily existence (see also Bourdieu 1977; Sahlins 1981). The major question is: how to link cultural forms to ongoing social life? The most trenchant statement of this perspective comes from a sociologist. Anthony Giddens (1984:173) speaks of the way in which culture compels human activity but also enables it; he asserts that human activity is necessary to carry culture forward either in reproduced or altered form (see also Bhaskar 1979). An older anthropology, such as the national character studies previously alluded to, generally saw culture as compelling only. Practice therefore was only epiphenomenal or artifactual.

Looking at the way in which culture gets practiced makes anthropology more sensitive to issues of power, domination, and human intention as they relate to the way in which constituted cultural beliefs work in everyday life. In this volume, although all the papers deal with practice because they deal with history, it is especially emphasized in several. Goldstein conveys the practice of culture in the very plots and comic ploys of an Iranian immigrant theater, which thereby dramatizes disadvantage in Israeli society. Dominguez shows the way in which the practice of a national ceremony can be shot through with (and to some extent, shot down by) the Israeli state's dominating intentions. Malkki indicates how cultural practice under the particular circumstances of exile and in the specific conditions of a refugee camp creates a novel historical consciousness among Hutu. Williams presents a case of "malpractice": a Guyanese national cultural practice is judged inauthentic and ruled out of existence as ethnic populations contest over cultural heritage.

For political economists, the problem has been opposite: when cultural beliefs are seen to serve social interests, it becomes difficult to recognize the formative character of culture, and it is all too easy to reduce culture to a set of manipulative or repressive strategies. The concepts of mystification and false consciousness attempt to solve this problem, but they seem to allow, or even require, some manipulative agent or agency—a class, the state or an individual ideologue—standing above and outside the culture. If culture is formative, then it is hard to see how any social actor could exist "above it all." The major question for political economy has been: how to link social inequalities to the formative capacity of culture, that is, culture's ability to define the way we see the world? The answer that seems to be emerging is to allow that existing cultural beliefs encode social inequalities. Just as culture is always practiced, it is also never neutral; it integrates and constitutes inequalities. These inequalities lie behind cultural integration and constitution—thus, integration is a variable related to the degree of successful domination in a society.

My reference here is obviously to the recent use of the concept of hegemony, in the reading Raymond Williams (1977:110) gives it. Hegemony, for Williams, is a process rather than a state. It happens as the system of domination and inequality in a society becomes so culturally encoded, that is, lodged deep in cultural belief, that it comes to appear natural and inviolate. All the papers deal with hegemony because they all locate national culture—whether fully achieved, partial or nonexistent—in power relations and the structure of inequality, and they all treat it as a process because they show it as developing, struggled for, or contested. Verdery gives special attention to it, however, when she shows that underneath all the disputation about national culture, there was an almost unquestioned agreement that such a nation existed. I try to show the process of hegemony building in the production of a new definition of India and Indian citizenship based on Hindu "traditions" and a Hindu homeland. Smith shows the most nearly complete hegemony, in Guatemala, as Indians confront Ladinos, each encased in a historically produced identity that now appears culturally impregnable.

These papers conserve the central problem that national character studies attacked two generations ago, but to do so they have had to adopt a very different image of the central concept of culture. We still wish to know about the production of national culture: where do the informing beliefs, the characteristic lifeways, and the diagnostic temperaments come from? It was much too easy to answer this question when anthropology was infused with psychological reductionism. Then, national culture could be the projection of childhood experiences into adult life. In an anthropology that now sees that cultural forms as obscure as headdress or haircut can be infused with world-systemic inequality (I think here of the British Indian army's support for Sikh orthodoxy, which requires the hair and beard to remain uncut), it is clearly not easy to specify the connection between cultural forms and material conditions, but neither is it possible to ignore either of them. The *trishul* (the trident symbol of the god Shiva) brandished by Hindu nationalists is both a symbolic and a material weapon, something to fight with and to fight over. The same is true of Williams's Guyanese Moharram, Goldstein's Iranian theater, Smith's ethnic categories, Dominguez's Independence Day ceremony, Malkki's Hutu history, and Verdery's Romanian Nation. These papers, in perhaps their most salient contribution, show that as people confront their material situations, they also contend with their cultural beliefs. Imagining new social worlds or legitimating the existing one, humans produce conquering ideas as well as dominating classes and ruling states.

Notes

Acknowledgments. I want to thank my fellow authors for their comments on this introduction, and especially Katherine Verdery and Brackette Williams for their many helpful queries and comments. Ernestine Friedl and Louise Lamphere gave useful suggestions.

I wrote this introduction as a Fellow of the John Simon Guggenheim Memorial Foundation and as a Resident Fellow of the School of American Research in Santa Fe. I thank both these institutions for their support.

1. All but the Malkki and Smith papers were read at the 1987 American Ethnological Society Annual Meeting in San Antonio. Malkki delivered her paper at the 1987 American Anthropological Association Annual Meetings in Chicago.

References Cited

Anderson, Benedict
   1983   Imagined Communities. London: Verso.
Barth, Fredrik
   1969   Ethnic Groups and Boundaries. Boston: Little, Brown.
Benedict, Ruth
   1946   The Chrysanthemum and the Sword. Boston: Houghton Mifflin.
Bhaskar, Roy
   1979   The Possibility of Naturalism. New Jersey: Humanities Press.
Black, C. E.
   1966   The Dynamics of Modernization. New York: Harper and Row.
Bourdieu, Pierre
   1977   Outline of a Theory of Practice. Richard Nice, trans. Cambridge: Cambridge University Press.
Cohen, Abner
   1969   Custom and Politics in Urban Africa. Berkeley: University of California Press.

Fox, Richard G.
   1985   Lions of the Punjab. Berkeley: University of California Press.
Fox, Richard G., Charlotte H. Aull, and Louis F. Cimino
   1981   Ethnic Nationalism and the Welfare State. *In* Ethnic Change. Charles F. Keyes, ed. Pp. 198–245. Seattle: University of Washington Press.
Geertz, Clifford
   1963   Agricultural Involution. Berkeley: University of California Press.
Giddens, Anthony
   1984   The Constitution of Society. Berkeley: University of California Press.
Gorer, Geoffrey, and John Rickman
   1949   The People of Great Russia: A Psychological Study. London: Cresset Press.
Greenwood, Davydd
   1976   Unrewarding Wealth. Cambridge: Cambridge University Press.
Hechter, Michael
   1975   Internal Colonialism. Berkeley: University of California Press.
Hertzfeld, Michael
   1982   Ours Once More. Austin: University of Texas Press.
Kapferer, Bruce
   1988   Legends of People, Myths of State. Washington: Smithsonian Institution Press.
Kardiner, Abram
   1945   The Psychological Frontiers of Society. New York: Columbia University Press.
Mead, Margaret
   1953[1930]   Growing Up in New Guinea. New York: Mentor.
Ortner, Sherry
   1984   Theory in Anthropology Since the Sixties. Comparative Studies in Society and History 26:126–166.
Ragin, Charles
   1979   Ethnic Political Mobilization: The Welsh Case. American Sociological Review 44:619–634.
Sahlins, Marshall
   1981   Historical Metaphors and Mythical Realities: Structure in the Early History of the Sandwich Islands Kingdom. Ann Arbor: University of Michigan Press.
van den Berghe, Pierre
   1973   Pluralism. *In* Handbook of Social and Cultural Anthropology. John J. Honigmann, ed. Pp. 959–978. Chicago: Rand McNally.
Williams, Raymond
   1977   Marxism and Literature. London: Oxford University Press.

2

An Innocent Abroad: How Mulla Daoud Was Lost and Found in Lebanon, or the Politics of Ethnic Theater in a Nation at War

**Judith L. Goldstein
Vassar College**

"There is no better starting point for thought than laughter."
—Walter Benjamin, "The Author as Producer"

Consider the following bare sketch of the plot of a play performed in Israel in 1985: two Israeli officers in Lebanon interrogate and threaten a prisoner they think is a Shi'i Iranian terrorist. The prisoner is innocent; the Israelis obtuse and insensitive. In the end, convinced they have made a mistake, the soldiers free the prisoner.

Despite appearances, this is not the outline of a drama produced by opponents of the Israeli government. Rather, it is a Persian-language comedy, performed by an amateur troupe of Iranian immigrants in Israel, and written by a man who supported Likud, the party in power during the Israeli invasion of Lebanon in 1982. The play invites us to consider a number of important issues related to the production of culture in a modern nation-state that encourages cultural pluralism on one hand, and a vision of cultural unity on the other. These issues include the relation between humor and cultural and political criticism, popular culture forms as loci of resistance to a dominant culture, and the effect of a national crisis on ethnic cultural production. I will argue that when the dominant discourse on the nation-state appears weak, the way is open for a hitherto minority discourse to address itself to those issues of general importance that were formerly the domain of the dominant culture. At this juncture, ethnic culture takes on an intellectual and political task that is far wider than, and different from, its prior function of representing diversity.

Whereas the discourse of ethnicity served, and was encompassed by, the national discourse, it now seems as if ethnic culture (which was part of a discourse of ethnicity that valued diversity within the context of an overarching unity) can move in a crisis beyond its former position and comment critically on the values and actions of the nation.

Laughter places everything in "cheerfully irreverent quotation marks" (Bakhtin 1981:55–56), and it is this aspect of humor that is useful in the production of culture in a situation of choice (pluralism) and dominance (cultural unity). This placing apart in quotation marks is in part what makes humor a good starting point for thought. It seems to me that quotation marks also provoke thought by functioning as question marks. They make cultural categories available for examination by saying, in effect, these are not "natural" categories, but rather what we call certain ideas that might be called something different, or indeed, might *be* rather different. The comedies I am considering here situate two Iranian immigrants, one somewhat acclimated and the other newly arrived, against a backdrop of cultural confusion and constant mistranslation. The farces play with a variety of identities. These identities, through performance, become "quoted" identities, available for examination and criticism. The farces thus can be said to deconstruct Iranian ethnicity in Israel.

Furthermore, because of the central place of the whole issue of identity and ethnicity in Israeli life, the plays present to the audience the possibility of constructing a political critique of Israeli society and the place of Iranians in Israeli society. I will argue that the most recent play "about" Lebanon, although it retains the form of popular ethnic theater, marks a crucial departure from previous plays performed by the troupe. By effortlessly and skillfully combining the form, characters and language of ethnic cultural performance, but by tackling national problems, the play makes the audience of Iranian immigrants a collective of sorts, and allows audience members to see that the domain of politics is not only accessible through ethnic discourse, but is indeed coextensive with that discourse.

In this way, the plays have what Benjamin (1979) calls an "organizing function," but their power must be understood (1) in relation to the creation of Iranian ethnicity in Israel—an ethnicity best understood as a varied set of responses to rapidly changing historical moments; and (2) in relation to the present political confusion that opens up the domain of politics to other voices and to forms of critique other than the strictly and narrowly political, by showing the extent to which the system in place may not be functioning. Thus, to continue with the metaphor of quotation, popular ethnic theater extends its mandate, perhaps even transcends itself, during periods of uncertainty when, as it were, that which quotation marks enclose changes. That is, we can begin to see quotation marks being placed around the previously dominant categories of Israeli society, such as ethnicity and politics, rather than around popular ethnic culture. What is subject to question are the verities of state discourse, and not the (presumed) vestigial and transitional pieties of ethnic discourse.

The play, in the context of the plays that preceded it, has allowed me to see that a fundamental shift is taking place. Whereas in the 1960s and 1970s academics and, according to them, Israelis more generally, can be seen as thinking of "Iranian" and "Kurdish" festivals taking place within the larger context of the Israeli nation, it may be more appropriate now to think in terms of an "Israeli" nation. In this "Israeli" nation "Israelis" of Iranian and other ethnic origins participate as critics *through*, rather than in spite of, distinctive cultural forms. In a period of instability, the more traditional categories of understanding can look more promising than the newer ones of national institutions, such as the schools or the political parties.

Distinctive cultural forms do not just serve or respond to hegemony, but at certain times can compete with it. At such times, ethnic culture attacks those issues that are usually approached exclusively through the terms of the dominant discourse. When the dominant discourse appears particularly weak, as I think it has since the invasion of Lebanon (which is the subject of the play), its claim to the exclusive right to analyze the "big" issues is undermined. Ethnic activities, already "in place," with their forms that have seemingly passed the test of time, can become commentaries on the "big" issues. In this way, I will argue, a popular culture form, in the hands of a very talented playwright, addresses high culture (which by definition was the domain of the dominant discourse) issues without becoming high culture, and without finding an audience broader than an ethnic audience. Rather than looking for broader audiences (at least yet), the play politicizes the audience it has, turning that audience into a collectivity with the right to address general political issues. Indeed, it transforms those issues, showing the ways in which ethnicity is political as well as cultural and, therefore, that ethnic theater can also be political theater.

I want to stress that this points to a certain inversion of the former roles of ethnic and national discourses. Part of the difference between ethnic forms and state forms was precisely that they addressed themselves to different spheres of life. Ethnic culture was "color," local tradition, particular meanings located in personal life histories. National (dominant) culture was what everyone shared. This national culture included the history of the Jewish people as a suffering and creative unified entity. National culture had to be taught to a first generation, but could be lived by a second generation in much the way ethnic culture was lived. Ethnic culture was both private culture—the customs of the home—and public culture—festivals, language, food, dress. Both the public and private forms of ethnic culture tended to be concrete, taking place at certain times (festivals) and in certain contexts (language use between two people of the same ethnic origin). National culture could also take the form of commemorations associated with the calendrical year but, in contrast with ethnic culture, it was the language of national debate. When ethnicity entered national politics, it was in the limited case of electoral appeal—was there an ethnic vote that the national parties could tap?

Iranian ethnicity has offered a particularly fertile ground for these modulations of ethnicity, culture, and politics because it has been comparatively unstable in the larger universe of Israeli ethnicity. Iranians in Israel have fallen between many opposed social categories (Ashkenazi/Oriental, upper class/lower class, religious/nonreligious), and the fact that their options have therefore been comparatively open has had a perpetually destabilizing influence on their cultural production. The plays I will discuss feature a main character who is a trickster figure, and I am attracted to the notion of Iranians in Israel as a trickster ethnic group.

Iranian Ethnicity in Israel

When Israel went through a period of ethnic activity in the 1960s, Israelis of Iranian origin took a wait-and-see attitude. Iranians in Israel had, until the late 1970s, what can be called a low ethnic profile. Classed neither with the Ashkenazim nor, in any consistent way, with the Sephardim, they never seemed able to decide if the ethnic route suited them or not. This changed during the Iranian Revolution, and I observed what I have called (after Schutz) the "constituting process" of Iranian ethnicity during the year 1978–1979 (Goldstein 1985). The self-conscious organization of ethnic activities, designed to appeal to a very diverse body of Iranians, was connected to demands Iranians wanted to make on the Israeli state, although they disagreed on those demands (these centered on what could or should be done about Iranian Jews in Iran). Iranian activists were convinced that ethnic visibility was a crucial dimension of political power. Community leaders, faced with a very diverse group of Iranians, searched for some way to define and organize a collectivity that would help the new immigrants join Israeli society, while also reflecting well on the Iranians already there. The activities that have been instrumental in constructing a sense of Iranian ethnicity include academic conferences on the subject of Iranian Jews; weekend retreats at vacation spots within Israel where Iranians come together to eat, pray, sing, dance, and attend lectures; and Iranian cultural performances that feature Persian-language comedies and Iranian music and dance. The comedies in the last category are the most completely "Iranian" of the cultural activities in form and content.

The diversity of the Iranians is related to differences in the times they emigrated to Israel. Major groups of Iranian immigrants arrived before 1948, from 1950–1951, after 1967, and from 1978–1979. The Iranian community in Israel today is composed of (1) veteran immigrants, most of whom arrived in 1950–1951; (2) young adults who were born in Iran or Israel, but who were raised in Israel; and (3) new immigrants who have come since 1978. Iranians in Israel differ along class lines, religious lines, in terms of Zionist ideology and in degree of corporate experience—some Iranians have led more communal lives in small towns, others come to Israel having spent their lives in more individualistic ways in Teheran; their lives in Iran were more varied than a nostalgic view of small-town life would suggest.

Most of the Iranians who came in 1950–1951 came as poor Jews from poor communities and arrived with few personal possessions. Symbolically, these immigrants often sold the few remaining "Iranian" objects they had—a copper bowl or tray, some silver, perhaps a rug—when they arrived. In the first decade or two the Israeli Iranians did better economically than the relatives they left at home, but recent Iranian prosperity (before the revolution) reversed this trend. The Iranian contingent pulled ahead, and Israelis saw the proof of their improved status when the Iranians came as tourists to Israel. Iranian Israelis who scrimped and saved over the years in order to purchase a small apartment were indignant over the ability of some recent Iranian immigrants to pay cash for housing in desirable neighborhoods. Their sympathy for those Iranians who now arrive having lost their wealth is tempered by their resentment over not being helped by their relatives during the years of plenty.

The families in Iran and Israel also grew apart in terms of religious observance. Ironically, it was often the relatives in the old country who became less religious, because of the different ways in which politics and religion were related in Iran and Israel. As the Iranian state became more secular, compared to the religious opposition, in the early 1970s the possibility of assimilation seemed to grow, and when I left the country after fieldwork in 1975, Jews in Teheran were worrying about the rate of intermarriage. One of Teheran's chief rabbis complained that the food at Jewish weddings was not kosher. In the meantime, while many Iranians in Israel may have become less observant, others were confronted with sizable numbers of Jews who by most definitions, including their own, were more religious than they were. Iranians in Israel, particularly those with whom I worked most closely in the religious neighborhoods of Jerusalem (Geula, Mea Shearim, Shuchunat ha Bukharim), saw religiosity as a way of upgrading their status, a way of emphasizing the social classifications "religious/nonreligious" over "Ashkenazi/Oriental." Increasingly too, religiosity was allied with political protest.

The Zionist ideology of veteran and new Iranian immigrants differs. The Iranian revolution caused a sudden influx of immigrants who might otherwise not have come to Israel. Many of the Iranian Jews who came during 1978–1979 were neither political nor religious Zionists and did not want to declare themselves Israeli citizens. They wanted a temporary haven until they could go back to Iran. They confront veterans of 30 years and their children, who have been educated in the Israeli school system. The differences are most obvious in young people: those who have gone through the Israeli school system have different ideas from those who did not. In any event, their definitions of Zionism are related to their conceptions of the past and their pasts are different. New immigrants in need of services and old immigrants (the term used is veteran immigrants) also differ in their relation to the modern state.

In sum, Iranian ethnic activity and the cultural construction of Iranian ethnicity has had to deal with all these different Iranians as well as with prevailing definitions of ethnicity, Judaism, Zionism, Arabs, Iranians, and Muslims. It is perhaps not surprising that one of the most successful ethnic activities was carnivalesque, a form that explicitly encompassed creativity and conflict and recognized the multiple forms of Iranian identity in Israel.

The Ethnic Carnivalesque:
The Plays and Immigrant Identity

The Persian-language comedies have been a forum in which these different identities have been presented. An examination of the comedies shows the changes in this ethnic discourse, all made within the rather short time of about a decade. My analysis of the plays will focus on the use of humor to delineate a relatively free space for cultural criticism, and to allow for exploring, in a flexible, improvisatory way, changes in individual and group identity. The concept of multivocality, of the intersection of many voices, focuses our attention on the representation of a variety of identities in the plays—the actors portray old and new immigrants, Iranian and non-Iranian Israelis—and offers a way into the relatively flexible positions of Iranians of different status in the Israeli social structure.

The plays are particularly interesting, not only for their use of humor, but also because they are produced for the consumption of Iranian immigrants only. This does not mean that what is produced is not influenced by the larger society, but it is not produced to be displayed and shared with nonethnic group members. In a multiethnic state such as Israel in which ethnic culture is encouraged, many groups express their "unique" traditions in similar ways. We can think of this public enactment of cultures as the museum model of ethnicity: we have a special food, you have a special food; we have a native dance, you have a native dance; we have traditional dress, you have traditional dress, and so forth. These are cultural traditions that have meaning in the marketplace as visible and divisible. These homogenized forms are not what they purport to be, but they do have a function in the politics of ethnic pluralism in which visibility is connected, or is thought to be connected, to political power. This aspect of Israeli ethnicity, as I have previously discussed (Goldstein 1985), generally goes unacknowledged. Israeli and non-Israeli social scientists have tended either to glorify ethnic cultural production as truly expressive of an authentic previous culture, or have resolutely opposed Ashkenazi culture to Sephardi or Oriental culture in such a way that the latter loses on every dimension—political, economic, religious, and cultural. Thus we have been offered a choice between a generalized culture seen incorrectly as continuous with many Middle Eastern pasts, or have been offered a people without culture, victims of a melting pot ideology of absorption in the 1950s and of ongoing discrimination.[1] In this context, what is most important about the plays is that they have an *intra*-ethnic, not an *inter*-ethnic function. When we enter into the production of ethnic culture at this level, we can finally see that, at the right historical moment, such culture is capable of challenging the dominant culture.

Because the plays are intra-ethnic they are a particularly interesting locus of cultural production. What is important about them is not only what they are—that is, their intrinsic value as a form of cultural criticism—but also what they are not (but could be). They are not ethnic festivals produced by one ethnic group in the context of competing ethnic groups; nor are they state-produced productions like those found in the schools and on television at times of national celebrations or historic commemorations.

In the comedies we can see the development of a counter-discourse, the establishment of unofficial perspectives, on the part of an ethnic group which, to be understood and to understand itself in context, uses the official discourse of ethnicity, but uses it in new ways. The multivocality of carnivalesque productions such as the plays can carve out an area for relatively independent cultural production, a place for thought, for a kind of collective thought that itself creates the collective. "When carnival goes the way it should, it would seem that its 'function' in relation to other social structures is itself ambivalent. It tests and contests all aspects of society and culture through festive laughter: those that are questionable may be readied for change; those that are deemed legitimate may be reinforced" (LaCapra 1983:306). The way these plays question is through mimicry and role-playing. This playing of other social roles through reversal and inversion is important, but since the plays, as I have argued, perform an intra-ethnic function, the role-playing includes versions of one's *own* (constructed) ethnicity. This taking of the position of others (not the Other) makes the plays critical examinations as well as comedies. I will use a closer examination of the plays themselves—and in particular the most recent play I saw in summer of 1985 which, since it is set in Lebanon, brings in yet another set of contrastive identities—to see how the plays resist and examine prevailing cultural assumptions.

The farces feature Mulla Daoud, a maladapted Iranian immigrant in Israel, and his only marginally better integrated friend and translator Nissan. Mulla Daoud is a new immigrant; Nissan has lived in Israel for a number of years. Mulla Daoud is a provincial Iranian Jew—his accent is that of an Isfahani—dressed in baggy trousers, a loose suit jacket, ethnic headgear, and shoes whose heels are crushed down to transform them to scuffs. He speaks to Hebrew and, with the help of his inept translator Nissan, misinterprets the doctors, custom officials, bureaucrats, and tax collectors whom he confronts in modern-day Israel.

For Iranians, the classification of Mulla Daoud is immediately apparent: he is a recent immigrant from a small town in Iran. His portrayal in the comedies, consisting as it does of his entire persona—his dress, speech, gesture, comportment, and assumptions about people and events—is more complex. In a sense, his whole is less than the sum of his parts. The character of Mulla Daoud is a caricature, but his behavior and speech ring true. The humor in the plays makes it possible for audience members to recognize their own past in Mulla Daoud's present, and forces them to confront the changes in the composition of their personal and ethnic identity that comes with immigration.

Although Mulla Daoud has different occupations from play to play, certain aspects of his representation remain constant. He is the new immigrant from the old country who is never going to really adjust. The most he can hope for is temporarily to turn the tables on his opponents. If Mulla Daoud represents the past in the present, then Nissan stands for the future in the present. Nissan apparently thinks that he speaks perfect Hebrew and is so well adjusted to his new country that he can offer expert help to his fellow Iranian immigrants. The depressing truth seems to be that Nissan too is frozen in his moment of inadequacy. He is less static a character than Mulla Daoud, but it would be illusory to interpret his movement as progress. Mulla Daoud knows no Hebrew; Nissan knows some Hebrew, but so little about Israeli culture that he lacks the background necessary to make correct translations.

In addition to his language problem, Mulla Daoud has trouble with nonlinguistic cues. He has no facility whatever in understanding the human panorama in Israel. He cannot recognize people in what are to him new social roles. He cannot tell an Iranian from a veteran Israeli, or even a new Iranian immigrant from a veteran Iranian immigrant. He decides other peoples' identities not from contextualized social readings, but in an *ad hoc* way based on their superficial physical appearance. Thus he assumes, based on physical resemblances, that a non-Iranian government official is a pupil he once taught in Iran, and is annoyed when he doesn't speak Persian.

Nissan understands who's who, but has his own trouble with what's what. His direct translations, devoid of any grasp of metaphor or the limits of translating idioms directly into another language, parallel Mulla Daoud's unmediated readings of people's social identity based on physical appearance. Nissan makes two major language mistakes. First, he translates idioms directly from Persian to Hebrew and from Hebrew to Persian, creating unacceptable combinations. For example, he translates literally the Persian idiom "eat the earth" for fall down when speaking in Hebrew, producing a phrase that is not idiomatic in the latter language. When introducing an Israeli named Dov, Nissan does not simply repeat the proper name "Dov," but, translating it, tells Mulla Daoud that the man in question is named "Bear."

Second, he assumes that phonetic similarity implies semantic similarity within Hebrew and between Hebrew and Persian, and thus switches the translations of Hebrew terms that sould alike or gives the Persian meaning for a Hebrew word that sounds like the Persian. The following exchange is typical.

Doctor: Ask him if he is married *(nesooi)*.
Nissan: OK. Honored Mulla, it seems as if the doctor has gone mad. He wants to know if you're the president *(nasi)*.
Mulla Daoud: Tell him, at my grave. Tell him I'm barely on the committee of the synagogue *(knisa)*.
Nissan (to the doctor): No, he's not the president, he's a member of parliament *(chaver knesset)*.

[*The New Immigrant*, from performance]

Nissan confuses the meanings of two Hebrew words that sound alike to him, *nesooi* and *nasi*, and then caps this by doing the same with the Persian word *knisa* and the Hebrew word *knesset*. The fact that his mistranslations often make some kind of sense only deludes him further and this makes his interactions even more surreal.

In terms of language, he has no grasp of metaphor or idiom. In terms of behavior, he has no grasp of social expectations. Lacking background information, he misses social cues. He misaligns social contexts, doing with behaviors what he did with idioms, as the following exchange illustrates. Nissan and Mulla Daoud are in a doctor's office.

Nissan: The doctor asked how old you are, may you stay healthy.
Mulla Daoud: I don't know. Tell him about 50.
Nissan: No, no, don't tell him the truth. If you say at once you're 50, he'll say it's nothing, go home. Make it a lot.
Mulla Daoud: Ok. Tell him what you want . . .
Doctor: Yes, how old is he?
Nissan: He's 195 . . .
Doctor: What's this 195, Adoni (mister)? A man lives maybe 90 years. What's 195?
Nissan: So what do you want him to be?
Doctor: Ask him again how old he is.
Nissan: Because you're a good man, let him be 90 . . .
Doctor: What is it to me, more or less. Ask him how old he is.
Nissan: So what do you want? Give me your hand, give me your hand. . . . To your health. Let it be 60. Y'Allah.

[*The New Immigrant*, from performance]

Mulla Daoud, like Nissan, behaves inappropriately in social situations, but he has the additional handicap of not being able to tell from appearance and dress who is Iranian and who is Israeli. In another play, the comedy revolves around his mistaking an Israeli tax collector for an Iranian who has come to arrange a marriage for him. The audience, of course, could make this distinction and roared with laughter when the "Israeli" came on stage wearing a neat short-sleeved shirt, sunglasses, and carrying a fat briefcase.

The malaise here runs deep. Mulla Daoud is expecting a traditional Iranian and his inability to distinguish basic categories for human types in Israel shows that he is alienated not only from non-Iranian Israelis, but from veteran Iranian Israelis as well. What he does have is a set of behaviors that he has brought with him. He tells the tax collector, who identifies himself as such in his first appearance, that he has no money, two wives, one in Israel and one in Iran, "etzel Khomeini" (chez Khomeini), and many children. When the tax collector returns for a second time, Mulla Daoud does not recognize him. Certain that he is the brother of the prospective bride because he looks just like her, Mulla Daoud tells the tax collector, through Nissan, that he is fabulously wealthy: he has money out on loan; owns valuable real estate on Dizengoff Street (an important commercial street in Tel Aviv); and keeps antiques and gold in the refrigerator. His deceptive presentation of self backfires in Israel, and he is told by the tax collector that he faces a prison term for witholding taxes.

The alienation depicted in this play goes even further. Mulla Daoud is a fortune-teller and his whole life is defined by falsehood. Because he is a fortune-teller, his alienated relation to other people is paralleled by his false relation to his environment. As depicted in the play, *The Fortune Teller*, he is involved daily in lying to others and in misrepresenting the link between human suffering and natural causality. When an attractive young Israeli woman comes to ask him how to have children and regain her husband's love, he enters into his divining routine, and one of the biggest laughs was generated by his list of traditional remedies. The traditional words, which have no Hebrew equivalents as they stand for flora native to Iran, are the linguistic or natural equivalents of Mulla Daoud's entire persona.

The young woman who comes to him for help is dressed in an outfit which clearly signals to the audience that she is a modern Israeli. She wears a one-piece jumpsuit with spaghetti straps and appears an altogether unlikely person to be consulting the likes of Mulla Daoud. After he fully incriminates himself by his suggested remedies, the woman reveals that she has come from the police department. Again, the limits of Mulla Daoud's world, and his relation to the modern Israeli state, have been redefined for him. If his conscience will not be his guide, the state will. It can take money from him, but he cannot take money from others on what are considered false pretenses.

The plays, as I have said, are a form of cultural criticism, and if they present the immigrants in a bad light, something similar can be said for how they depict the overarching Zionist ideology, which is what permits the state to make demands on new immigrants and punish them for noncompliance with these demands. Some of the language jokes are based on mistranslations, which, when analyzed, are revealed as a form of critique. Thus Nissan tells Mulla Daoud that when he first came to Israel, they (government officials) were going to send him to Ramat ha Gola, but he ended up in Naveh Yaqoob. Mulla Daoud, in turn, offers that he lives in Mahalleh Yehuda. Ramat ha Gola should have been Ramat ha Golan, as Naveh Yaqoob should be Neve Ya'acov, and Mahalleh Yehuda, Maxane Yehuda. I would argue that these mistakes have a sting in their tails. They transform a place in Eretz Yisrael to a place in exile *(galut)*.[2] The term Ramat ha Gola does this explicitly—the Golan becomes gola, a form of *galut*—while the terms Naveh Yaqoob and Mahalleh Yehuda achieve the change implicitly. The Hebrew Ya'acov is replaced by the Persian personal name Yaqoob (and even in Persian a place name does not take the more informal spoken pronunciation). Mahalleh is the Persian word used to indicate the Jewish quarter in Iranian cities. Many Iranian Jews live in Maxane Yehuda. The neologism "Mahalleh Yehuda" combines the historic sense of being Jewish in Iran with the current sense of being Iranian in Israel, and also paradoxically seems to state that one can be in *galut*, in exile, in the land of Israel.

As the new immigrant, Mulla Daoud's creative misuse of language can be a profound statement about the modern bureaucratic state, as the following exchange indicates.

> Nissan: Shalom Aqa Daoud. May God bless you, what are you doing here?
> Mulla Daoud: How do I know, may I be your sacrifice. I got into a taxi. I wanted to go to the *Kotel Ma'aravi* (Western or Wailing Wall). Whatever I did, however I tried to remember where I was going, I couldn't think of the word. Without language, I tried to make the driver understand, "There, the place where they cry," and he brought me here. But this isn't the Kotel.
> Nissan: May I be your sacrifice. This is the *misrad ha shikun*, the Housing Office. They give out apartments here.
> [*The Apartment*, from scenario]

Here again, Mulla Daoud's misunderstanding is a form of critique. Eretz Yisrael, the Land of Israel, and Medinat Yisrael, the State of Israel, are shown to be at odds with one another. In the modern state, the poor Jew cries as much for four walls as he did for centuries at the Wailing Wall. In Eretz Yisrael, appeals are aimed at God; in Medinat Yisrael, they are directed at the *pakid*, or bureaucrat.

Tricksters at War: The Plays and Israeli Identity

The newest play presents a different, and perhaps prophetic, kind of ethnic critique. In the most recent play we move from the new immigrant's focus on the bureaucracy to the more veteran Israeli's concern with the body politic. The play, *The Prisoner*, which takes place in Lebanon, marks a departure from the other comedies because it is the Israelis who mistake the identity of the Iranian immigrant, rather than the reverse. The play's set is that of an Israeli army camp in Lebanon. A soldier brings in a blindfolded prisoner wearing a camouflage jacket. The prisoner is Mulla Daoud. The Israelis are on the trail of a terrorist who has set off a number of bombs within Israel. Mulla Daoud speaks no Hebrew or Arabic, just Persian. The head officer sends for Nissan, who is working in the kitchen.[3] Nissan comes out wearing a metal colander reversed on his head like a helmet. He immediately recognizes Mulla Daoud ("What, you again? Everywhere I go I see you, like a minaret"), but does not tell the Israelis this because he does not grasp that the problem is one of mistaken identity. Told that the prisoner's name is Mulla Daoud, the Israelis think they have captured the notorious Abu Daoud. Through a series of mistranslations of the kind I have described, Mulla Daoud concedes that he has set off a number of bombs, and hijacked a plane.

The Israelis finally realize they have a recent Iranian immigrant when they examine his documents. They ask in surprise if he is an Israeli. Mulla Daoud responds, "What am I, a goy?"[4] Nissan adds, "Yes, he's a Jew, my friend." When the officer asks Nissan why he didn't say anything sooner, he answers, "You didn't ask us."

The problem we confront here is not just that of mistaken identity on an individual level; it is a problem of noncongruent group categories. This time it is the Israelis who are confused by superficial signals; Mulla Daoud is wearing a camouflage jacket he picked up somewhere and is speaking Persian. Iranian Shi'ites were fighting against the Israelis in Lebanon. Mulla Daoud was picked up in Lebanon, therefore he must be an Iranian fighter. For Mulla Daoud, his chief identifying factor is religious—he cannot understand that anyone could take him for anything but a Jew, his primary identity in Iran. When asked if he's an Israeli, he does not say, "What do you take me for, an Iranian (or an Arab)?" He says, "What do you take me for, a non-Jew?" as if the answer is evidently negative. I think it is also the fact that this mistaken identity indicates a "worst case scenario" for Iranian Jews in Israel, who indicate here that they are afraid of being taken for the enemy. Whereas North African and Middle Eastern Jews in Israel may worry about being confused with Arab Muslims, Iranians now have their version of that problem with the expansion of hostilities to include Shi'ites and Iranian Muslims in Lebanon. The mistake poses the question of whether ethnicity in Israel can be constructed without references to non-Jews within and outside of Israel.[5]

Very apologetic, the Israeli officer asks Mulla Daoud how he came to be in Lebanon. He answers that he saw buses, asked if they were going to Jerusalem, thought he got an affirmative response, and then fell asleep on the bus. When he awoke he saw tanks and soldiers and thought the Shah was supposed to come. I am tempted to see a criticism of the Israeli state here that is not unlike the one made when Ramat ha Golan became Ramat ha Gola, when a place in Eretz Israel became a place in *galut*. If one was meant to be in Jerusalem, then why was one in Lebanon? And if one was in Israel, then why should one be expecting the Shah? Of course, it is a sign of his political obliviousness that the oldtimer thinks the Shah is still alive at all, but the play seems to be criticizing Israel's presence in Lebanon as well as the Israeli establishment's inability to distinguish adequately between Iranian Muslims and Iranian Jews, and between Iranian Israelis and Arabs. There is a clear and pointed inversion here of the other plays in which the Iranians cannot distinguish among the different types of Israelis, and of the dominant Israeli modes of definition of persons that separate Jews and non-Jews, but mix up and mix together their cultures of origin.

I see this placing of Israelis in the position formerly occupied by the ignorant Iranian immigrants as a move that expands the relevance of an ethnic discourse. This is a move that results in the challenge of the political establishment by people formerly defined and limited by an ethnic definition of self and group. To stress "politics" rather than "culture" for the moment, phase one of the construction of Iranian ethnicity in Israel was ethnic group building, the creation of ethnic visibility suitable to a politics of interest groups. The critique implicit in this newest play may mark phase two, in which Iranians think they can move into the present political disarray and attract a constituency broader than their ethnic group. They can mobilize people on the basis of interests more inclusive than ethnicity, a basis that does not limit them the way ethnicity does.

What I am suggesting here is a move from a discourse about ethnicity and alienation to one about ethnicity and political participation. Let me tell a short story that illustrates the move from a more ethnic to a more explicitly political discourse and the speed of the move. In 1978 I met a politician of Iranian birth at an Iranian ethnic event. He was rediscovering his roots, as it were. He was the mayor of a development town. He became visible nationally during the year of the Iranian revolution. He is now a member of the Cabinet. But the widening of relevant space from local to international is perhaps best illustrated by his appearance in a recent editorial piece (translated from a Hebrew newspaper article) in the *New York Times*, in which he was offered as an ideal candidate for Prime Minister. No specific mention of his Iranian background was made; he was presented as one of the most promising of a group of talented young politicians of Middle Eastern background who were moving up in Likud.

I began by calling Iranians a trickster ethnic group, and it is with the ambiguity of the trickster and the carnival world that I wish to end. When we enter this new more political discourse, I have to posit what might be called a political multivocality, a display of multiple voices, even more complex than that which mimics Israeli officers, Iranian immigrants, and presumed terrorists. As I have said, the playwright supported the Israeli entry into Lebanon. He thought it was absolutely necessary that the Israelis do something to get rid of the arms amassed along Israel's northern border. He wrote the first version of the play in the summer of 1982. I remember visiting him in his store while he was on temporary leave from *miluyim* (army reserves), wearing his army uniform, and writing the play at his desk when he had no customers. He had been posted in Lebanon, and would be returning to his post there.

I asked him many times how it was that he wrote a play that seemed critical of the Lebanese War when he supported it. As far as I could tell he found the question completely uninteresting.[6] Finally, exasperated by my persistence, he said to me, "It's my job to write the plays. It's your job to analyze them." So be it, I thought, although I definitely suspected the presence of the carnivalesque in his statement. But I see now that he also did my job for me because, if my analysis is correct, the play was pointing to the failure of official discourses, including the academic discourse, at this time in Israel. The task of the playwright was not to answer my questions, but to show that popular ethnic theater could enter the big time and pose its own questions about what the important issues were. I think that ethnic culture in Israel, then, is not just fighting, as it has in the past decade, for the right to define itself. It is beginning to compete in an increasingly public sphere for the right to define the nation. More specifically, ethnic forms of expression and protest have begun to compete with what have been valued and institutionalized cultural categories to redefine the nation not as an elite bastion of Western liberal ideologies working to convert the more conservative "East" within, but as a nation that potentially holds within it a new and powerful alignment of "Eastern" culture and a different, and more religious, "Western" culture.

Notes

Acknowledgments. Fieldwork in Israel was done in 1975, 1978–1979, and summers of 1982 and 1985 with support from the National Institute of Mental Health, and Mellon grants from Vassar College. I am very grateful to Suleiman Mottahedeh for his hospitality and for all the time he spent helping me understand the plays. I thank Greg Acciaioli and Daniel Segal for sending me written comments on the paper, and Faye Ginsburg, Stephen Lewis and Yehuda Moradi for discussing some of the issues in it with me.

1. This is not to say that I have not learned a great deal from other anthropologists working in Israel, or that I do not consider myself part of their community. Anthropologists who have worked in Israel and Israeli anthropologists have done a lot of work aimed at understanding ethnicity as a cultural category. The recent collection edited by Alex Weingrod (1985) includes many of these anthropologists, and Kevin Avruch and Henry Rosenthal have also contributed to this debate. However, the assumption that ethnic festivals are "revivals" has meant that ethnic cultural production has not been analyzed for what it says about contemporary Israeli society. Indeed, I think it could be argued that the almost exclusive attention anthropologists have paid to ethnic group members has itself helped to marginalize them as quaint rather than to take them seriously as political actors.

2. This parallels a reverse use in Iran: at times when Jewish life was easy, Jews said, "There was no *galut*," when, in terms of the usual definition, any place outside Israel was in *galut*.

3. Of note here is the relative position of Iranian and non-Iranian Israelis—Nissan works in the kitchen in the army, and is the translator or patient, but not the doctor in the hospital. Class differences as depicted in the plays are an issue I will deal with in another paper, but wish at least to mention here.

4. He uses the term *goyim*. In the Persian of Jewish speakers the Hebrew plural *goyim* is used as singular. This is particularly funny now for audience members who still use the form *goyim* in Persian, but as Hebrew speakers use the grammatically correct *goy*, and know that *goyim* is "wrong."

5. This is a question, I might add, that academics, following the Iranians, should ask more often. Anthropologists tend to build upon the differences between *edot*, ethnic groups, or Jews, and *miyutim*, minority groups, or non-Jews, without asking about the intersection of these categories.

6. The question was also puzzling, perhaps, because one cannot be said to be simply "for" or "against" a war in Israel. The issue was whether or not the war in Lebanon was a defensive one necessary for national survival.

References Cited

Bakhtin, M. M.
    1981   The Dialogic Imagination. Austin: University of Texas Press.

Benjamin, Walter
    1979 The Author as Producer. Reflections. New York: Harcourt, Brace, Jovanovich.
Goldstein, Judith L.
    1985 Iranian Ethnicity in Israel: The Performance of Identity. *In* Studies in Israeli Ethnicity. Alex Weingrod, ed. New York: Gordon and Breach.
LaCapra, Dominic, ed.
    1983 Bakhtin, Marxism, and the Carnivalesque. *In* Rethinking Intellectual History. Ithaca: Cornell University Press.
Weingrod, Alex, ed.
    1985 Studies in Israeli Ethnicity. New York: Gordon and Breach.

3

Context and Consciousness: Local Conditions for the Production of Historical and National Thought among Hutu Refugees in Tanzania

Liisa Malkki
Harvard University

This paper is a part of a larger study that explores the interrelationships between historicity and national consciousness, refugeeness and exile, and the making of categorical order and liminality among Hutu refugees from Burundi living in western Tanzania.[1] At its broadest, this essay suggests, through the description of a particular ethnographic case, how the study of historical consciousness among refugees, the stateless, and other displaced peoples can offer an illuminating, anthropological view into the often interrelated transformations in historical and national consciousness. More specifically, it explores the ways in which a particular, localized setting, a refugee camp, came to be an enabling device in the elaboration of deeply categorical forms of consciousness that centered upon nation-ness and historicity.

The argument to follow is based on field research[2] among the Hutu who fled Burundi in 1972 as a result of a genocidal massacre, and who have since lived as refugees in rural western Tanzania.[3] The majority (150,000) live in highly organized refugee camps in rural areas, while some 20,000–30,000 Hutu refugees are so-called "spontaneously settling refugees," and live interspersed with local Tanzanian citizens in and around Kigoma Township on Lake Tanganyika, as well as throughout the Kigoma Region. (Armstrong 1986b:41; cf. Tanganyika Christian Refugee Service 1984).

This paper will explore how these two radically different settings shaped conceptions of "the past" and relationships with history among the camp refugees and the town refugees. While field research was evenly divided between these two very different settings, here the "camp refugees" are the dominant focus.[4] It will be argued that the camp played an important, generative role in the elaboration of a form of consciousness that was both national and historical, and that vividly contrasted with the much less historical and national forms of consciousness found among the town refugees on Lake Tanganyika.

This study was initially generated by a set of questions concerning the place occupied by refugees in the contemporary system of nation-states, and the techniques that have emerged for containing and controlling these displaced and therefore marked peoples. Despite the objective modernity of nations, which only emerged as a categorical system toward the end of the 18th century, nations are now subjectively perceived as a categorical order of some antiquity (Anderson 1983:14). Nations—never experienced as "mere" historical artefacts—have come to be perceived as an organic and necessary order, and it is in this sense that they constitute a powerful, hegemonic categorical system (cf. Anderson 1983; Handler 1988; Herzfeld 1987:13; and, from a different perspective, Kapferer 1988).[5] Refugees, the stateless and the displaced represent a challenge to this system. They are, in other words, a "categorical anomaly" and hence "dangerous" in both a political and a symbolic sense.[6] Precisely because refugees are interstitial in the order of nations, or liminal as Mary Douglas (1966) might put it, states have developed systematized, "routine" techniques for dealing with the permanently growing number of refugees in the world,[7] and have, in the process, created a new and distinctive object of knowledge, "the refugee," as a generic and essentialized figure.[8]

The last years of the Second World War in Europe mark the moment at which the refugee camp emerged as the principal technique or instrument for ordering, administering, and controlling refugees.[9] Since the war, the refugee camp has become emplaced as a systematized and generalizable "technology of power" (Foucault 1979), "standard equipment" routinely deployed in dealing with large, displaced refugee populations around the world.[10] In this interpretation of the camp as a technology of power, the key term, power, is not intended merely as a negative or normative term akin to "repression," "coercion" or "domination," but rather, as something that *produces* and generates (Foucault 1979:194). As Foucault writes, power "produces reality; it produces domains of knowledge and rituals of truth" (Foucault 1979:194).

A close ethnography of a particular contemporary case, that of the Hutu refugees in camp and town in Tanzania, revealed that the camp as a device of power had in fact helped to produce an unintended effect of some significance: it had created the conditions that promoted an extremely historicized, historicizing form of social existence. The camp as a technology of power (Foucault 1979) was implicated in and even constitutive of the elaboration and intensification of historical consciousness. The more extensive study mentioned above (Malkki 1989) is a detailed exploration of this historical consciousness in the process of production. Here, it will be more briefly mapped out how, in the particular case of the Hutu, history is constructed, how it is deployed or used, and why at a certain moment and not at another, history seizes center-stage in everyday thought and practice in the present.

This should not, of course, be taken to imply that the Hutu were previously "without consciousness" or "without history,' nor, indeed, that any social group can be described as "having" or "not having" historical consciousness. It seems more accurate to think in terms of transformations of consciousness, as opposed to a more totalizing (and essentializing) "formation" of consciousness that would imply a unidirectional trajectory. This analytical shift allows for the conceptualization of historical consciousness as a situational, localized process that does not necessarily constitute a unified whole. It also suggests that a heterogeneity of forms of consciousness can exist at once among particular groups of actors.

The history in question here is a kind of collective narrative of the Hutu refugees' past, which heroizes them as a distinct people with a historical trajectory setting them apart from other peoples.[11] Embedded in the creation of this collective history is another process, the creation of nation-ness and national identity. The Hutu refugees' construction of a collective past where the Hutu are the principal actors is also essentially a construction of a "national past," of the past of the Hutu as a "People," and as a *"moral community"* (cf. Anderson 1983:15; emphasis added).[12]

Living historically, as these refugees do, implies the creation of nation-ness and, conversely, the elaboration of the construct, "nation," is necessarily historical. The twin processes of the production of historical and national consciousness represent a transformation that is in part a creation of the refugee camp itself. It is this transformation in its local context that is central here.

The foregoing is intended to situate the project in a wider, more general context, and to indicate the direction of the argument to follow. A brief outline of the ethnographic context will perhaps also be helpful.

Setting

In April and May of 1972, generations of political inequality and conflict in Burundi between the ruling ethnic minority, the Tutsi, and the dominated majority, the Hutu, culminated in a cataclysmic massacre in which perhaps as many as 100,000 or more Hutu were killed.[13] At this time, some 180,000 Hutu fled across the eastern border of Burundi into neighboring Tanzania. The Government of Tanzania, the United Nations High Commissioner for Refugees (UNHCR) and the Tanganyika Christian Refugee Service (TCRS; a local arm of the Lutheran World Federation), entered into a "Tri-Partite Agreement"—the purpose of which was, first, to provide immediate relief to the Hutu refugees, and, second, to settle them in three long-term, organized refugee settlements or camps in different regions of Tanzania.

For the 1985–1986 fieldwork two sites were selected. The first half-year was spent in Mishamo refugee camp in Mpanda District, Rukwa region, in western Tanzania. This is one of the three refugee camps reserved for the Hutu from Burundi. Mishamo is a highly structured agricultural settlement widely considered by refugee agencies to be a "success" (Armstrong 1986a:33–34) and a "prototype of a new generation of refugee settlements" (Armstrong 1987:5) in Africa at large. The infrastructure and other facilities in Mishamo are substantial in relation to other areas of rural Tanzania. The cost of the camp[14] to date is estimated to exceed US $30 million (Armstrong 1987).

Carved out of thick, tse-tse-infested forest by the refugees brought there in 1979, Mishamo is the most recent of the three Hutu camps. It still remains physically quite isolated from any other population in the region. In fact, prior to the creation of Mishamo, this area was inhabited only by small groups of Wabende hunters. The closest town to the south, Mpanda, is a three- to four-hour drive away, while the closest village to the north, Uvinza, lies a two-hour drive away. The refugees, who must have Leave Passes[15] to travel legally beyond the camp, do not have access to reliable motor transportation and often walk great distances. The population of 35,000–36,000 in Mishamo is spatially and socially more isolated than those of the other two camps.[16]

Mishamo spreads over a vast area of 2050 square km, equal to the area of the island of Zanzibar (Armstrong 1986a, 1987). The settled area in the camp consists of 16 villages separated from each other by forested buffer zones. The 16 villages are virtually identical in spatial layout. Every village has a "village center" and a series of numbered five-hectare plots, each of which is assigned to a single household. The villages, the "main roads" connecting them, the "feeder roads" within the villages and the household plots are all numbered. The overall effect of the camp is one of precise order.

An important factor adding to the organizedness of the camp is that each village has been systematically formed as an *ujamaa* village in accordance with Tanzania's Villages Act of 1975 (see Hyden 1980; McHenry 1979; Mwansasu and Pratt 1979:13). Thus, in each village there are the offices of the Village Chairman, Village Secretary, Road Chairman, Ten-cell Leader, and so on. These offices are occupied by refugees who act as intermediaries between the refugees at large and the camp authorities who are government employees and live in the so-called Settlement Headquarters. Individual refugees are elected to office at the village level by the refugee communities themselves, but the election process is closely supervised by the Settlement Commandant. The ultimate authority in the camp is in the hands of the Settlement Commandant. He and his staff administer "rural development," cooperatives, health care, family planning, law enforcement, and other areas.[17] The hierarchical structure of relationships between the refugees and the government staff will figure in more detail below.

The second six months of the fieldwork were spent in and around Kigoma Township on Lake Tanganyika among the "spontaneously settling" Hutu refugees (Armstrong 1986b:41; Tanganyika Christian Refugee Service 1984). They often live in rented quarters interspersed with local citizens, Zairean refugees, and numerous other categories of resident. Many town refugees have intermarried within the nonrefugee population. They practice mostly farming, petty trading, fishing, or some combination of these.

One of the most vivid contrasts between camp and town is that while the camp and its inhabitants were an object of abundant documentation, surveying, and monitoring, the town refugees were not readily accessible to intervention. For the most part, they had no contact with the refugee agencies, governmental or nongovernmental, and tended to circumvent bureaucratic entanglement wherever possible. The inaccessibility of the town refugees was related to the fact that they were largely invisible as a collectivity. They did not compose discrete "communities" of refugees, nor did they tend to define themselves as a distinct collectivity.

The Camp as the Locus of Mythico-Historical Narratives

In virtually all aspects of their contemporary life in the refugee camp, Mishamo refugees made reference to a shared body of knowledge and belief about their past in Burundi. Everyday events, processes, and relationships in the camp were spontaneously interpreted by evoking this collective past as a kind of moral blueprint. The striking preoccupation with renarrating and reconstructing the past seemed to be a universal social fact about life in the camp. The Hutu refugees as a collectivity were intensively and continually engaged in a kind of historical ordering and reordering of their past. This historicity was not a form of specialized knowledge wielded only by the very old or by the political activists in the camp. Nearly everyone was knowledgeable about this history, and capable of adding to it and discussing it in authoritative detail.[18] When asked to talk about their lives, the refugees regularly slipped from the domain of personal life history into the wider field of the collective history. The wider, more collective domain seemed to help them express and interpret facts about their individual lives both in Burundi in the past and at present in the camp. The personal and the collective fused into one dynamic discourse that was recorded from different persons and in varying contexts. The impassioned, even relentless, preoccupation with this particular form of history presented itself as a social fact to be explained.

This historicity of identity and everyday practice was expressed in highly narrative forms, and it is principally on these narrative forms that this analysis is based. A series of dominant, frequently recurring themes began to emerge from the exhaustively detailed historical narratives. As "event history" (cf. Comaroff 1985:17ff.), these substantially corresponded to records of events, processes and relationships published in colonial and postcolonial historical texts on Burundi.[19] This history, however, went far beyond accurate recording. It represented not only a description of the past, nor even merely an evaluation of the past, but a subversive recasting and reinterpretation of it in fundamentally moral, categorical terms. In this sense, it can be described as a "mythico-history," *not* because it is "untrue," but because in it the history of "the Hutu" and their status as a distinct "People" were heroized and placed within a more encompassing moral ordering of the world. The mythico-history is most fundamentally concerned with the reconstitution of a *moral, categorical order* of the world. It seizes upon historical events, processes, and relationships, and reinterprets them within a highly moral scheme of good and evil. In this grand, metahistorical narrative, the historical actors are categorical. The Hutu and the Tutsi—the minority ethnic group in power in Burundi—are the two principal categories locked in an oppositional, agonistic relationship with each other.

One of the most surprising and unexpected aspects of these narratives was their degree of standardization. Both the mythico-historical narratives of the past in Burundi and the mythico-history of the present in the camp tended to undergo standardization into thematically comparable and interrelated forms. This was particularly visible with regard to events that occurred in the camp during fieldwork. That is, certain events became subject to a standardizing telling and retelling and, in the process, became inserted into the more overarching mythico-historical ordering processes. These events became transformed into mythico-historical events. The fragments of narratives presented below are such "standard versions," and were told by many informants in substantially the same form.[20]

The following account begins with some reflections on the construction of the history as a collective discursive practice and suggests how it has a mythico-historical structure. It then maps out some of the ways in which this mythico-historical discourse was put to use by the refugees in interpreting their life in the refugee camp, and how the mythico-history served as a blueprint for acting in the present. Finally, it is suggested that the structure of everyday life and the exigencies of the present as lived in the camp helped to promote or give form to the mythico-history that was in the process of production. In other words, a three-tiered process will be described—or rather, a larger process that can be interpreted as incorporating three simultaneous processes. Together these three processes represent a transformation that is occurring in the Mishamo refugee camp and is not occurring among other Hutu refugees who live in Kigoma, outside of the spatially and sociopolitically highly structured environment of the camp.

The Mythico-History

It would be impossible to encapsulate in this paper all of the interrelated themes that compose the Hutu mythico-history. Here, the scope of these themes will be preliminarily outlined in synoptic form. It will then be possible to explore in more detail a circumscribed list of some of the paramount themes to illustrate what this collective recasting of a past entails, and what it does.

The mythico-history starts by constructing the "origin" and "foundation" of ancient Burundi as a primordial nation and asserts that the Hutu, through their ancestral links with the Twa "pygmies," are the aboriginal first people of the nation. The aboriginal nation is defined as a pristine, just social order. The narratives then document the arrival of the "pastoral," "Nilotic"[21] Tutsi "from the North" a "mere" 400 years ago, and chart the Tutsis' seizure of power from the autochthons by deception and trickery.[22] The egalitarian, primordial social order is thus corrupted and hierarchized, and the autochthons are transformed from "human beings" into "servants" of the Tutsi.[23] The narratives emphasize that before the arrival of the Tutsi, the Hutu were not Hutu at all. They were *abantu*, a word signifying not only the "Bantu peoples" but also "human beings." The name *"hutu,"* the narratives emphasize, is a "Tutsi word" signifying "servant" or "slave." The mythico-history continues into the Belgian colonial period, and casts the category of "the Belgians" as protectors of the Hutu, the underdogs—protectors against the "trickery" of the Tutsi. The postcolonial era is reconstructed as the era following the defeat of the colonialists by the ruse of the Tutsi, and here it is believed that in the absence of the mediating category of "the Belgians," the "evil" or "malign-ness" of the Tutsi was unleashed. It is asserted that the ruling Tutsi had, and still have, a "secret plan" to eliminate all Hutu from Burundi (see Leclercq 1973:13). The culmination of a chapter in the mythico-history was the massacre of untold numbers of Hutu in 1972. This slaughter, along with the techniques of killing, is meticulously described and elaborated in the mythico-history.

But as will become evident below, the moment of exile does not signify the end or closure of the mythico-history. The mythico-historical discourse has no absolute closure. It is open-ended and in perpetual transformation because new elements are being cumulatively inserted or incorporated into it in the sociopolitical present of the refugee camp, and because its earlier themes are put to use in interpreting current everyday practice in the camp. Thus, exile has become the next chapter. Before this mythico-historical construction of the lived-in present in exile can be meaningfully presented, it is necessary to look in greater detail at some central themes in the mythico-historical construction of the past, the past signifying the era prior to flight into Tanzania in 1972.[24]

The first cluster of themes concerning "the past" revolves around the "origin" and "foundation" of Burundi. Here, the question of who were the original, primordial occupants of Burundi is central to the Hutu claim to rightful precedence over the Tutsi and the Hutu peoples' status as the "true members" of the "primordial nation," the "aboriginal homeland." The narratives state:

> It was one hundred years before Jesus Christ that we [the Hutu] came to Burundi. We came from central Africa. . . . We came as hunters, cultivators, and herders. The Batwa ["autochthons"], their work was to hunt quite simply. They knew neither cultivating nor herding. . . . We came as Bantu. We were not Hutu. . . . Our ancestor whose name was Burundi had to leave Katanga in pursuing the hunt with his dogs, and he arrived in Burundi. . . . In his time, the country had no name. . . . After

his hunting expedition, [Burundi] lost his way. He met some Batwa who lived in the place where he had lost his way. He mixed with them. He married the woman of the Batwa. He produced children with her. It was a very big relation between the Bahutu and the Batwa. . . . [He eventually brought his original family from Katanga to the place that is called Burundi today.] He had already had a wife in Katanga. . . . He distributed his family in several regions of the country because the country was good to live in. After his death, his children named the country in the name of their father. That was the first birth of the country of Burundi. There! The Batutsi, when they came in the sixteenth century, they kept the name Burundi because the citizens of Burundi were very numerous, and their language was Kirundi . . . and because they [the Hutu] had mixed with the Twa and spread over the surface of the country. [Malkki 1989:124–125]

The foundation narrative is linked to several other central themes in the mythico-history. The ancestral link to the Twa, who are still the smallest minority in Burundi, is significant because it further bolsters the precedence of the Hutu and Twa as interlinked peoples over the Tutsi, who came much later, "only four centuries ago," and who are a "different race" of people. The Tutsi are thus constituted in the mythico-history as imposters who abused the hospitality offered to them by tricking their way into power, and "stealing" the nation:

What have they stolen from us? First of all, our country. The Tutsi are of Nilotic provenance. They came from Somalia. And then [they stole] that which exists in a country—the livestock, cows, chicken, domestic animals, . . . let us say, the living things—even the birds, the fish, the trees, the banana fields, whatnot. All the wealth of the country, you understand, was ours. Because we were the natives of the country. They came perhaps four or five hundred years ago—that is approximate. . . . There are all the things in the country, X, Y, Z. They stole all that. [Malkki 1989:147]

This introduces the second theme discussed briefly here. There are several narratives showing how the Tutsi, possessed of innate cleverness in the art of deception, *tricked* the original inhabitants of Burundi into servitude by the gift of cows.[25] In this cluster of themes belongs an elaborate story of how the ancestors of the Hutu, in accepting the cows from the Tutsi, were caught in servitude under the Tutsi. The servitude was not only lifelong but extended from generation to generation. This relationship *(ubugabire)* has been described by scholars as a feature of the "traditional" societies in both Burundi and Rwanda.[26] In the mythico-history, the Hutu refugees have radically "denaturalized" and "decanonized" this relationship by stating that this was one of the first in a long series of tricks that the Tutsi deployed in order to gain power (cf. Lemarchand 1970:9). They are thus stripping this relationship of the legitimacy of "tradition" by locating its foundations in ill-gotten power. This is just one of the many themes which together constitute a commentary on the hierarchical inequality in Burundi. In the dominant "Tutsi versions" of Burundi's history, which are also shared by some colonial historians of the country, the asymmetrical social structure is taken as an organic order.[27] A central dynamic of the mythico-history is the deconstruction and denaturalization of this hierarchy. In the mythico-history, there is a transformation from *homo hierarchicus* to *homo aequalis*. This is also tellingly expressed in the refugees' comment that before the Tutsi came, the Hutu were not Hutu at all; they were simply *abantu* which, as mentioned earlier, is interpreted by the refugees as meaning "the Bantu peoples" or simply, "human beings." The name Hutu, they say, was imported by the Tutsi from their home "in the North" and means "slave" or "servant." Thus, "we became their Hutu" is equivalent to "we became their slaves."

The subversion of the natural "caste" hierarchy[28] is also embedded in the third and last theme described here, because this last theme, perhaps more than any other, expresses how the categorical negation of the humanity of the Tutsi occurs. The Tutsi category here becomes the embodiment of evil, the "strange" and "foreign" element in the moral community being narratively created in the mythico-history. They are "the other" irrevocably and necessarily pitched in opposition to the "self," the Hutu. The Tutsi at this point are not only "other," but "enemy." This last theme centers around the significance of racial and physical differences between "self"/Hutu and "other"/Tutsi. In the camp, precise and lengthy descriptions of physical differences between Hutu and Tutsi abounded. It was clearly important that this difference be prescribed as categorically unambiguous. These meticulously crafted maps of physical difference were superimposed in the mythico-history with analogous maps of innate moral character differences between Hutu and Tutsi. In their broad outlines, these two kinds of maps reproduce many of the descriptions of Hutu and Tutsi found in historical records of the colonial period (cf. Menard, cited in Gahama 1983:275ff.); the Tutsi are supposed to be the tall, stately, thin people, and the Hutu the short, stockier peasants.[29] The mythico-history provides a grotesquely elaborated replay of these highly conventionalized and stereotyped distinctions. Color of tongue and gums, size of pupils, prominence of ankle bones, protrusion of calves, lines on the palm of the hand are all markers of difference. These markers are superimposed on moral and social difference.

> [The] Tutsi are taller generally, . . . at the same time, thinner . . . they are of a beautiful stature. They cannot do painful chores, for example,

constructing houses in brick, in wood. . . . Their hair is not kinky, their eyes are a little round . . . also, their noses are more or less long. . . . They are real drinkers of no matter what drink. . . . The Hutu: This is a vigorous man, being long or short. He likes to work very much—painful jobs are play for him. . . . The Tutsi did not know how to cultivate—up until today they have not learned. . . . The Tutsi are tall and light of build, and they are incapable of strenuous physical labour. They also have an aversion to hard work because they are lazy, and wish only to engage in the secret art of statecraft, "administration," and chiefly duties. The whites of the Tutsis' eyes are whiter because they do not bend over hot, smokey fires.[30] [Malkki 1989:165–166]

In such body maps are inscribed not only assertions of "racial difference" but of political and social inequality. These body maps are also put to other uses in the mythico-history: According to the refugees, these physical markers served as clues during the 1972 massacre as to who was Hutu and who Tutsi, and, thereby, who would be killed. The differences therefore signaled the difference between life and death.

The body maps described here are articulated with another set of very physical maps, maps charting the techniques of mutilating and killing used in the massacre. These maps for destroying the body were taken as diagnostic signs or "symptoms" of political efforts by the Tutsi to render the Hutu powerless, or impotent. For example, piercing the brain by penetrating a sharpened bamboo stick into it through the anus is taken as a humiliation of the intellect, and as a squashing of the Hutus' efforts to gain higher education. Similarly, the disemboweling of pregnant Hutu women is interpreted as an effort to destroy the reproductive capability, "the new life," of the Hutu as a people.

These maps were systematically elaborated with careful detail, and occupied a central role in the mythico-historical narratives. Their significance appeared to be multifold. On the one hand, the accounting of details seems to be a means of asserting the veracity of events that informants had experienced, witnessed, or heard about retrospectively. On the other hand, these narratives served to further negate the very humanity of the Tutsi category, and to constitute this category as essentially evil.

The physical and moral difference between the Hutu and the Tutsi that is constructed and encoded in the body maps also reinforces a theme already mentioned. By emphasizing this difference, the mythico-history reinforces the point that Burundi as it is today is *not* and never can be a single harmonious nation and that the ruling Tutsi are the foreign, discordant, evil element in it. They are "the impostors from the North." Thus, Burundi—although it may be a political entity—is not a *"true nation,"* not a moral community. The enemy of the "authentic" nation of Burundi, then, is the category of "the Tutsi."

One further point should be made about the massacre as a major theme in the mythico-history: The massacre is interpreted as an attempt by the Tutsi to eliminate the Hutu, or at least to equalize the population on a statistical scale. All informants in Mishamo were able to recite the statistical configuration of Burundi: the Tutsi are 14%, the Hutu 85%, and the Twa, 1%.[31] The Tutsi, they say, tried to change these numbers by killing as many Hutu as possible. This, it is claimed, has been the Tutsis' secret goal all along, but it is only the massacre that brings the ultimate illumination of these secrets.[32]

The Uses of History in the Refugee Camp: Living in the Present in Historical Terms

This section outlines the way in which the mythico-history of the past was put to use in Mishamo camp, and how transformations in historical consciousness were intimately articulated with, and even produced by, the everyday life of the camp. This articulation seemed to have two aspects. First, the mythico-history of the past served as a political ideology for the present. It served as a means of interpreting in historical and meaningful ways the relationships that were being lived in Mishamo. It therefore structured social action in very concrete ways, as the following will attempt to demonstrate. But there was also a second level of articulation between past and present: The present experiential world of the camp, in turn, served to objectify and constitute the mythico-history. That is, experiences in the camp were inserted cumulatively into the mythico-history, and these experiences also clarified further aspects of the refugees' past in Burundi. Certain key events in the camp were seen as analogous to events that had occurred in Burundi, and the perception of this analogy seemed to help in interpreting both ends of the historical spectrum in a meaningful way. Here, the analysis of the ways in which the past and the present reflexively constituted each other in the mythico-history in the camp must rely on a limited number of examples.

Certain distinctive features of the Mishamo refugee camp were constitutive of it as a technology of power (Foucault 1979). These include the particular structure of formal authority in the camp, the spatial isolation and concentration of the refugees in it, the organization of the refugee villages into *ujamaa* villages, the restriction of mobility by roadside check points and Leave Passes, the organization and control of production, refugee registration and identification, the absence of possibilities for secondary education in the camp, and the formal definition of what a "refugee" should and should not be.

Here, particular attention will be given to four of these constitutive features: first, the constitution of the figure of the refugee by the international and government agencies involved, and the uses to which the refugee status was put by the refugees themselves; second, the refugees' conception of the camp authorities; third, the organization and control over the refugees' agricultural production; and, finally, the blockage to higher education in Mishamo.

The first theme centers on the struggle over what it means to be a refugee. The figure of the "refugee" is a distinct marked category in the discourse of the international refugee agencies and governments concerned with refugees as their principal object of knowledge and practice. In this discourse, a "refugee" is nearly always cast as an object of technico-practical problem solving that is a systematically synchronic, ahistorical operation. The refugees' past, containing the events that made them refugees in the first instance, is avoided because it is intrinsically political. In order for the technical problem solving to function, it seems necessary to obliterate history from the figure of the refugee. National governments concerned with refugees require the same for reasons of their own—such as "national security," "law and order" and agricultural productivity. Much of the discourse of "humanitarian concern" shares in this dehistoricizing, depoliticizing discourse.[33] In order to understand more fully the implications of "living historically" as a refugee, it is important to keep in mind this dehistoricizing operation. In this context, historicity is an act of defiance in the camp. Talking publicly about history, about relations with the Tutsi in Burundi or about the possibilities of regaining "the Homeland" was interpreted as dangerous and undesirable, a sign of trouble, by the camp authorities.

For the Hutu refugees themselves, the official status of refugee has become incorporated into the mythico-history as an integral part of their transformation from natural servants (cf. Leclercq 1973:11–12) of the Tutsi into categorical enemies of the Tutsi. By becoming refugees, they have been ejected from the concretely lived asymmetric relationship with the Tutsi, and they now stand outside the hierarchy in the antagonistic separateness of exile as enemies and as equals. Yet, at the same time, the Hutu now find themselves in another set of hierarchical relationships in the refugee camp with the Tanzanian camp authorities. By insisting on their official status as refugees, the Hutu are thus resisting incorporation and asserting that their exile in Tanzania is only temporary. The following narrative can be seen as a re-

Context and Consciousness 45

fusal to become incorporated and "naturalized" into yet another hierarchy.

> They try to make us immigrants quite simply. We cultivate, we are taxed, like immigrants. They get a lot of benefit and money from us. Yes, they want us to be "integrated" because we are beneficial to them. But this is only on the economic level, not otherwise. . . . We do not *want* citizenship. And neither do we want to be immigrants. . . . As refugees we have at least some rights. We will wait and then we will return to our home country. [Malkki 1989:358–359; emphasis in original]

Similar themes are evident in the next narrative fragment, which further underscores the significance of refugee-ness as a historical condition defining the Hutu, and as an official status that protects their liminality in exile.

> And further, [the Tanzanians] invite us to nationalize ourselves. We *refuse! Yes!* With this really . . . tsk! tsk! . . . they are not happy. They want us to stay as their slaves like. . . . Have we come here uniquely to have ourselves nationalized?! Did we not have our own country? The best that we have now, it is that we are still in the hand of . . . [the] U.N. . . . But once we accept the nationality of here, we will be like what? One will oblige us like one obliges their dogs and cats, or no matter what domestic animal. [Malkki 1989:359–360; emphasis in original]

Narratives such as those above suggest that actions in exile were considered to be intimately related to the affirmation and maintenance of a symbolic link to the "Homeland." Being a refugee signals the possibility of an ultimate, if distant, return to a new Burundi. Thus, the resistance to "putting down roots" in exile is a part of what exile is all about, and it is central to the refugees' formation of a collective identity based on the past and the "Homeland" conceived as the imagined aboriginal nation that existed prior to the arrival of the Tutsi. Finally, being a refugee means being categorically "pure," and maintaining essential boundaries between "self" and "other"—be the "other" the Tutsi or the Tanzanian category. In this context, the refugees frequently employed biblical themes to indicate the moral and symbolic significance of being refugees in exile. They evoked, for example, the story of how the Jews wandered in the desert for 40 years in search of the Promised Land. One person said: "Even Jesus was a refugee in Egypt. When his enemy, Herod, died, he came back. Herod was pursuing him. Then, when Herod died, Jesus did not stay in Egypt. He returned to his country. We are Hutu, natives of Burundi. We will never be natives of Tanzania, never" (Malkki 1989:384). Another person showed his listeners an article on the Israeli airlift of the Falashas from Ethiopia in a much-read issue of the magazine, *Africa*

(1985:164:25–27), saying: "Look, the Ethiopian Jews were refugees for who knows how long—hundreds of years! Now they have finally returned to the country of their ancestors. They were 'airlifted'; the Jews of Israel arranged it" (Malkki 1989:384).

The refugees see their own exile as an analogous period. Their exile is also interpreted as a kind of diaspora. The trials and tribulations of exile or diaspora are constituted in the mythico-history as a test of virtue and strength that the Hutu as a "People" have to endure in order to become truly worthy of regaining the aboriginal "Homeland." Through processes and relations explored elsewhere (Malkki 1989), the refugee camp has become the locus of this ideological and moral purity.

Ironically, although these linkages between exile and "Homeland," liminality and purity, refugee-ness and antagonistic equality were seen as troublesome and dangerous by the camp authorities, they were in large measure enabled by the camp itself. The physical demarcation and objectification produced by the camp helped to transform its inhabitants into "the refugees" as a collective body, a categorical "we" standing apart from "others." As will become apparent, this objectifying transformation did not define the social setting of the town refugees in Kigoma.

The second contemporary theme discussed involves the structuring of the relationship between the camp authorities in Mishamo and the refugees as two distinct and hierarchically nested categories. As was already mentioned, the past provides the model for current relationships between the refugees and the Tanzanians and the Tanzanian state. The Tanzanian camp authorities who have such palpable power over the lives of the refugees are frequently said to be like the Tutsi, to be "tutsianized" and "malign." (See below.) Here, two key events, which became "standard versions" expressing something about the relationships between the refugees and the camp authorities, will be outlined.

The first of these "standard versions" can be entitled "The Beating of the Bride." Every year, the camp authorities together with District authorities from Mpanda circulate in the camp collecting a "Development Levy" *(kodi ya maendeleo)*. This is a nationwide levy of 200 Tanzanian shillings, which at the time of fieldwork was about a quarter of a month's minimum wage, or US $11. The refugees saw the levy as a form of taxation and claimed that by international law, refugees are not required to pay taxes. (They misinterpreted the law here; it only says that refugees cannot be taxed beyond what citizens are taxed. In any case, this was what the refugees acted on.) Many of them were also unable to pay this per-head tax, which applied to everyone of 18 and over. In this particular year, 1986, the District authorities brought with them armed soldiers to enforce payment of the levy. Many refugees hid in their houses, in the forests and on river banks for several weeks in order to escape payment. During this time, a young woman coming from a celebration with her fiancé was struck with a rifle butt because she was unable to exhibit proof of payment immediately. This story caught everyone's attention and became what has here been called a "standard version." It was incorporated into the mythico-history and mapped onto key events of violence and atrocity between the Hutu and the Tutsi in Burundi.

The second "standard version" was generated by a tour of the District Commissioner in all 16 villages in the camp. His message in each village was that the refugees should cultivate more industriously and that they should abandon hopes of returning to Burundi to make a revolution. The contents of the District Commissioner's speech became standardized, and were taken as symptomatic of an alliance between these authorities and the Tutsi-dominated government in Burundi. The refugees said that "They [the Tutsi] have sold us to the Tanzanians" and further, that the Tanzanian authorities like the Tutsi do not want "us Hutu to be political—they just want us to work and them to do politics." The main point to be drawn here from these "standard versions" is that the Hutu-Tutsi relationship served as a model for current relationships with the "others," with the camp authorities, in the camp. In the camp, the Hutu refugees did live in a hierarchical and in many ways oppressive setting, and it is perhaps not surprising that the categories of "the Tutsi" and "the Tanzanians" should often be conflated in the mythico-historical narratives. In the course of everyday conversations, the meaning of "they" shifted between the two categories of oppositional "other," between the "past" and the "present."

The foregoing themes suggest the next theme to be mentioned, that is, the refugees' perception of the organization of agricultural production in the camp. Mishamo has been used by the Tanzanian government as a kind of "pioneering settlement," established to domesticate formerly unproductive regions of western Tanzania, and the refugees are very aware of their role in this process.[34] They frequently make the claim that without them, international agencies would not have invested millions of dollars into developing this area which now, according to the refugees' conception, is one of the most productive in Tanzania. A part of the evolving mythico-history concerns the heroization of the Hutu as cultivators and as hard workers, in distinction to the Tutsi who—as was said earlier—are characterized as somehow innately lazy and incapable of strenuous physical labor. The refugees often said, talking both about the past and the present: "They eat a lot, we cultivate a lot."

> And we left Burundi for this? Nothing has changed. In our native country, we were 85% of the population, we the Hutu. The Tutsi were 14%, and the Twa, 1%. The Twa are more or less like the Hutu. In Burundi, it is we who are the cultivators. It is the Hutu who cultivate the coffee, the tea, the cotton, the palm oil, . . . All this is exported and foreign exchange is received. That is to say that the Tutsi, the minority, receive it. They, they do not cultivate. . . . So, we cultivate for the whole country. And here, what is different? We are granaries of the Tanzanians. If we have a sack of beans, we cannot sell it to our friend. The government says to us that it is to be sold at two and a half [shillings] to the cooperative shop of the village. Same with the maize. Then the trucks of the NMC come to buy them. . . . We are the granaries of the Tanzanians. . . . We are qualified workers, and they know it. They are savage. They are tutsianized. . . . They do not want us to leave their country. We cultivate a lot, they eat a lot. [Malkki 1989:219–220]

Here, the term "they" merges Tutsi and Tanzanian, making them into categories that stand in opposition to the Hutu, and fusing past and present. The themes of parasitism and the sapping of labor power were a domain in which the two categories of "other" became virtually interchangeable.

The last mythico-historical theme here centers upon the perceived blockage of the Hutu from higher education. Each village in Mishamo has a primary school, but there is no secondary school, and UNHCR or government stipends for study elsewhere, are very few. According to some estimates, only 1–2% of the refugees are able to get any kind of training beyond the primary level.[35] Informants frequently said that when they do manage to obtain training outside the camp, it is "always for becoming a mechanic, or a carpenter." The following narrative makes a direct analogy to the past in Burundi.

> There were two categories of school—one for the children of the Tutsi chiefs, another for the Hutu children. The Hutu were taught, were prepared for agriculture, and the Tutsi are prepared to govern. . . . The Tanzanians also have schools for themselves where they learn—how is it called?—the social rights—for example, the politics of the country. For the Hutu, it is the *métiers* like mechanics, construction, and carpentry. These are their chosen schools for us, the technical schools. [Malkki 1989:241]

Echoing common sentiments, one person asked: "What if I wanted to study philosophy?" Education and intellectual achievement are very highly valued by the Hutu refugees in the camp. They see the situation in the camp as a kind of replay of the situation in Burundi where the study of the higher arts of statecraft and administration, politics and philosophy, were the domain of the Tutsi elite. The refugees interpret both cases as a secret plan to keep them working hard as peasants, to distance them from politics and administration.

These themes have been schematically laid out here in order to suggest how the refugees' past provides a model for current relations in the camp and a vehicle for meaningfully interpreting and acting upon events of the present, and how, in turn, key events of the present are transformed into mythico-historical events. These articulations underscore not only the "present" being lived in the camp and in exile, but also, the continual transformative elaboration of the "past" in Burundi. Neither "past" nor "present" are simply stable, structurally fixed models shaping social action; rather, they are generated in everyday practice, and are therefore more accurately described in deeply processual terms.

The Town Refugees: Assimilation as Loss of Categorical Purity

As suggested above, it is the camp that has become the privileged locus for the mythico-historical construction and subversion of categorical orders, and for the heroization of the national, categorical history of the Hutu as a "people." It might be expected that the Hutu refugees in town would produce mythico-historical narratives similar to those produced in the camp, since they had also lived in Burundi and experienced the massacres that led to their flight. This was not the case, however. This difference between camp and town must be explored, and not least because it is central in trying to arrive at a contextual understanding of the mythico-historical ordering processes of the camp. This short section does not do justice to the complexity and dynamism of the different, rival constructions found among the town refugees.[36] It serves mainly to show that conditions in the refugee camp provide a favorable setting for the production of the mythico-history, whereas the Kigoma town setting does not.

The relationship between camp and town is not simply one of analytic comparison, but also one of opposition as defined by the refugees themselves. Condensing for the sake of clarity, it may be said that the town refugees represent for the camp refugees an "enemy from within," a dangerously irresponsible group consumed by mundane and trivial preoccupations such as wealth, pleasure and comfort. They are on several levels outside the mythico-historical locus of moral and ideological purity. The assimilation of the Kigoma refugees into Tanzanian social life in an individualistic way is regarded in the camp as a loss of purity, or a loss of virtue, which endangers the goal of ultimate return to the "Homeland." The relationship between these two groups of Hutu refugees is thus animated by opposition, but this opposition is an asymmetrical one. For, while the "town refugees" are an important categorical actor in the mythico-history of the camp, the "camp refugees" are not an equally pivotal, preoccupying figure in the daily lives and conversations of the town refugees.

The linkage of the Kigoma refugees to impurity occurs through specific or concrete accusations of "pollution" such as prostitution, drunkenness, vagrancy, laziness, avoidance of hard work in the fields, petty theft and, more seriously, smuggling ivory to Burundi, to the enemy, and finally,—most dangerously of all—acting as paid informers of the Tutsi government in Burundi. All of these accusations, varying in gravity, are at some level linked with the dangers of assimilating into the "Other," and in this case, the wider Tanzanian society—in other words, the dangers implied in the "mixing of categories." From the vantage point of the camp, the Kigoma refugees are not only mixing with the Tanzanian category, but also with the Tutsi, the categorical enemy.

The town refugees are also considered to shame themselves by "hiding their identity," by pretending not to be "Hutu" or "Refugee," but choosing, rather, to manipulate their identities in such a way as to allow their social and economic advancement in the wider society and, importantly, to safeguard themselves against the stigma and uncertainties of publicly acknowledged, collective refugee status. In the camp—where virtually every person is by definition a refugee—refugee status is valued as an indicator of purity in the overarching symbolic and political order being constructed and expressed in the mythico-history. And there, as was suggested earlier, refugee status is put to positive uses.

From the point of view of Kigoma, however, the camp-town relationship looks radically different. The camp is for them an ever-present spectre of the loss of freedom and mobility. The Kigoma town refugees expressed fears that they, too, might one day be transported into a camp and subjected to its rigours and isolation. The camp signals undesirable forms of control not only from the camp authorities, but also from the camp refugees, who are seen by many in town as somewhat naïve and moralistic in their categorical worldview.

For ethnic, linguistic, and historical reasons, it has been relatively easy for the Kigoma refugees to blend in with the local population of the town and its surroundings.[37] The refugees there have made use of this fact and have assimilated to such a degree that they are not a discrete, marked category and, therefore, not accessible to formal interventions—such as refugee registration and control of mobility—as are the refugees concentrated in camps. In contrast to the self-definition of those in the camp as "Hutu" and as "refugees," the Kigoma refugees managed a series of different identities. Some claimed immigrant status, others said they were Waha (the main ethnic group of the Kigoma area) and hence Tanzania citizens, and yet others staked a claim to citizenship through religion. One informant, for example, confided:

> I do not like the name "refugee," particularly here in town. That is why I have even changed my name. If you ask for me by my Christian name [Albert] here, they will say that they do not know him. For now my name is Hamisi. This name, I like it, but that is not to say that I am a Muslim; it is only a fashion of living. I go to mosque often. If I do not go, it might become known that I am a liar. [Malkki 1989:308]

In Hamisi's case, being Muslim served as an indicator of citizenship.[38] Another person explained: "I do not like to be called a 'refugee.' That word, 'refugee,' I *detest* it. But also, I do not want to be a Tanzanian citizen. I like that one should call me a 'Murundi Tanzanian citizen' " (Malkki 1989:302).

Hence, while in Mishamo identity was heroized, in Kigoma it was subject to intensive management. Moreover, when the Kigoma refugees *did* talk about themselves as a distinct collectivity, it was not usually in the ethnic terms of "we the Hutu" but, rather, in the conventionally national terms of "we the Burundians." This flexible, pragmatic management of identities corresponded to a significant contrast with the Mishamo refugees with regard to the valuation of the mythico-historical national identity as described earlier, and through it, the collective identity as a "People." The role of history as an interpretive device, as an ideology for the present, appeared to be nearly irrelevant in Kigoma. This has at least in part to do with the fact that in Kigoma, relations with "others" are not so systematically nested in a hierarchy as they are in the camp, or as they were in Burundi. Thus, in the life of the town refugees, a concrete transformation from hierarchy as a hegemonic, organic order to relative equality in Kigoma has occurred. It is ironic that this transformation is not elaborated by them, as it is by the camp refugees for whom such a complete transformation has not occurred. For, as indicated above, the relations between the Mishamo refugees and the camp authorities are hierarchical and interpreted by the refugees as such. Hence, the refusal of any kind of incorporation. It seems, then, that a degree of experiential, lived equality in Kigoma renders irrelevant the continual ideological challenge to asymmetry that is so evident in Mishamo.

For these and other reasons, therefore, the connection to the past is not as essential to the Kigoma refugees, and the dynamic elaboration of historical consciousness that is going on in Mishamo is not happening among them. They are much more firmly rooted in the present, and there is considerable individual debate over whether a return to Burundi will ever be possible or, indeed, desirable.

Conversations and debates about these and other issues revealed that "past" and "present" were defined very differently in camp and town. In the former, the past was located in Burundi and the present in exile. For those in town, the years spent in Tanzania since 1972 were not a perpetual "present," but already a historical trajectory in its own right. People very readily described the "early days" and the initial difficulties of their life in Tanzania, and contrasted these to their current, more settled and successful circumstances. Chronicles of individual trajectories, of hard work and vagaries of fortune, were very popular and can perhaps be likened to "Horatio Alger-stories."

These vivid differences between camp and town suggest that for the town refugees, living in Tanzania was not necessarily being "in exile" at all. In the camp, exile was meaningful as a liminal condition, a temporary trial ultimately culminating in the return of the "nation" to the "homeland." The very condition of exile was linked to a "there-ness" (Said 1986:28). In town, by contrast, proscriptions against "putting down roots" on "foreign soil" were not as powerful.

In sum, it seems accurate to characterize the town context as one where the categorical orders of the camp were irrelevant. The mythico-historical categories of the "Hutu people" opposed to "others" were routinely transgressed, challenged, mixed, and ultimately dissolved into a noncategorical, cosmopolitan practice. This dynamic cosmopolitanism was particularly often expressed in discussions about lovers and marriage. Choice of partners was explained not in terms of categorical prohibitions but, rather, other considerations such as "beauty," "God's will," "love," "comportment," "disease" and "luck." One man who had "had two fiancées, one citizen and another Hutu," explained:

> If truth be told, I loved them both, and it was difficult to choose one and leave the other. But, as in our Christian religion it is prohibited to be a polygamist (to have more than one wife), I decided to marry with the citizen because it seemed to me that she loved me more than the second one. For this I can say that it is love quite simply. [Malkki 1989:324]

Others explained that they had married "with citizens" for reasons of "security." Intermarriage was a form becoming a *"de facto* citizen" without being obliged to apply for official, legal "naturalization." In discussions of marriage, as in the other domains mentioned, it was evident that categorical purity, as defined in the mythico-history, was not a meaningful principle in town.

The camp refugees' narratives manifested a vivid understanding of these differences between themselves and the town refugees. Those in camp frequently said that they would prefer all Hutu refugees in towns and outside of camps to be transported into camps. Once within the camp, the town refugees, too, would perhaps be incorporated into the moral community that is in the process of construction there.

Conclusion

Some of the themes outlined here may already suggest why this process of historical reconstruction and innovation in the camp is appropriately termed "mythico-historical." The Hutu refugees' collective narrative is similar to myth in that it is concerned with order in a very fundamental sense. It is concerned with the ordering and reordering of social and political categories, with the defining of self in distinction to other, with evil and good. It is most centrally concerned with the reconstitution of a *moral* order of the world. It seizes historical events, processes, and relationships, and reinterprets them within a moral scheme of good and evil. It would be missing its significance if we tried to make an essentialist evaluation of the extent to which the themes and ideas of the mythico-history are "true" or "distorted" representations of reality, fact or fiction, scientific or fantastical (Comaroff 1985:4; Comaroff and Comaroff 1987:193). Mythico-history, like myth, is a system of communication, a mode of signification (Barthes 1972). But it is the difference between myth and mythico-history that is most interesting here. Barthes, for example, characterizes myth as follows:

> What the world supplies to myth is an historical reality . . . and what myth gives in return is a *natural* image of this reality. . . . Myth is constituted by the loss of the historical quality of things: in it, things lose the memory that they were once made. . . . A conjuring trick has taken place; it has turned reality inside out, it has emptied it of history and has filled it with nature, it has removed from things their human meaning so as to make them signify a human insignificance. [Barthes 1972:142; emphasis in original]

But the reverse is happening in the processes just described. The refugees' mythico-history seizes upon the exigencies of the past (and the present) and objectifies them, makes them strange and *unnatural*.

For example, the hierarchy of Burundi and the asymmetric relationship between the Hutu and the Tutsi is denaturalized and historicized, and its status as a "traditional," organic order is taken apart by the insertion of particular historical events and relationships. Thus, the mythico-history creates new, meaningful connections and significations between things where they did not exist before, while at the same time "making strange" relations that were formerly natural.

Another aspect of Barthes's conception of myth is also inverted in the case of the mythico-history. Barthes writes:

> Men do not have with myth a relationship based on truth but on use: they de-politicize according to their needs. [1972:144]

The refugees *do* in fact have with their mythico-history a relationship based on use. But they do not *depoliticize; they politicize according to their needs*. Thus, while *myth,* as Barthes defines it, depoliticizes by naturalizing, the mythico-history politicizes by denaturalizing. The mythico-historical discursive practice in which the refugees are so impassionedly involved, politicizes their past in Burundi and their present in the refugee camp. The mythico-history is an expression of transformations in a politicized historical consciousness. The past as constituted in the mythico-history serves as a political ideology for the present, while the lived-in present provokes the past into narration, transforming it in the process. In this sense, both past and present are mythico-historical, and both are in continual transformation.

One of the central conclusions that can be drawn from the case presented here is that nationality and history are produced and elaborated where particular conjunctures of processes and relations, specific local contingencies and events in everyday practice, render them meaningful. In other words, collective histories flourish where they have a meaningful, signifying use in the present, as they do in the camp. In contrast to the evolutionary view of historical consciousness as a capability typifying a particular stage of development, it is being argued here that actors produce historical consciousness in the thick of everyday life (cf. Appadurai 1983; Comaroff 1985; Comaroff and Comaroff 1987; Lan 1985; Rosaldo 1980).

Further, it has been argued that the construction of the mythico-historical discourse, which is an integral part of the production of historical consciousness in the camp technology, is inextricably tied to the constitution of an imagined moral community, an aboriginal and therefore "authentic" nation (cf. Anderson 1983). Nation-ness as a form of consciousness creates a single figure with historicizing forms of consciousness and historicity of identity.

Anderson (1983), Handler (1988), Hobsbawn and Ranger (1983), Nairn (1977), Wright (1985) and others have demonstrated how national traditions come to be invented by states, and how these traditions serve to legitimate and idealize, or heroize, the state apparatus, or statehood.[39] The case of the Hutu refugees is different in that the creation of a "national tradition"—indeed, of a nation-ness—is happening in the absence of a corresponding state apparatus and territorial base.[40] The Hutu mythico-history is in the process of constructing an alternative nation-ness that challenges the state. It directly challenges the politico-moral legitimacy of the contemporary state of Burundi and, in a different way, it also challenges the Tanzanian state by generating issues of "national security" and "international relations" between Tanzania and Burundi. In a wider context still, the mythico-historical, categorical construction of the Hutu as a "People" being "born" in and through exile signals the production of a nation-ness in the interstices of the contemporary order of "nation-states." At this level, Hutu nation-ness also presents an analytical challenge to those theories of nationalism that posit a one-to-one correspondence between nation and state (and national territory), as Giddens (1987:116, 119) seems to do, for example.[41]

It is not an accident that these issues should have emerged as central in fieldwork among refugees. It is precisely their interstitiality and liminality in the contemporary order of nation-states that pushes issues of nationality and national identity to the forefront among refugees. For refugees, as for stateless and other "displaced" categories of people, nation-ness is problematized (cf. Abu-Lughod 1971; Arendt 1973[1951]:294, 297, 300; Said 1986).

Exploring the conditions and effects of the liminality of refugees in the classificatory order of national "units" opens up ways of studying nation-ness that are at once new and classically anthropological. Most studies of nations and nationalism imply an "ideal" or "normal" state of affairs where the sovereign territory, the state and the nation become complementary principles, united in the single figure of the nation-state. Studying nation-ness as a situational form of categorical consciousness necessitates the analytical subversion of these complementary units as a natural order of things.[42]

Notes

Acknowledgments. Many friends and colleagues have contributed careful readings and valuable comments to earlier versions of this paper. I would like to thank, in particular, Jim Ferguson, Sally Falk Moore, Jean and John Comaroff, Stanley J. Tambiah, F.M. Rodegem, Olli Alho, George Bisharat, Nur Yalman, Charles Lindholm, Jennifer Robertson, and John Borneman.

1. The present paper is a subsection of a larger study (Malkki 1989) in which fuller historical and ethnographic documentation can be located.

2. One year of fieldwork, from October 1985 to October 1986, was funded by a research grant from the Council for the Humanities, Academy of Finland.

3. An attempted Hutu uprising in April of 1972 was squashed by government forces and, within a few weeks, government "reprisals" for the failed uprising became systematic, genocidal killing (Lemarchand and Martin 1974; Melady 1974:15; Weinstein 1976:xi). The death toll has been impossible to fix. Estimates vary between 80,000 and 250,000 (Chomsky and Herman 1979:109; Kay 1987; Kuper 1982:164; Lemarchand and Martin 1974:5). Lemarchand and Martin (1974:15) have characterized the massacres as "selective genocide" because they targeted "all the educated or semieducated strata of Hutu society." See also Chomsky and Herman (1979:106); Greenland (1973:443–451); Kuper (1982:163); Weinstein (1976). The events of 1972 have been difficult to document reliably. A part of the difficulty in writing about these massacres appears to be that neocolonialist discourse readily appropriates them as a manifestation of "the old African problem of tribalism," as opposed to recognizing them as a product of stark inequalities of power and elaborate domination.

4. This essay, concerned with national and historical consciousness, gives a dominant role to the camp refugees in favor of the town refugees because it was among the former that nation-ness was a crucial issue. This is not to imply an "absence" of transformations of consciousness among the town refugees.

5. The hegemonic quality of national thinking is evident not only in "folk" categories and nationalist ideologies, but also in theories of nations and nationalism, as Handler (1988), for example, argues. See also Anderson (1983); Hobsbawm (1983); Sollors (1989).

6. Compare Arendt (1973[1951]:285): "statelessness spread like a contagious disease."

7. Compare Turner (1967:98) who notes that those classified as liminal ("neophytes" in his example) are "ritually polluting" and "commonly secluded, partially or completely, from the realm of culturally defined and ordered states and statuses." The spatial "seclusion" and collecting of refugees into camps is a comparable practice. Refugees are a "betwixt and between" category in the cultural order of nation-nesses perceived as discrete, bounded "units."

8. See, for example, Kismaric (1989) on "the refugee."

9. Malkki (1985); and compare Marrus (1985). See also Arendt (1973[1951]:284).

10. Foucault's exploration of the prison as a "technology of power" (1979) might be compared to van Onselen's (1976) careful study of the "compound system" on the mines of colonial Southern Rhodesia, and also to Goffman's work on "total institutions" (1961a,b). These possible analogies to the refugee camp as a "technology of power" have been discussed elsewhere (Malkki 1985, 1989).

11. To insist on defining the Hutu refugees as "merely" an ethnic group would not only reject the camp refugees' self-definition; it would also force a shift of the whole focus of study from exile back within the boundaries of the internationally "recognizable" nation-state, Burundi. This study, however, is located entirely in the observed processes in exile, not in Burundi. In this context, it should also be noted that while this project is intimately concerned with the history of Burundi through the historicizing narratives of the Hutu refugees, it cannot claim to stand as a contribution to the historiography of Burundi. It concerns historicity as a contemporary phenomenon in the present.

12. Anderson (1983:15) has suggested that the term "nation" defines an "imagined political community." It can be added without contradiction that when a group like the Hutu refugees in question form a collective sense of themselves as a "People" they are also creating a specifically and primarily "moral community."

13. Estimates of the death toll vary. See note 3.

14. The organizations involved referred to Mishamo as a "settlement," but the refugees called it a "camp." The two terms are used interchangeably here.

15. Leave Passes are valid for 14 days.

16. Population estimates vary. See Armstrong (1987).

17. Mishamo was "handed over" to the Government of Tanzania in August of 1985, at which time the direct role of the UNCHR and TCRS in the project came to a virtual end.

18. The role of women in producing the mythico-historical narratives, and in the fieldwork project, is discussed elsewhere (Malkki 1989).

19. These texts are reviewed in Malkki (1989).

20. The issue of standardization and the methodological challenge of representing this accurately without thereby obliterating variation and difference is discussed in Malkki (1989).

21. The "Nilotic origins" of the Tutsi are claimed in the mythico-history. The term, "Tutsi," is likewise the term universally used by the refugees. According to Trouwborst (1962:120), two subcategories of Tutsi are distinguished in Burundi: Tutsi-Abanyaruguru and Tutsi-Hima, and the latter are considered an "impure caste." The Abaganwa (*ganwa*) or "princes of the blood" are members of the royal family and are generally not considered as Tutsi (Trouwborst 1962:120). Compare Weinstein (1976:ix,1); Lemarchand (1970). The "gradual infiltration" of pastoralists, from the east as well as from the north, began before 1520 (Vansina 1972:192). These immigrants are thought to have been the ancestors of the Tutsi.

22. Most scholars agree that any history of the settlement of the area must remain hypothetical due to the scarcity of reliable evidence, but some hypotheses are reviewed in Richards (1960:28ff.). As Vansina (1972:192) notes, it is generally thought that the Twa were the first inhabitants, and were followed by the Hutu and, later, by the Tutsi and the Hima. See also Lemarchand (1970:19); Vansina (1966:34,91); Weinstein (1976:ix).

23. Vansina (1972:5) describes the pronounced hierarchy of social categories in Burundi as a "regime of castes."

24. The refugees have lived in exile from 1972 up until the present, but these 17 years appear to be seen as a perpetual present. The past is located in Burundi.

25. Compare Lan (1985:84) for an interesting analogy.

26. See Maquet on "the *buhake* agreement" in Rwanda (1961:129ff). On *ubugabire* in Burundi, see Vansina (1972:195).

27. See Leclercq (1973:11-12), who also mentions the attribution of a quasi-divine quality to this hierarchy.

28. For discussions of the use of the term, "caste," see, for example, Lemarchand (1970:4-5ff.); Vansina (1961:215n.7, 1972). See also Richards (1960:30).

29. Indeed, these constructions also inform the "Watusi" of Hollywood.

30. This "body map" is composed of several persons' narratives, as are some of the longer quotes in this paper. All of the quotes here derive from Malkki (1989), where their precise transcription and uses of narratives are explained.

31. These figures appear widely in the literature on Burundi, but they are not based on a population census (F.M. Rodegem, personal communication).

32. The reverse of this theme appears in the "White Paper" presented by the Permanent Mission of the Republic of Burundi to the United Nations, 6 June 1972 (Burundi 1972). In this peculiar document, it is charged that the danger was the elimination of the "Tutsi ethny." Kay (1987:3) charges, however, that "the Micombero government started to plan the massacres through carefully calculated provocations and misinformation as soon as it overthrew the monarchy in November 1966."

33. See, for example, the photographic essay by Kismaric (1989).

34. See Armstrong (1986a:33-34): "Tanzania has also benefited from her hospitality. By directing major refugee settlements like Mishamo to this thinly populated and most inaccessible of western regions, it has found a way, both generous and ingenious, to promote regional development and expand food production. In doing so, it was able to mobilize international aid to meet the bulk of the sizeable investment involved."

35. UNHCR officials, Dar-es-Salaam and Kigoma, personal communications. See also Armstrong (1987:35-36).

36. These are explored in more detail in Malkki (1989).

37. The town population includes immigrants from Burundi who came during the colonial period; Tanzanian Ha people whose language, Kiha, is mutually intelligible with Kirundi; Zairean refugees; and a diversity of other groups of residents and visitors (Lugusha 1981; Malkki 1989; Nindi and Mbago 1983; Richards 1960:212ff.).

38. Informants explained that this tactic was efficacious because there are very few Muslims in Burundi and many among Tanzanian citizens.

39. And Corrigan and Sayer (1985), in turn, examine state formation as cultural revolution.

40. Compare Abu-Lughod (1971); and Said (1986) on territoriality.

41. The work of Gellner (1983); Giddens (1987); Kemiläinen (1964); Kohn (1955); Nairn (1977); Seton-Watson (1977); Smith (1986), and other scholars of nationalism is more fully reviewed in Malkki (1989).

42. Good directions for such a denaturalization are mapped out by van Binsbergen (1981). See also Appadurai and Breckenridge (1988); Hannerz (1987); Hebdige (1987:156-159); Sollors (1989).

References Cited

Abu-Lughod, Ibrahim, ed.
   1971   The Transformation of Palestine: Essays on the Origin and Development of the Arab-Israeli Conflict. Evanston: Northwestern University Press.
Africa
   1985   We Want the Falashas Back (Interview with Mengistu Haile Mariam). 164:25–27.
Anderson, Benedict
   1983   Imagined Communities: Reflections on the Origins and Spread of Nationalism. London: Verso.
Appadurai, Arjun
   1983   The Past as a Scarce Resource. Man (NS) 16:201–219.
Appadurai, Arjun, and Carol Breckenridge
   1988   Why Public Culture? Public Culture, Bulletin of the Project for Transnational Cultural Studies 1(1):5–9.
Arendt, Hannah
   1973[1951]   The Origins of Totalitarianism. New York: Harcourt, Brace, Jovanovich.
Armstrong, Allen
   1986a   Mishamo ou la nature domptée. Réfugiés [Mishamo: Taming the Wilderness. Refugees] (UNHCR) 25:33–34.
   1986b   Tanganyika Christian Refugee Service (TCRS). Refugees (UNHCR) 32:41.
   1987   Developing New Refugee Settlements: An Evaluation of Mishamo's Establishment and Operation. Dar-es-Salaam: Lutheran World Federation (LWF) and Tanganyika Christian Refugee Service (TCRS). Mimeograph.
Barthes, Roland
   1972   Mythologies. New York: Hill and Wang.
Burundi, Republic of
   1972   The White Paper on the Real Causes and Consequences of the Attempted Genocide Against the Tutsi Ethny in Burundi. New York: The Permanent Mission of the Republic of Burundi to the United Nations.
Chomsky, Noam, and Edward S. Herman
   1979   The Washington Connection and Third World Fascism. Boston: South End Press.

Comaroff, Jean
　1985　Body of Power, Spirit of Resistance: The Culture and History of a South African People. Chicago: University of Chicago Press.
Comaroff, John, and Jean Comaroff
　1987　The Madman and the Migrant: Work and Labor in the Historical Consciousness of a South African People. American Ethnologist 14:191–209.
Corrigan, Philip, and Derek Sayer
　1985　The Great Arch: English State Formation as Cultural Revolution. Oxford: Basil Blackwell.
Douglas, Mary
　1966　Purity and Danger: An Analysis of the Concepts of Pollution and Taboo. London: Routledge & Kegan Paul.
Foucault, Michel
　1979　Discipline and Punish: The Birth of the Prison. New York: Vintage.
Gahama, Joseph
　1983　Le Burundi sous administration belge. Paris: Karthala.
Gellner, Ernest
　1983　Nations and Nationalism. Ithaca: Cornell University Press.
Giddens, Anthony
　1987　The Nation-State and Violence. Berkeley: University of California Press.
Goffman, Erving
　1961a　Asylums. New York: Anchor.
　1961b　On the Characteristics of Total Institutions: The Inmate World. In The Prison. D. Cressey, ed. Pp. 15–67. New York: Holt, Rinehart, and Winston.
Greenland, Jeremy
　1973　Black Racism in Burundi. New Blackfriars 54(641):443–451.
Handler, Richard
　1988　Nationalism and the Politics of Culture in Quebec. Madison: University of Wisconsin Press.
Hannerz, Ulf
　1987　The World in Creolisation. Africa 57(4):546–559.
Hebdige, Dick
　1987　Cut'n'mix: Culture, Identity, and Caribbean Music. London: Methuen.
Herzfeld, Michael
　1987　Anthropology Through the Looking-Glass: Critical Ethnography in the Margins of Europe. Cambridge: Cambridge University Press.
Hobsbawn, Eric
　1983　Introduction: Inventing Traditions. In The Invention of Tradition. Eric Hobsbawn and Terence Ranger, eds. Pp. 1–14. Cambridge: Cambridge University Press.
Hobsbawn, Eric, and Terence Ranger, eds.
　1983　The Invention of Tradition. Cambridge: Cambridge University Press.
Hyden, Goran
　1980　Beyond Ujamaa in Tanzania: Underdevelopment and an Uncaptured Peasantry. Berkeley: University of California Press.
Kapferer, Bruce
　1988　Legends of People, Myths of State: Violence, Intolerance, and Political Culture in Sri Lanka and Australia. Washington: Smithsonian Institution Press.

Kay, Reginald
   1987   Burundi Since the Genocide. London: The Minority Rights Group.
Kemiläinen, Aira
   1964   Nationalism: Problems Concerning the Word, the Concept, and Classification. Jyväskylä: Jyväskylän kasvatusopillinen korkeakoulu.
Kismaric, Carole
   1989   Forced Out: The Agony of the Refugee in Our Time. New York: William Morrow.
Kohn, Hans
   1955   Nationalism: Its Meaning and History. Princeton: Van Nostrand.
Kuper, Leo
   1982   Genocide: Its Political Use in the Twentieth Century. New Haven: Yale University Press.
Lan, David
   1985   Guns and Rain: Guerillas and Spirit Mediums in Zimbabwe. London: James Currey.
Leclercq, C.
   1973   Les racines du mal . . . ou la triple mystification. La Relève 28(13):11–15.
Lemarchand, René
   1970   Rwanda and Burundi. London: Praeger.
Lemarchand, René, and David Martin
   1974   Selective Genocide in Burundi. London: The Minority Rights Group.
Lugusha, E.A.
   1981   Final Report of a Socio-Economic Survey of Barundi Refugees in Kigoma Region. Dar-es-Salaam: Economic Research Bureau, University of Dar-es-Salaam.
Malkki, Liisa
   1985   The Origin of a Device of Power: The Refugee Camp in Post-War Europe. Unpublished manuscript.
   1989   Purity and Exile: Transformations in Historical-National Consciousness Among Hutu Refugees in Tanzania. Ph.D. dissertation, Harvard University.
Maquet, Jacques
   1961   The Premise of Inequality in Ruanda: A Study of Political Relations in a Central African Kingdom. London: Oxford University Press.
Marrus, Michael
   1985   The Unwanted: European Refugees in the Twentieth Century. Oxford: Oxford University Press.
McHenry, Dean E.
   1979   Tanzania's Ujamaa Villages: The Implementation of a Rural Development Strategy. Berkeley: Institute of International Studies, University of California.
Melady, Thomas
   1974   Burundi: The Tragic Years. New York: Orbis Books.
Mwansasu, Bismarck, and Cranford Pratt
   1979   Tanzania's Strategy for the Transition to Socialism. *In* Towards Socialism in Tanzania. Bismarck Mwansasu and Cranford Pratt, eds. Pp. 3–15. Toronto: University of Toronto Press.
Nairn, Tom
   1977   The Break-Up of Britain: Crisis and Neo-Nationalism. London: Verso.

Nindi, Benson, and Maurice Mbago
    1983   A Final Report of a Survey of Zaireans Living Along Lake Tanganyika. Dar-es-Salaam: Departments of Sociology and Statistics, University of Dar-es-Salaam.
Richards, Audrey, ed.
    1960   East African Chiefs: A Study of Political Development in Some Uganda and Tanganyika Tribes. London: Faber and Faber.
Rosaldo, Renato
    1980   Ilongot Headhunting 1883–1974: A Study in Society and History. Stanford: Stanford University Press.
Said, Edward
    1986   After the Last Sky: Palestinian Lives. New York: Pantheon.
Seton-Watson, Hugh
    1977   Nations and States: An Enquiry into the Origins of Nations and the Politics of Nationalism. London: Methuen.
Smith, Anthony
    1986   The Ethnic Origins of Nations. Oxford: Basil Blackwell.
Sollors, Werner
    1989   Introduction: The Invention of Ethnicity. *In* The Invention of Ethnicity. Werner Sollors, ed. Pp. ix–xx. New York: Oxford University Press.
Tanganyika Christian Refugee Service
    1984   TCRS: Twenty Years. Dar-es-Salaam: Tanganyika Christian Refugee Service.
Trouwborst, Albert
    1962   Le Burundi. *In* Les anciens royaumes de la zone interlacustre méridionale: Rwanda, Burundi, Buha. Marcel D'Hertefelt, Albert Trouwborst, J. H. Scherer, eds. Pp. 113–169. Tervuren: Musée Royal de l'Afrique Centrale.
Turner, Victor
    1967   The Forest of Symbols: Aspects of Ndembu Ritual. Ithaca: Cornell University Press.
van Binsbergen, Wim
    1981   The Unit of Study and the Interpretation of Ethnicity. Journal of Southern African Studies 8(1):51–81.
van Onselen, Charles
    1976   Chibaro: African Mine Labour in Southern Rhodesia 1900–1933. London: Pluto Press.
Vansina, Jan
    1961   Oral Tradition: A Study in Historical Methodology. Chicago: Aldine.
    1966   Kingdoms of the Savanna. Madison: University of Wisconsin Press.
    1972   La légende du passé: traditions orales du Burundi. Tervuren: Musée Royal de l'Afrique Centrale.
Weinstein, Warren
    1976   Historical Dictionary of Burundi. Metuchen, New Jersey: The Scarecrow Press.
Wright, Patrick
    1985   On Living in an Old Country: The National Past in Contemporary Britain. London: Verso.

4
Hindu Nationalism in the Making, or the Rise of the Hindian

Richard G. Fox
Duke University

In India today, an ethnic majority—an "underprivileged" population hitherto unknown in the Subcontinent—appears to be in the making. Its identity rests on a Hindu consciousness and on a nationalism that constructs India as a Hindu nation. "The majority appears to have developed a minority complex" announces *India Today* (31 May 1986, p. 32). Since about 1980, the public media and the "educated classes" in India have increasingly recognized a growing Hindu nationalism, and many Indians have begun living it, or at least, with it. While some Indians lead crusades to reclaim what they take as Hindu sacred land now occupied by mosques (van der Veer 1987), others organize mass meetings across the country for Hindu unity (see list in Seshadri 1984:143–157), and still others decry "the thundering voice of arrogant Hinduism" (Chitta Ranjan 1981).

Hindu nationalists maintain that "Hinduism is in danger" (*India Today*, 31 May 1986, p. 30) and that India is endangered, too. Many Indian Hindus believe their nation grows ever weaker under Sikh, Muslim, Untouchable, and Christian demands. Bullied by these ethnic groups, the state capitulates, and the just expectations of the majority go unfulfilled, so it is said. At a grassroots level, new associations espousing Hindu nationalism have sprung up and existing ones have grown more militant. There have been numerous confrontations between them and Sikhs, Muslims, and Untouchables even in places, such as the Punjab, where Hindu nationalist associations have hitherto been weak (for Punjab, see *India Today*, 15 April 1986, pp. 14–15; for Hindu-Muslim conflict in Gujarat, see Baxi 1985; Fera 1985; Sayed 1986; and in Bombay, see *Economic and Political Weekly* 1984; for massacres of Untouchables by Hindus in Bihar, see *India Today*, 31 December 1986). Government estimates in 1987 placed the number of communal organizations (including Hindu, Sikh and Muslim associations) at over 500, whereas in 1951 they numbered fewer than a dozen. They had an estimated membership in 1987 of several million. In 1961 only 61 Indian districts (out of 350) experienced communal violence, but by 1979 there were 216 districts affected by it, and the estimate for 1987 was 250 districts (*India Today*, 15 June 1987, pp. 17, 19). Political parties are said to exploit Hindu nationalist sentiments, and even to compete for electoral support on this basis (*India Today*, 30 November 1986; Vanaik 1985:78). As nonviolent participants in Hindu unity processions *(yatras)* criss-crossing India; as trident bearers (the trident [*trishul*] is a symbol of the Hindu god Shiva) in mass protests *(bandhs)*; and, at the worst, as militants able even to kill in defense of their creed—in these various roles, Hindu nationalism involves a large and committed population.

Hindu nationalists often use two terms, *bharat* and *bharatiya*, to express their concept of the Indian nation and their ethnic majority consciousness. Bharat, the half-brother of the god Rama, appears in the epic *Mahabharata* as an able ruler. After independence, the government adopted his name as the official title for the country whenever the indigenous *devanagari* script is used (as, for example, on postage stamps). I translate the terms *"bharat"* and its adjectival form *"bharatiya"* as "Hindia" and "Hindian," respectively, and use them in the following paper to reference this nationalist ideology and the national consciousness it hopes to produce.

I deal with the recent construction of Hindu nationalism for three purposes:

1. To show that the making of this ideology involves a struggle through and over cultural beliefs about Indian nationalism. Through this struggle, Hindu nationalism works toward dominance or hegemony over national consciousness. My general proposition is that what may end up as *the* national culture starts out as one contending nationalist ideology among several. No nationalism is natural; they are all constructed through confrontation.

2. To show the appropriation and reconstitution of Gandhian ideas by Hindu nationalists, who hope in this way to commandeer potent public symbols. I wish to illustrate this process of appropriation and reconstitution as evidence for the reality of struggle among national ideologies. In confrontations over cultural beliefs, "ideology transplant" (Devdutt 1981:204) or "hijacking" (modified from Baxi 1985:2) is an old and time-honored maneuver.

3. To analyze the collectivity behind the production of Hindu nationalist ideologies. My aim is to explain Hindu nationalist consciousness in the making in terms of changing material conditions and class

relations in India since independence and especially since the mid-1960s. Without this class analysis, I could only say that nationalist ideologies are cultural constructions—which is not very illuminating by itself. With a class analysis, I can also specify the agents and agencies behind the construction. Hindu nationalism, as I show below, represents the consciousness of a part of the Indian population living through and laboring under the changing material conditions of the last 20 years.

Hindu Nationalism's History

Hindu nationalism arose early in the 20th century, initially in Bengal (see Broomfield 1968; Kopf 1969, 1979; Sarkar 1973) and Bombay (see Wolpert 1961), where westernization was strong and Brahmans were politically and culturally dominant. This provenance communicates two important characteristics of early Hindu nationalism: it began as a form of cultural resistance to westernization and British colonialism and its agents came predominantly from the high caste of Brahmans. This early Hindu nationalism represented a "liberal communalism," as Bipan Chandra (1984:323–330) calls it. It was liberal because it looked forward to an India free from imperialism and was not yet avowedly anti-Muslim. Vivekananda (French 1974), Sister Nivedita (Foxe 1975), Aurobindo (Broomfield 1968:31–34), Besant (1904, 1913), Malaviya (Chandra 1984:328–330), Tagore briefly (Hay 1970), even Savarkar (Raghavan 1983), and other leading cultural nationalists of the early 20th century defended Hindu cultural traditions against a pejorative Orientalism from abroad, not against Islam or other Indian minority traditions within.

Hindu nationalism turned against perceived indigenous enemies, especially Muslims, beginning in the 1920s. The Hindu Mahasabha, for example, had existed since the early 20th century, but it only adopted an impassioned anti-Muslim stance in the 1930s, under Savarkar and Bhai Parmanand (Dixit 1986:131–135; Raghavan 1983). The Rastriya Swayamsevak Sangh (RSS), however, because it started up in 1925 (Anderson and Damle 1987:34), held strong reservations about Muslims from the beginning. These associations were predominantly Brahman in caste composition; lower-middle by class (that is, middle-level merchants, professionals and civil servants) (Anderson and Damle 1986:45), urban in locale (Raghavan 1983), and north Indian in provenance.

Although Hindu national associations became increasingly militant in the quarter-century before Independence in 1947, a Hindu nationalism remained throughout this period only one nationalist ideology among others, and a relatively unsuccessful one at that (Cleghorn 1977; Raghavan 1983). Other competitors were Nehru's democratic socialism, Gandhian *sarvodaya* ("welfare for all"), M. N. Roy's communist revolution, and Muslim, Dravidian and other ethnic nationalisms. Hindu nationalism enjoyed less political legitimacy and more state repression than many of these other nationalist ideologies, especially after 1948: Hindu nationalism was blamed for the assassination of Mahatma Gandhi and for the Partition-period communal riots. Also, its image of a modern India could not have been further from the Nehru government's (1947–1964) commitment to secular democratic socialism. Although, therefore, today's Hindu nationalists trace a relatively long pedigree, back to the 1920s, their burgeoning consciousness is very recent in fact, no earlier than the late 1970s.

Hindian Identity and Hindu Nationalism

I have much too briefly noted the history of Hindu nationalism in order to devote more space to its recent character, mainly as put forward in newspaper and periodical accounts of the leading Hindu cultural organization—the RSS—and the political parties—the Jana Sangh and its successor after 1980, the Bharatiya Janata Party (BJP)—which have broadcast Hindu nationalist appeals (or at least wrestled with other political parties for control over them). The RSS interlinks more or less closely with many other Hindu nationalist associations, each pursuing common goals but in quite different ways. These affiliated associations include an erstwhile scholarly undertaking, the Deendayal Research Institute; an organ of Hindu evangelism, the Vishwa Hindu Parishad; many local-level rural development programs (see *Manthan* 1984:9–103); and a youth wing, the Akhil Bharatiya Vidyarthi Parishad (Anderson and Damle 1987:108–156). Since about 1980, other Hindu national organizations have appeared, especially various militant paramilitary societies such as the Shiv Senas, the Bajrang Dal, and others that may have some connection with the RSS, but it is not clear of what sort (*India Today*, 15 October 1986 overviews these *senas*, or private armies, and speculates on their connections).

These diverse associations, I believe, share a basic nationalist ideology. (Perhaps their agreement is one instance of the "unity in diversity" they espouse as an essential Indian characteristic.) Their guiding notion is that India will be a Hindu nation, otherwise it will be no nation at all. They call for a *Hindu rashtra* ("Hindu way") and a *bharatiya* ("Hindian") society. Their appeal is not sectarian, however, because of the way they define *bharatiya*. No adequate translation of *bharatiya*, as used by Hindu nationalists, exists. It refers to India at once as a geographical region and as a cultural realm with deep-rooted traditions (cf. Dixit 1986:131–135 and Raghavan 1983 on the concept of "Hindutva" put forward by the early Hindu national Savarkar). It thus combines what the English terms "Indian" and "Hindu," as a cultural, not sectarian, label imply (cf. Advani 1979). I try to translate this meaning by the neologism "Hindian." Hindu nationalists maintain that underneath the superficial diversity of India's sects and castes lies an essential unity, a "unity in diversity." Anyone who recognizes India as a geographical homeland and as a cultural heartland is a true Indian, that is, a Hindian. Hindus, Muslims, Sikhs, Untouchables, and Christian Indians, no matter their superficial sectarian identities, partake of this essential Hindian unity, if they would only put aside their squabbles and recognize it.

The former head (Sarsanghchalak) of the RSS gives an apt example of the way in which the concept of Hindia lends Hindu nationalism an aggressive attitude toward Indian minorities. G. S. Golwalkar maintained that a devout Hindu must show respect for other ways of worship. Therefore, he claimed, the RSS respected Islam and Christianity, but required that Christians and Muslims remember that they are children of the soil of Bharat, which is the nation of the Hindu. They therefore must serve that nation and not be loyal to foreign lands (Golwalkar 1966:127–128). They should "come back and identify" with the Hindu way of life "in dress, customs, building houses, performing marriage ceremonies and funeral rites and such other things" (Golwalkar 1966:131).

National success will ultimately depend on development in accord with inherent national characteristics, Hindu nationalists assert. A cultural essentialism underlies this notion—that a nation must have a character, that this character derives from some cultural underpinning, ancient and deeply rooted, and that India's must rest on a Hindian one. Deendayal Upadhyaya, perhaps the most thoughtful RSS leader, spoke of a nation's *chiti*, or essence (see Upadhyaya et al. 1979:34ff.; also see Golwalkar 1966:1–10).

Hindu nationalism posits the following Indian cultural essentials: (1) a deep spirituality, growing out of stern physical discipline—in opposition to the crude materialism and never-ending consumerism of the West (cf. RSS leader Deshmukh 1979:16); (2) the corporate body, family, village, or nation is placed before and above the individual, so that loyalty to the nation must be based on consensus and not self-interest (Upadhyaya et al. 1979:16–22). By pursuing the common good, individuals, no matter how imperfect they may be, attain a collective, national perfection (Golwalkar 1966:38). Given these essential cultural differences, "therefore both democracy and socialism need to be Indianized" (Deshmukh in Raje 1978:36). National development toward a future utopian Hindia must sponsor individual spiritual revolution first (Seshadri 1984:80), then worry about institutional changes, such as redistribution of property and wealth.

For Hindu nationalism, India's current wounded condition rests on: (1) failure to recognize Hindian cultural essentials—and so there is the rag-tag nation of many sectarian and special interests; for example, Sikhs and Muslims confuse their sectarian practices with their essential cultural identity, which is Hindian, whatever *they* may think; (2) lack of patriotism, as, for example, among Indian Muslims, whose primary loyalty, Hindu nationalists maintain, is to Islam; (3) the misguided mimicry of Western culture; (4) the contemporary machinations in India of America and the Soviet Union; (5) the policies of national leaders whose cultural identity has been twisted by foreign influences, as, for example, Nehru's commitment to a Western socialist model inappropriate to India (Upadhyaya 1969:129–132); (6) a rampant national corruption and personal selfishness due to the lack of spiritual discipline and national commitment.

Hindu nationalists foresee a future, perfected Hindia arriving through a new spiritual dedication. To quote Golwalkar:

> The Rastriya Swayamsevak Sangh has resolved to fulfill that age-old national mission by forging, as the first step, the present-day scattered elements of the Hindu Society into an organised and invincible force both on the plane of the Spirit and on the plane of material life. [1966:10]

The RSS works toward this spiritual revolution by organizing local-level *shakas*, or branches. These cadres wear uniforms, drill army fashion, learn to wield cudgels *(lathis)*, sing patriotic songs (which are also devotional), and study Hindian traditions (Anderson and Damle 1987:1; Mishra 1980:52–55). Caste is no bar to membership, but the leadership has always been from the Brahman or other "forward castes" (see below). The intent is to develop a national physical and mental discipline to make Hindia strong (cf. Balasaheb Deoras, present head of RSS, quoted in *Organiser* 1975; also see Golwalkar 1966:52–54).

Hindu nationalists, for example, believe that the 1983 Ekatmata Yajna, which consisted of Hindu processions criss-crossing India, achieved a major national spiritual revolution. Hindu pilgrimages have generally been for individual or family merit *(punya)*. In the Ekatmata pilgrimage, personal merit "[was] sublimated into" social *(samajik)* and national *(rashtriya)* merit "towards giving a social and national direction to the people's devotion." The other revolution was that the "numberless" pilgrimage places not only were identified as *"Punya Bhoomi"* or holy land but also as *"Matru Bhoomi"* or motherland (Seshadri 1984:174–175). Whether or not the Ekatmata Yajna accomplished all this, Hindu nationalists labor hard at raising (what they take to be) such a revolutionary consciousness.

Hindu nationalists also work for: (1) doing away with the government program of "reservations," or affirmative action programs for Scheduled Castes and Tribes (that is, for Untouchables or Dalits and for Adivasis) and for Other Backward Classes (see Galanter 1984:179–187); (2) limiting the state's involvement in social welfare programs, such as rural development, and depending on private initiative; (3) avoiding "Russian-style" socialism, that is, excessive state centralization; (4) reclaiming Hindu temple sites from mosques; (5) resisting Christian conversions of Untouchables; (6) destroying separatist movements, such as the Khalistan agitation by the Sikhs, that threaten Hindia's integrity; (7) giving respect to Hindu cultural traditions, such as *sati* (see *India Today*, 15 October 1987, pp. 60–61); (8) deemphasizing English education and giving greater resources for primary education where "Indian religio-cultural content, quality, and spirit" could be inculcated (*Manthan* 1986:4–7); (9) legalizing a common civil code for all Hindians—Muslims are not now covered by the Indian civil code (Seshadri 1984:xv).

Gandhian and Hindian

In the middle 1970s, an unforeseen ideological and organizational conjunction—an ideological hijacking—occurred that gave Hindu nationalism a new legitimacy (see Fox 1987 for details). Hindu nationalist ideology merged with another nationalist ideology, Gandhism, which in 1981 became the BJP's reigning policy under the label "Gandhian socialism" (see Abraham 1981:8). In so doing, Hindu nationalism appropriated public symbols enjoying wide currency and substantial authority in India. Gandhian socialism, based on the Mahatma's notion of *sarvodaya* (welfare for all), proposed that India could follow a developmental path different from both Western socialism and capitalism. This alternative modernization would build on the presumed essential spirituality and corporativeness of India.

There were major areas of overlap in belief between Hindu nationalism and Gandhism, especially in the acceptance of an Orientalist notion that East and West were innately different. They shared the view that India was spiritual, organic and incorporative against the materialism, individuality and competitiveness said to characterize the West. Even on the issue of nonviolence, there is agreement, at least in principle if not necessarily in action. RSS chief Golwalkar (1966:248-249) embraced a nonviolence from strength, obviously modeled on Gandhi's *satyagraha;* his successor, Deoras, reaffirmed this commitment in 1979 (*Organiser* 1981:15). Gandhism and Hindu nationalism also celebrate India's traditions, distrust state centralization, affirm "appropriate" technology and discount class struggle.

There are also major differences, perhaps most fundamentally, in the conclusions drawn from the common view of Indian society as having "unity in diversity." For Hindu nationalism, this idea subsidizes the belief that underneath sectarian and caste differences, all Indians are Hindus in essence—Hindians, as I have called them. If Muslim and Sikh Indians do not recognize the Hindian substrate, they threaten the nation, and they must either be (forcibly) reminded of it or removed as a threat. For Gandhi, too, there was one Indian nation underneath the many separate caste and sectarian identities. At base, however, was consanguinity—all Indians were kinsfolk—and at an even deeper level, they shared a common humanity that even transcended India and linked them to people around the world. Thus, Hindu nationalism redefines what Gandhi spoke of as God and Truth and makes it a Hindu truth alone. Hindu nationalism can therefore be intolerant of all social identities other than Hindian.

The ideological transplant also produced hybrid beliefs: the amendment of Gandhi's notion of *satyagraha* against colonialism to legitimate mass civil disobedience against an elected Indian government, the transfer of Gandhi's moral self-abnegation to moral condemnation of corruption in public officials, and the reconstruction of Gandhi's notion of nonviolently shaming an opponent into capitulation *(ahimsa)*, into physically intimidating an opponent short of violence (as in the *gherao,* where an opponent is "mobbed" and not permitted access to food, water or other needs).

The organizational conjunction involved the merger of cadres from the Hindu nationalist association, the RSS; its political arm at that time, the Jana Sangh party; and other Hindu national groups with Gandhians *sarvodaya* workers, that is, those involved in Gandhi's voluntary program of rural uplift and social regeneration. This merger had a complex history.

The centennial of Gandhi's birth in 1969 made *sarvodaya* leaders face some harsh realities: almost all aspects of their Constructive Programme, from voluntary land reform to homespun cloth, had failed or, what was worse, existed only through government subsidy (see Ostergaard 1985:70ff.). Indeed, under the Nehru government the utopian vision of the *sarvodaya* movement had been domesticated into local welfarism and had been tightly leashed to the Congress Party. In 1969, however, the Congress Party came apart, as Indira Gandhi challenged the old leadership and constructed her own political following by personalistic and populist appeals to the poor, such as her famous slogan of *garibi hatao* ("End Poverty!") (see Church 1984:236; Mayer 1984:144). Sympathetically, the *sarvodaya* movement also split. One group adopted an activist program of social regeneration and soon confronted the Indira Congress government, which they saw as corrupt and Communist.

These *sarvodaya* activists were the initial agents of the merger of Hindu nationalism and Gandhism. Led by Jayaprakash Narayan (known as "J.P.") and his call for *sampurna kranti* or Total Revolution based on Gandhian principles, a mass social protest against the Indira Gandhi government broke out in Bihar in 1974–75 and threatened to spread over northern India. In response, Indira Gandhi declared the emergency suspension of civil liberties, which lasted from 1975 to 1977. Hindu nationalist organizations were major supporters of J.P.'s movement, and they began in 1974 vigorously to champion his Gandhian approach and appropriate certain elements of it as their own (details in Fox 1987).

This ideological transplanting has continued up to the present and produces such anomalies as these: the RSS, the very organization once banned under suspicion of involvement in Gandhi's assassination, now invokes his image as an ancestor figure (literally, see photo of Gandhi in *Manthan* 1984:13). Gandhi's name and his program are vainly taken by organizations that turn a blind eye to street violence against Untouchables in Gujarat (Baxi 1985:6). And political parties, at one time avowedly secular, now compete *sotto voce* for the Hindu nationalist vote.

Historical contingencies underlie the split in the *sarvodaya* movement, J.P.'s mass protest and the resulting emergency. But there was a solid base of support for J.P.'s appeal, and afterward, the movement generated or served as a vehicle for the growing consciousness of particular elements in the population. Support for the J.P. Movement in the mid-1970s and for subsequent Hindu nationalism has generally come from Hindus rather than Muslims or Sikhs; from the urbanized rather than the rural; from young people, especially students; from the lower-middle class—that is, professionals, teachers, petty manufacturers, traders, civil servants and the like; and from the "forward castes" rather than the "backward castes" or the Scheduled Castes. Collectively, these attributes define the emerging Hindian consciousness and the national culture it proposes.

One attribute, caste, requires some clarification. Caste categories in contemporary India are quite complex because of the intersection—and sometimes interference—of folk perceptions, legal classifications and political rhetoric. The Scheduled Caste category is the cleanest cut: it generally consists of castes once called Untouchable or Harijan, now "scheduled" (that is, "listed") by government for affirmative action benefits, and often now self-labeled "Dalit." "Backward castes" and "forward castes" are much more ragged categories. Other Backward Classes, which is what I mean by the label "backward castes," is a legal classification used in many Indian states to refer to castes above Scheduled but still deserving of affirmative action (Galanter 1984:179–187). These castes are generally rural and intermediate in caste rank, and they have a long history of political action—earliest in southern and western India, where they merged politically to foster "non-Brahman" movements; most recently (since the Green Revolution) in the north, where their political ambitions have often led to violence (as, for example, Koeris and Kurmis in Bihar and Sikh Jats in Punjab).

The "forward castes"—the caste base for Hindian identity—approximate to the "educated classes" of Brahmans, Kayasthas, Khatris, and other urbanized high castes who obtained English education and staffed the British colonial enterprise and who have continued to dominate government and the professions even after independence. It also includes the somewhat lower ranking castes of merchants, moneylenders, and small-scale entrepreneurs, collectively known as "Vaishyas" or "Baniyas," who dominate trade, manufacturing, banking, and other commercial activities.[1]

This Hindian population, still inchoate, entered public life on a large scale in the second wave of mobilization by the Congress movement for independence, when Gandhi turned it into a mass endeavor. They profited greatly from the postindependence regime in the 1950s and 1960s, which some scholars (Fox 1984; Mitra 1977; Raj 1973), following the Polish economist Kalecki (1972), call an "intermediate regime." An intermediate regime differs from a capitalist state, with a dominant bourgeoisie, and also from a socialist regime, where the proletariat in theory rules. Intermediate regimes, because of their colonial histories, have neither a well-developed indigenous bourgeoisie nor proletariat, and they are therefore dominated by the lower-middle class, which has prevailed under colonialism. In India, to a large extent, the lower-middle class and the urban forward castes are congruent and form a single social grouping. This caste/class population rose to national prominence and forged the independence movement under British colonialism and have dominated the postindependence intermediate regime.

The decades immediately before and after independence in 1947 saw the fluorescence of the forward caste/lower-middle class. This regime limited foreign capital's penetration (Bardhan 1984:44) and regulated indigenous large capital (Vanaik 1985:59) to preserve the dominance of the indigenous lower-middle class against either an Indian or foreign bourgeoisie. Economic development came from a large "public sector" under government control or a "private sector" licensed and supervised by the bureaucracy. The mixed economy, with ostensible socialist leanings but a true capitalist tilt, favored the urban forward caste/lower-middle class in several ways. As government necessarily burgeoned, so too did employment opportunities for the lower-middle class. Opportunities for bribes, kickbacks, university placements, jobs, and other forms of corruption and chicanery also increased, creating entangling but profitable alliances among bureaucrats, politicians, traders, manufacturers, lawyers and other professionals. The result was, in Salman Rushdie's phrase, a land of *chamchas* ("spoons," nested front-to-back)—a land of back-scratchers. More formally, Bardhan typifies it as "a patron-client regime fostered by a flabby and heterogeneous [class] coalition preoccupied in a spree of anarchical grabbing of public resources" (Bardhan 1984:70).

Hindian Identity and Class Relations

Why should this caste category/economic class have come to feel threatened over the last 15 years? And why should Hindu nationalism serve as a proper vehicle for its inherent interests and emerging consciousness under this threat?

Since the mid-1960s circumstances have turned much less favorable for these Hindians in the making and the Hindia they have made. Other emerging classes, whose consciousness is often envehicled in sectarian or caste identities (on this point, see Fox 1985:163–164; Sarkar 1983:31), have now come to the fore.

1. Perhaps the most important factor has been the growth of a vocal rural rich farmer class, usually drawn from intermediate ranking castes (commonly, the official Other Backward Classes) like the Jats in Punjab and U.P., the Patidars in Gujarat, or the Yadavs, Koeris, and Kurmis of Bihar (Bardhan 1984:54; Blair 1980:64, 1984:197; Brass 1983: 331; Breman 1985:433). This rural lower-middle class was on the rise in favored agricultural locales even before independence, and land reform (*zamindari* abolition) in the 1950s also served its interests. Since the mid-1960s the Green Revolution, first in the wheat-growing regions of Punjab and Western U.P. and thereafter in the rice-growing

areas of eastern and western India, has swollen their ranks, increased their wealth and given them great political leverage.

This wealthy peasant class in the making is also lower-middle class (it stands between rural wage laborers and large landlords), but rural, and often opposes Hindian, that is, urban lower-middle class/ forward caste, interests on that basis. Sharad Joshi, the Mahasthrian farm leader, refers to a war between Bharat and India or between the rural and the urban. Charan Singh, representing Jat farmers in Uttar Pradesh, spoke against urban lobbies and a parasitic intelligentsia. Rural and urban fight over the terms of trade between rural agriculture and urban manufacturing or the urban salariat's cost of living. The level of commodity supports has been a hot political issue for all parties even though the government purchase price seems to have exceeded the cost of production since the mid-1960s for wheat, and since the mid-1970s for rice (Bardhan 1984:54–55).

This confrontation is therefore not a class struggle but a competition within a class.[2] This newly empowered rural population sometimes demands subsidies, which would come from urban lower-middle class profits, for their advanced capitalist agriculture. Water, electricity, and fertilizer subsidies are important here. Other times, especially in Bihar and other regions where the Green Revolution is recent, these newly wealthy peasants want freedom from government and the law, in order to exploit Untouchable landless laborers. Still other times, their rural youth agitate against their lack of access to education and urban employment. The most significant of these rural movements led by rich peasants of intermediate caste rank is the agitation for an independent Khalistan, led by the (Sikh) Jats of Punjab, which by its own sectarian form authorizes an equivalent Hindian backlash.

2. The second most important attack on Hindian interests comes from the reservation policies originally introduced by the Nehru government in the 1950s. This, the most extensive affirmative action program in any nation, reserved places in colleges, civil service and government for Scheduled Castes and Tribes. At the state level, the reservations program expanded in the 1960s and 1970s to include new, supposedly deserving caste communities, the Other Backward Classes, who usually represented the newly wealthy farmers alluded to above.

By the 1970s the first generation to profit from these reservations had begun to argue for greater concessions. Indira Gandhi's program to end poverty also made reservations an important policy plank. As the rural rich farmers used their new political clout to gain more concessions (through bribes very often) and as Hindians perceived that reservations deeply cut into their access to education, one of the main demands of Hindu nationalism became increasingly attractive: namely, that reservations should be done away with because they institutionalize sectarian and caste differences that are only superficial. Baxi (1985:1–2) finds that the reservation policy in Gujarat does not threaten the forward castes very much in reality, but he sees the street violence against Muslims and Untouchables as "anticipatory class warfare" and a "symbolic politics" of repression. This is, in part, a class confrontation (forward castes against Untouchables) but it is also partly an intra-class competition (between intermediate caste/lower-middle class farmers and forward caste/lower-middle class urbanites). Whenever the confrontations involved class, they have engendered extensive mass violence, especially in states like Gujarat and Maharasthra where there is both a large forward caste population and a large politically aggressive Scheduled Caste population. The confrontation between urban forward castes and rural intermediate castes, by comparison, has been relatively benign.

3. Petro-dollars, earned by Indians Muslims through wage labor in the Gulf States, adds another dimension of conflict, in this case, also a class conflict. Muslim artisans and skilled laborers are pitted against the Hindu urban lower-middle class employers and consumers. Extramural remittances have helped subsidize a rising sense of injustice among Muslims in India (see *India Today*, 15 October 1986; 15 June 1987, pp. 17, 19), and also a forceful suppression by Hindians, especially in Gujarat and Bombay where the new Muslim wealth has been most apparent.

4. An intermediate regime, with the lower-middle class dominant, cannot continue indefinitely. Its very success in keeping foreign capital at bay eventually leads to the formation of a powerful indigenous bourgeoisie. Even though the Indian government has slowed the growth of big capital through public sector development, licensing and other controls, indigenous large capital has been growing slowly (Vanaik 1985:59) and there is increasing alliance between big business and big bureaucracy. Pressed by this development, the urban lower-middle class finds Hindu nationalism's emphasis on "Gandhian" economic decentralization, small-scale enterprise, "appropriate" (to the lower-middle class) technology, and government deregulation most appealing. If this program were to be implemented, it might retard the erosion of the lower-middle class's perquisites or at least pay them off in consumerism for their loss of political power.

5. As other nationalist ideologies became more radicalized, were hijacked by other interests, or failed in practice, there was no longer any strong ideological justification for the forward caste/lower-middle class. Nehru's democratic-socialist nationalism, which had in fact leg-

itimated the intermediate regime earlier, became much more radical as Indira Gandhi manipulated it after 1967. She was responding to the fact that the Indian poor had demonstrated a new political consciousness and political participation in the 1967 elections (Mayer 1981:145–146). Gandhism, as interpreted after independence by Vinoba Bhave and the Sarva Seva Sangh, had also legitimated the intermediate regime. For example, Gandhian programs like "voluntary" land reform (the *bhoodan* movement) were set up expressly to curtail class conflict and revolutionary movements in the countryside. By the late 1960s, Vinoba's version of Gandhism had quite obviously failed. Because it no longer effectively disciplined the poor, it also no longer legitimated the intermediate regime. Hindu nationalism, as put forward by the "ideological professions" like lawyers, doctors and college professors (Baxi 1985:2), is attempting to substitute. It has succeeded so well that alienated Hindian youth, the "educated unemployed," or "semi-literates" as Vanaik (1985:65) calls them, have flocked to the RSS, even from ultra-left parties.

Conclusion

Will Hindu nationalism prevail? Will a new dominant nationalism and a new national consciousness, in the image of Hindia and the Hindian, replace today's India? Hindu national organizations have played a very subtle game of alliances with political parties. Up until the early 1980s, Hindu nationalists, at least in the form of the RSS cadres, were quite firmly allied with opposition parties like the Jana Sangh or the BJP. That situation changed in the two or three years before Indira Gandhi's assassination. Her government came into increasing conflict with Punjab Sikhs, and Indira Gandhi responded by ever more openly plugging Hindu appeals into her political rhetoric (Seshadri 1984:138; Vanaik 1985:78). Her son and her party took such appeals even further in the 1985 election (Brass 1985 vol. 2:19; *Organiser* 1985). Hindu nationalist organizations realized they could fellow-travel with the Congress Party in power (Abraham 1983; *India Today*, 15 January 1985). So now there is less clear identification of one party with Hindu nationalism, as suport for this nationalist ideology ramifies. If this development continues, and it would seem from Rajiv's 1985 electoral appeal to Hindu sentiments that it will, Hindian consciousness may become culturally dominating and therefore may come to define India's national culture.

In this paper, I have tried to show the making of Hindu nationalism in India today within a field of class oppositions and intra-class competitions, often carried forward by caste and sectarian consciousness. I have also explored the way in which Hindu nationalism appropriated meanings from Gandhism in the mid-1970s in order to gain greater public authority. In my portrayal, struggle and competition among people appear alongside related confrontations among nationalist ideologies. In the event, national culture gets produced, but not in some quiet artisan way and with a precision tool kit, but, rather, ragged and rough hewn, as people, very often unskilled except by experience, work up their cultures as they work out their lives.

Notes

1. Some writers classify the trading castes as "intermediate" or even "backward" (see, for example, Vanaik 1985:60–65), but then they have to differentiate a "higher-intermediate" category (as Vanaik 1985:78 does) to represent the urban trading castes as against the other "intermediate" castes, the mainly rural "backward castes" in the north, recently empowered by the Green Revolution. This confusion comes about because of failure to recognize that the urban provenience of trading castes also made them "forward" in an economic and political sense quite early, much as other, higher-ranking caste categories like Brahmans and Kayasthas were. Also, their urban location gives them very different interests from rural intermediate castes, although there have been attempts to forge political alliances (as between the Lok Dal and the BJP political parties) linking them. These alliances have generally been unsuccessful and short-lived.

2. An equivalent intra-class competition exists between these newly powerful "backward" castes and the old rural forward caste/landlord class in places like Bihar (see Brass 1985 vol. 2:11; *India Today*, 31 December 1986, p. 42).

References Cited

Abraham, A. S.
　1981　BJP's Gandhian Socialism: Formula for Ideological Amorphousness. Times of India 8(2 January):col. 3–5.
　1983　BJP's Declining Fortunes: Internal War of Attrition. Times of India 8(22 July):3–5.
Advani, L. K.
　1979　In Defense of the RSS. Illustrated Weekly of India 100(27, 7 October):7, 8–11.
Anderson, Walter K., and Shridhar D. Damle
　1987　The Brotherhood in Saffron. Boulder: Westview Press.
Bardhan, Pranab
　1984　The Political Economy of Development in India. Oxford: Basil Blackwell.

Baxi, Upendra
   1985   Reflections on Reservation Crisis in Gujarat. Mainstream (June):1–17.
Besant, Annie
   1904   Hindu Ideals for the Use of Hindu Students in the Schools of India. Benares: Theosophical Publishing Society.
   1913   India's Mission Among Nations. *In* Essays and Addresses, vol. 4. London: Theosophical Publishing Society.
Blair, Harry
   1980   Rising Kulaks and Backward Classes in Bihar, Social Change in the Late 1970s. Economic and Political Weekly 15(12 January):64–74.
   1984   Structural Change, the Agricultural Sector, and Politics in Bihar. *In* State Politics in Contemporary India, Crisis or Continuity? John R. Wood, ed. Pp. 197–228. London: Westview Press.
Brass, Paul
   1983   Caste, Faction and Party in Indian Politics, vol. 1. Faction and Party. Delhi: Chanakya Publications.
   1985   Caste, Faction, and Party in Indian Politics, vol. 2. Election Studies. Delhi: Chanakya Publications.
Breman, Jan
   1985   Of Peasants, Migrants and Paupers. Delhi: Oxford University Press.
Broomfield, J. H.
   1968   Elite Conflict in a Plural Society: Twentieth-Century Bengal. Berkeley: University of California Press.
Chandra, Bipan
   1984   Communalism in Modern India. New Delhi: Vikas.
Chitta Ranjan, C. N.
   1981   The Revivalist Menace. Mainstream 20(8, 24 October):1–3.
Church, Roderick
   1984   Conclusion: The Pattern of State Politics in Indira Gandhi's India. *In* State Politics in Contemporary India, Crisis or Continuity? John R. Wood, ed. Pp. 229–250. London: Westview Press.
Cleghorn, B.
   1977   Leadership of the All-India Mahasabha 1920–39. *In* Leadership in South Asia. B. N. Pandey, ed. Pp. 395–425. New Delhi: Vikas.
Deshmukh, Nana
   1979   RSS, Victim of Slander. New Delhi: Vision Books.
Devdutt
   1981   The BJP and Gandhian Socialism: A Case of Ideology-Transplant. Gandhi Marg 3:200–213.
Dixit, Prabha
   1986   The Ideology of Hindu Nationalism. *In* Political Thought in Modern India. Thomas Pantham and Kenneth L. Deutsch, eds. Pp. 122–141. New Delhi: Sage.
Economic and Political Weekly
   1984   Editorial. Unlearnt Lessons of 1970. 19:826–828 (19 May).
Fera, Ivan
   1985   A City Aflame. Illustrated Weekly of India. 106(1):14–15 (12 May).
Fox, Richard G.
   1984   Urban Class and Communal Consciousness in Colonial Punjab: The Genesis of India's Intermediate Regime. Modern Asian Studies 18:459–489.

1985 Lions of the Punjab: Culture in the Making. Berkeley: University of California Press.
  1987 Gandhian Socialism and Hindu Nationalism: Cultural Domination in the World System. Journal of Commonwealth and Comparative Politics 9:233–247.
Foxe, Barbara
  1975 Long Journey Home, A Biography of Margaret Noble (Nivedita). London: Rider.
French, Harold W.
  1974 The Swan's Wide Waters. Port Washington, NY: Kennikat.
Galanter, Marc
  1984 Competing Equalities, Law and the Backward Classes in India. Delhi: Oxford University Press.
Golwalkar, M. S.
  1966 Bunch of Thoughts. Bangalore: Vikrama Prakashan Chamarajpet.
Hay, Stephen N.
  1970 Asian Ideas of East and West, Tagore and His Critics in Japan, China, and India. Cambridge: Harvard University Press.
India Today
  1985 January 15. A Historic Mandate. Pp. 16–29.
  1986 April 15. Fighting Back. Pp. 14–15.
  1986 May 31. Militant Revivalism. Pp. 30–39.
  1986 October 15. Militancy on the Move. Pp. 32–36.
  1986 November 30. A Wounded City. Pp. 71–79.
  1986 December 31. Area of Darkness. Pp. 40–43.
  1987 June 15. Danger Signals. Pp. 17, 19.
  1987 October 15. A Pagan Sacrifice. Pp. 58–60.
Kalecki, Michael
  1972 Selected Essays on the Economic Growth of the Socialist and the Mixed Economy. Cambridge: Cambridge University Press.
Kopf, David
  1969 British Orientalism and the Bengal Renaissance. Berkeley: University of California Press.
  1979 The Brahmo Samaj and the Shaping of the Modern Indian Mind. Princeton: Princeton University Press.
Manthan
  1984 The All India Workshop on "Development: Concept and Grassroot Experiment." 4:9–103.
  1986 Editorial. Wanted: A Quiet Moral Revolution. 6:3–8.
Mayer, P. B.
  1984 Congress (I), Emergency (I): Interpreting Indira Gandhi's India. The Journal of Commonwealth and Comparative Politics 22:129–150.
Mishra, Dina Nath
  1980 RSS: Myth and Reality. Ghaziabad: Vikas.
Mitra, Ashok
  1977 Terms of Trade and Class Relations. London: Frank Cass.
Organiser
  1975 Balasaheb Asks PM to Shed Bias Against RSS. 28:7(30, 8 March).
  1981 Gandhi and BJP: Two Emanations of the Same Spirit. 33:15(23, 25 October).
  1985 BJP Has Retained Its Base. 37:1 (27 January).

Ostergaard, Geoffrey
   1985   Nonviolent Resistance in India. New Delhi: Gandhi Peace Foundation.

Raghavan, T. C. A.
   1983   Origins and Development of Hindu Mahasabha Ideology: The Call of V. D. Savarkar and Bhai Parmanand. Economic and Political Weekly 18(15, 9 April):595–600.

Raj, K. N.
   1973   The Politics and Economics of "Intermediate Regimes." Economic and Political Weekly 8(27, 7 July):1189–1198.

Raje, Sudhakar, ed.
   1978   Destination. New Delhi: Deendayal Research Institute.

Sarkar, Sumit
   1973   The Swadeshi Movement in Bengal 1903–1908. New Delhi: People's Publishing House.
   1983   "Popular" Movements and "Middle Class" Leadership in Late Colonial India: Perspectives and Problems of a "History From Below." Calcutta: K. P. Bagchi.

Sayed, Ashraf
   1986   Calling Out Army Overdue in Gujarat. Times of India 5(15 July):1–4.

Seshadri, H. V.
   1984   Hindu Renaissance Under Way. Bangalore: Jagarana Prakashana.

Upadhyaya, Deendayal
   1968   Political Diary. Bombay: Jaico.

Upadhyaya, Deendayal, Sri Guruji, and D. B. Thengdi
   1979   The Integral Approach. New Delhi: Deendayal Research Institute.

Vanaik, Achin
   1985   The Rajiv Congress in Search of Stability. New Left Review 154:55–82.

van der Veer, Peter
   1987   "God Must Be Liberated!" A Hindu Liberation Movement in Ayodhya. Modern Asian Studies 21:283–301.

Wolpert, Stanley A.
   1961   Tilak and Gokhale: Revolution and Reform in the Making of Modern India. Berkeley: University of California Press.

5
The Production and Defense of "the Romanian Nation," 1900 to World War II

Katherine Verdery
Johns Hopkins University

For several centuries, certain persons calling themselves "Romanians" have given speeches and written treatises, tracts, and histories in which they spoke of an entity they called "the Romanian nation."[1] Their speeches and tracts addressed what this entity was, how one would recognize it if one came upon it, who its enemies were, and what was good for it. The enemies were usually seen as peoples having other identities—Hungarians or Austrians, who oppressed Romanians living in the region of Transylvania, or Turks (sometimes also Poles and Russians), who oppressed Romanians in Moldavia or Muntenia;[2] what was good for Romanians was sometimes but not always seen as requiring liberation from these foreigners. Later, when the foreigners had been expelled (usually with the help of still other foreigners), those seen as the nation's enemies might be the *native* leaders, now portrayed as deracinated; they generally returned the accusation and defended their claim to act in "the nation's" behalf.[3]

I call these centuries of arguing about the Romanian people, its mission, its enemies, and its interests the production and defense of the Romanian Nation, and I see this as the basis for producing and reproducing a Romanian national ideology. Perhaps it is better to call the result not an ideology but an ideological process, on the view that ideologies are not most helpfully seen as bodies of thought and imagery but, rather, as social processes that form particular human subjectivities and senses of being in the world (see Therborn 1980:1–2). A very important part of such processes is the development of an elite discourse (with associated concrete practices) concerning the Nation.[4] This elite discourse creates ideological effects by setting up a field of arguments and claims that rest, for the most part, on premises rarely brought to light. As these arguments, claims, and premises become deeply lodged in the institutions in which they take place, they may serve to develop the national ideology further.

The present essay is an interpretive exploration into how a national discourse that was initially a handy medium for pursuing certain kinds of contests took on a kind of life of its own, entering thereby into the very constitution of political processes. My discussion is partial: it treats only a small piece of the long-running process by which a national ideology has been (and continues to be) formed in Romania. Although the piece I describe comes from earlier in this century, it has considerable contemporary relevance, for nationalism remains a distinguishing characteristic of Romania's Communist Party leadership. The contemporary sequence deserves its own analysis,[5] but that, in turn, presupposes an understanding of how the national ideology developed in the period of its greatest elaboration, the half-century between about 1900 and World War II. I present a subset of some debates carried on in Romania during these years, especially during the years between the two World Wars: debates concerning the Romanian "national essence."[6] In looking at these debates, I will first give the reader a hint of their flavor, emphasizing their character as responses to structures of power beyond Romania's borders; second, I link the debates to the internalization of national symbols and to changes in Romania's interclass relations; and third, I point to some very material effects of the debates, as they helped to institutionalize academic disciplines and thereby to create for the participants formidable redoubts in which a national discourse became so deeply embedded as to be very difficult to dislodge.

My objective is to inquire into how certain intellectual arguments served as part of the material through which social actors affected the balance of social forces—the transformation of institutional structures and class relations—as they struggled in discourse to create more solid and autonomous platforms of power. Their actions had a number of important consequences, particularly for the processes of state-building in Romania. To see this, we might analytically separate "nation-state formation" into two components: the building of organizational and institutional structures and arenas, related to governance within fixed borders and to interactions across them—state building—and the production of a community imagined as a single social body (ideally contained within actual or possible state borders)—nation-building.[7] For western nation-states, these two components are generally assumed to have been complementary. In the Romanian case—exemplifying, I suspect, a larger set of cases—the relationship between them was more complex. The manner in which Romanian national ideology arose partly facilitated and partly opposed the centralization of state power (see Verdery 1990a). Talk about the Romanian Nation served partly to consolidate state power by constructing a nation subject to state policies; it also represented the masses in a way that silenced them and opened them to surveillance, control, and reform by the state and the intellectuals. At the same time, the discourse on the Nation created an ongoing potential for opposition to the activities of those in power, as it entrenched intellectuals within partly autonomous institutions from which they could argue against the direction of state-making, justifying their arguments as a defense of the Nation's interests. Through the national discourse they also sought to displace other institutions, such as the Orthodox Church, that had been central creators and defenders of the Nation in earlier times.[8]

This essay primarily concerns representations of Romanian identity, leaving aside (for lack of space) both the policies whose shape such representation often aimed to influence and the sociopolitical environment within which the debates occurred. Nevertheless, the general reader requires a brief account of why representations of Romanianness—and the authority to speak that was implied in them—were such crucial issues during the first few decades of the 20th century, most especially the 1920s and 1930s. To begin with, Romania's international situation included the struggle of newly unified Germany to support its capitalist development, like France and Britain, through colonial expansion; excluded from most overseas regions by the prior activities of fellow Europeans, much of the German expansion would occur *within* Europe. The Balkan region and resource-rich Romania were particularly important in this pan-European competition, which involved not only France, Germany and Britain, but also the Habsburg and Ottoman Empires. In the different orientations of Romanian intellectuals, many having been educated in France or Germany, one could see the competition's intellectual facet. Romanian policy-makers felt another facet, as each country attempted to influence the Romanian economy toward or away from preserving its agrarian export structure. Although in global comparison with England and France the Austro-German presence remained weak, in interwar Romania German interests triumphed, securing it within Germany's economic orbit by the late 1930s. These international events help to account for the salience of representations of the West in Romanians' national discourse and for their attention to western models of economic development.

In the second place, the aftermath of World War I vastly complicated Romania's internal situation, from the national point of view.

Territorial settlements had nearly doubled its territory and population, fulfilling nationalist dreams but also bringing tremendous problems of reorganization and unification. Higher industrial capacity in the new territories posed very acutely the possibility of developing Romanian industry, and this complicated economic decision-making. Unification of the fiscal, jural, religious, and administrative apparatuses—already an overwhelming task—was impeded by the sizable national minorities of Germans and Hungarians who now resided within Romania's borders; the Hungarians waited impatiently for restitution of the old territorial borders, which would deliver them from Romanian rule. Thus, Romanian representations of national and territorial unity took place against the constant threat of territorial dismemberment. The threat was realized in 1940, when the Soviet Union annexed Bessarabia and Hitler gave northern Transylvania back to Hungary. The 1920s worsened the situation: the Communist International openly supported minority struggles for national liberation even where these jeopardized the integrity of already-constituted states. This challenge to Romania's sovereignty over the new lands caused the government to ban the Communist Party as a deadly peril to the country's unity. Interwoven tacitly with the Romanian national discourse, therefore, were arguments about socialism and efforts to come to terms with it, in part through national means.

These conjoined problems—of economic development and neocolonialism, institutional reform and integration, and the world socialist movement as it affected Romania's internal politics—provided an environment rich in possibilities for change in the social situation of various groups. A major idiom for discussing the alternatives was talk about the Nation and its identity; those who utilized this idiom were members of political, religious and intellectual elites. While their social origins and affiliations were diverse, those active chiefly in religious and cultural life rather than in politics were more likely to come from middling and professional families, the politicians descending more often from families of greater wealth rooted in the old landed nobility.[9] Because social actors circulated in and out of formal political office, however, it is difficult to separate "intellectuals" categorically from "politicians."[10] I generally use the term "intellectuals" in reference not to persons with specific occupational or educational characteristics but to a structural situation: that segment of the societal elite who did not directly hold political or economic power—or, in Alexandrescu's words (1983), the fraction of the dominant class that was out of power.

Despite their diverse origins and affiliations, the political and intellectual elites discussed below all participated in a common universe of discourse, in which the Nation and the Romanian people occupied a central position. The changed conditions of Romanian society following World War I gave this discourse both greater scope and greater urgency; an exponential rise in the already large volume of writings on the Nation shows how widely the urgency was perceived.

Defining the Nation between East and West

A contemporary Romanian scholar has observed,

> From the middle of the last century, that is since the beginning of modern Romania, systematically every two to four decades the drama of alternatives has been unleashed. The problem posed during it was, invariably, what path of development to follow. The dispute would flare up overnight and last a good while, then subside in favor of one of the camps. . . . But then some major socio-political event would unleash the confrontation again in a new phase of this unbreakable cycle. [Ornea 1980:100]

One participant in that cycle remarked, "West or East, Europe or the Balkans, urban civilization or the rural spirit?—[since 1860] the questions are still the same" (Sebastian, cited in Livezeanu 1984:313). The questions posed in this "drama of alternatives" were central to discussions that produced and perpetuated the Romanian national ideology. At the heart of the discussions were debates concerning the national essence of Romanians as a people.

The debates on the national essence began in the mid-1800s and spread through virtually all political and intellectual discourse. From 1900 on, there was scarcely a politician, regardless of party, and scarcely a thinker, whether in economics, psychology, sociology, ethnography, philosophy, literature or art, who did not directly or indirectly have something to say about Romanians' essential character. The preconditions of the debate lay in Romantic notions about the "spirit" of different peoples *(Volksgeist)*, each people being thought to have its own special and original "genius" and its mission in the world. These notions entered widely into Romanians' intellectual exchanges. They also entered into the lexicon of politics and political economy, through a major tenet of Herderian Romanticism: the idea that a clear understanding of the national essence is prerequisite to formulating a politics suited to the Nation, for if politics follow interests that have *not* taken account of the people's essential character, the people will suffer, its natural mission will remain unfulfilled, and the policy will necessarily fail. Therefore, arguments about the national essence included policy questions about whether to preserve or to change what were seen as Romania's traditional social, economic, political, and cultural forms, and if they should change, in what direction and to what extent.

These arguments continued already venerable practices—different, of course, in form, context and meaning—that went back to the 1500s. Despite the differences in context and meaning, however, one basic question was common to earlier and later efforts to define the Romanian Nation: is the Romanian character occidental or oriental, and what is the basis for that affinity? Focusing on answers to this basic question will help convey a sense of the debate, even if at the cost of oversimplification. There were three principal positions on the matter of claimed affinities, with countless minor variations in each of them. One, which I call the pro-western or westernizing position, viewed Romanians as the heirs to, and participants in, a western tradition descended from Rome. This view emerged from a historiographical interpretation that found Romanian origins in the Roman legions that had entered the territory around AD 100, defeating the native Dacians. A second, pro-oriental position affiliated Romanians with the traditions of the East. This position had both a strictly religious variant—Romanians are oriental because of their ties to the Byzantine empire and Eastern Orthodoxy—and a more generally historical one—Romanians are oriental from their eastern-derived Thracian forebears, more ancient than the Romans. The third view, indigenism or autochthonism, emphasized local values over affinities with either East or West and preferred the Dacians as the principal ancestor. Indigenists came in great variety; some of them leaned ever so slightly eastward or westward, while still emphasizing qualities they thought peculiar to Romanians and wished to protect from the corrupting effects of imported civilizations, particularly the western one. This spectrum of views parallels similar options in many other countries of the world, among them the debates between Russian "Westernizers" and "Slavophiles."

The positions are best illustrated through the words of some of the participants themselves. First, a pro-oriental voice:

> If the mission of the Romanian people is to create a culture after its image and likeness, this implies as well how its orientation should be resolved. Whoever recommends an orientation toward the West speaks nonsense. *Orientation* contains within itself the notion of *Orient* and means directing ourselves toward the Orient, in accord with the Orient. Altars face toward the Orient; the icons of the hearth face us from the Orient; the peasant who kneels in his field faces toward the Orient. Everywhere it is said that light comes from the East. And for us, who find ourselves geographically in the Orient and who, through our Orthodox religion, hold to the

truths of the eastern world, there can be no other orientation than toward the Orient, that is, toward ourselves. . . . Westernization means the negation of our orientalness; Europeanizing nihilism means the negation of our creative potential. [Crainic 1929:3]

This same author often voiced the opinion that the contemplative style characteristic of "orientals" made Romanians unsuited to industrial work.

Next, an indigenist who often played up the oriental connection:

We think ourselves merely latins—lucid, rational, temperate, lovers of classical form—but willy-nilly we are more than that. [A] significant percent of Slavic and Thracian blood seethes in our veins. The Romanian spirit may be dominated by latinity, a peaceful and cultured force, but we have also a rich latent Thraco-Slavic foundation, exuberant and vital, which, no matter how much we oppose it, sometimes detaches itself from the nether realms and rises up powerfully in our consciousness. Our latin symmetry and harmony are often battered by a storm that rages in the Romanian spirit at near-metaphysical depths; and this storm is the revolt of our non-latin soul. . . . Why should we violate our true nature, corset ourselves in a formula of latin clarity, when so many other possibilities for development lie within us in that barbarian unconscious? [Blaga 1921:181–182]

Next, a "pure" indigenist firmly opposed to western influences and to eastern affiliations as well (not evident in this quote):

Our whole social life is shot through with illusions. We have adopted civil and political laws unsuited to our traditions; we have organized a public education useless to the large majority of the people; we have imitated the bourgeois technique of economic production in which neither the qualities of our people nor the wealth of our country can bear fruit; we have done everything in our power to falsify the traditions and the aptitudes given us by nature . . . [thinking] ourselves obligated to be to Europe's taste. . . . For better than a century, the Romanian people has not been faithful to itself. Let us have an end to experiments with laws for the [so-called] "Belgium of the Orient." [Rădulescu-Motru 1936:31, 118, 35]

In contrast, here is a moderate westernizer:

In the twentieth century, history has set Romanians the following problem: will Romania continue to be a semi-asiatic, oriental country or will it enter the ranks of European peoples and European culture. This problem has been answered by history. For various reasons, Romania could not exempt itself from the European influence [that] penetrated into our country. It penetrated through the very fact of its superiority. [Ibrăileanu 1909:261]

While this writer seems *resigned* to accepting western influence, another openly *embraces* it, envisioning the people's deliverance in such an embrace:

> Under the banner of Orthodoxy and tradition some persons flourish the ideal—static and immobilized in hieratic byzantine-muscovite forms—of a primitive [Romanian] culture without development or prospects. *Our* cultural ideal [in contrast] is dynamic, eager for growth, renewal and fructification. . . . We mean to propagate a sense of culture that is European. Our light comes from the West. We see our deliverance in the occidentalization of this country, many of whose vital organs are putrefying even before it has reached maturity. Balkanism, our cherished and idealized orientalness . . . now shelters all the brigands who have impeded political purification and opposed uplifting the people from the cultural cesspool in which it flounders. . . . [We seek] the affirmation of our genius and specific character in the forms of European culture, in the harmonious and shining framework of the culture of the West. . . . We have faith that soap, comfort and urbanism, the telegraph and civil law in no way threaten the purity of our race. [Filotti 1924:2–4]

Even this cursory exposure to the arguments on the national essence reveals the tensions among peasantism and urban cosmopolitanism, stasis and dynamism, agriculture and industrialization, all summarized in the contrast between affiliation with Orient or Occident. The preoccupation with this contrast betrays an elite transfixed between more powerful countries and larger hegemonic discourses. That one of them—the western one—has overtaken the other is visible in the "orientalist" representations (see Said 1978) given the East even by its partisans. A final example will highlight the western stereotypes in terms of which East and West are presented:

> All of occidental civilization can be reduced to a single phrase: *an aptitude for creation*. . . . The psychology of the Orient is exactly the opposite. It reduces ordinarily to *passive resignation*. The Occidental imposes himself on the environment, the Oriental submits to it. . . . Fatalism . . . seems to him the only solution. . . . If we observe closely our people's habits, institutions, way of reacting and of living, we will easily conclude that its psychology enters into a conduct equidistant between the activist voluntarism of the occident and the fatalistic passivity of the orient. [Ralea 1943:103, 104–105, 106–107; emphasis in original]

Participants in the debate speak in terms of active and passive, will and fatalism, and so forth; nearly all see the West as rational, ordered, productive and the East as irrational, stagnant, impulsive, disorderly; and they depict the East as, at best, a realm of *spiritual* values, in contrast to the *material* civilization of the West. The constellation of views that emerges in the arguments reveals the difficulties of defining a national voice in a period of western political, economic, and ideological hegemony.

The struggle was not merely to define a national voice, however, but to establish a satisfactory relation to western capitalism, a problem implicit in the terms of the debate. Whether or not Romania would be receptive to capitalism is apparent not only in the arguments about whether the peasant and agrarian essence of the Romanian character, and its spiritual as opposed to material values, make it unsuited to capitalism and other western forms. It appears also, less visibly, in underlying assumptions about such things as how the Nation would be recruited. Recruitment is implicit in the question of how Romanian national identity and its essence were acquired and how vulnerable they were to outside influence. Among the several conflicting opinions were that the Romanian essence is something ineluctable (a "fatality," in one writer's terms), that it is a matter of customary, unmeditated behavior (language, traditions), or that it comes from conscious and willful adherence. Here are two divergent views on that question:

> *To wish to be* Romanian does not also mean *to be* Romanian. Being Romanian is a natural state, having a certain make-up, from which, with absolute necessity, flow certain attitudes and gestures. Our will has no say under these conditions, because we cannot normally transcend ourselves except by ceasing to be ourselves. [Ionescu 1937:197; emphasis in original]
>
> The ethnic soul is the result of a culture, of a certain social life. Change the culture and habits and slowly the soul of the people will change as well. . . . The ethnic soul is constantly changing. A single and uniform ethnic soul does not exist. [Ralea 1943:89, 90]

The second view recognizes the potential malleability of the national essence and therefore relativizes it somewhat. This is quite different from those theorists who rooted it in unchanging, uninfluenceable unconscious or racial structures. Adherents of the second view believed that the essence could be changed without ceasing to be national; opponents saw any change, especially assimilation to foreign ways, as jeopardizing it. The more open, relativized conception generally rested Romanian identity on behavioral manifestations, rather than blood, and saw it as susceptible to historical and environmental modification.

This "malleable-essence" view was associated with westernizers and, I would argue, with capitalist industrialization, while the "fixed-essence" view characterized anticapitalist indigenists and pro-orientalists. The link is what each view implies for recruitment into the Nation and, by extension, the national labor force. The "malleable-essence" view is inclusive: it makes aliens potential members of the community, and it embraces new ways into the Romanian repertoire. Recruitment into the group becomes more flexible. To see Romanian identity and essence as inborn, on the other hand, as carried by blood, creates a collectivity very closely delimited by genealogical links, a genetic community into which recruitment is rigid. Both conceptions entail mechanisms for eliminating or incorporating outsiders (genetic relations can be disavowed or fictively created just as behavior and consciousness can be changed); but the greater flexibility of the nongenetic conception is perhaps more suited to a world in which the availability of resources (and the labor for working them) contracts and expands frequently, as in a capitalist economy, while the genetic view suits a relation to resources that fluctuates less widely. The two conceptions thus bear implicitly upon political choices that would welcome or resist capitalism.[11]

It would nevertheless be a mistake to see the debates as constructing a Nation that would be automatically tied to a more or less capital-friendly state. To the contrary: participants of all stripes were apt to express the view that the Nation was theoretically separate from and even superior to the state. This possibility had also been voiced by people such as Herder, who saw the state as artifice and the Nation as natural; nobles in Hungary had brandished arguments of this sort, in their struggle to break free from the nation-smothering artificial Habsburg state (Verdery 1983:117). In seeking their accommodation with western hegemony, Romania's interstitial elites constructed a kind of Nation that lacked a necessary and integral connection to the state. The nation-building of these elites would bear a more contradictory relationship to the process of state-building, therefore, than we believe true of the western experience, with its supposedly organic link between national ideologies and the rise of the nation-state. In the Romanian case, the Nation could be invoked—through claims to defend its interests—*against* the processes of state-building. If we see the state as helping to secure the conditions for capitalist production/reproduction and as also, itself, further consolidated by its ties to capitalism, then any political argument that successfully presents the Nation as *un*suited to capitalism will impede the unfolding of this functional complex.

Arguments that rooted the Romanian essence in the peasantry, that extolled the past and promoted the values of spiritual over material civilization, had precisely this effect. In so doing, they faithfully enacted the intention of other European Romantics upon whose imagery these Romanian thinkers drew so heavily. To struggle over the definition of the Romanian Nation, and to claim defense of its interests on the basis of that definition, then, was an integral part not just of directly producing Romania's relation to capitalism but also of strengthening or weakening its state, with the indirect effects this would have upon the country's capitalist prospects.

The Nation as Subject

The possibility that such anti-state defense of the Nation would be more than simply rhetorical, potentially contributing real political support for these counterelites from at least some members of Romanian society, would depend on whether or not Romanian identity and its symbols became internalized. The ideological production I have been discussing did indeed move toward its own internalization, I believe. At issue is the process whereby a national ideology comes to be experienced as part of a sense of *self as ethnic;* that is, how it constitutes ideological subjects who regard themselves as *national* and who cathect that identity as a meaningful element of the social person. This goes beyond the elite's creation of external symbols, such as the heroes of Romanian history that historical writing had taken great pains to publicize to the masses. It involves creating a subjectivity of a national kind that responds emotionally when such symbols are flourished.[12]

In my view, the debates on the national essence began this process by exploring what it means to be Romanian as—among other things—an *inner state of being.* That is, the debates were instrumental in constructing a notion of *Romanian inner self.* They accomplished this in part through the overriding concern of many participants with the notion of Romanian *spirituality,* seen as inner essence, a preoccupation that emphasizes an interior space and implies an inward migration of identity into a form of subjective consciousness. To talk about spirituality amounted to recognizing areas internal to the human person, areas of subjective experience that might welcome inside themselves the symbols of Princes Michael the Brave and Stephen the Great, upon whom historians had worked diligently. How did the debates imply such a development?

While much of the discussion did no more than define the national essence loosely in terms of habits of mind or a collective ethnic psyche, it also included arguments about the specific *traits* of which the essence is comprised. The concern with an interior lurks at the margins of these arguments: some writers characterized Romanians by their "resignation" or "serenity," for instance, while others insisted that discussions of Romanian culture should rest upon understanding Romanian consciousness and "the life of our soul," best achieved through a form of psychological inquiry. There were disagreements over whether or not the Romanian soul is inherently "mystical"; whether or not Romanian religiosity is interior or a matter of external adherence to ritual forms; and whether the national soul was best described through externalities like customs and language or, instead, through inner sensibilities or tonalities of sentimental expression.

Perhaps two specific examples will make the point. First, a Transylvanian ethnographer writing in 1939 criticized ethnography for busying itself with collecting and cataloguing *objects* and *sounds* as if it were the science of the retina and eardrum. He proposed the following remedy:

> Thus reduced to the exterior aspect of our popular culture, ethnography and folklore have collected . . . a huge material that will arouse the admiration of posterity. The collections, however, no matter how voluminous and perfect, comprise a material from which the *spirit* is largely lacking. To proceed further, ethnography will have to move from *studying the surface* of our popular culture to a *depth perspective*. . . . Popular culture is in the first place *the soul;* this is dressed in certain material forms, but it has itself *created* them, as well. The researcher cannot limit himself to the study of these material forms without trying to understand the soul that gave them birth. [Pavelescu 1939:460–461; emphasis in original]

Second, two influential writers argued over whether it was adequate to define the essence of Romanianness as "adaptability," a capacity to adapt quickly to any new situation. One said yes; another objected, talking instead of qualities like "serenity" and "equanimity," which imply a process of contemplation "proving interiority and conflict in the Romanian soul" rather than the orientation to the *outside* world that was basic to the notion of "adaptability." Labeling his concern with an interior "accommodation," this writer argued:

> Accommodation presupposes an indifference for external conditions. It implies much interiority. Adaptation, by contrast, implies not interiority but a certain rootlessness of soul, a spiritual and physical nomadism. It presupposes alienation and an immediate alignment of oneself with external conditions. [Comarnescu 1985:219]

He concluded by suggesting that the essence of being Romanian is to be *internally* Romanian no matter where one is placed: thus, territory and language are of less importance, ultimately, than a particular inner disposition.

I am not in a position to argue that intellectual efforts to define the national essence caused this inner disposition, this interior subjectivity, to emerge full-blown for all Romanians. Such an argument will require much more research. I do contend, however, that from arguing about the inner or exterior character of Romanian identity, an inner space of an ethnic kind became real for the intellectuals engaged in exploring it. This resulted not so much from the fact that some intellectuals (the pro-orientalists and indigenists) insisted upon it but from the whole field of argumentation in which an inner space became an explicit premise. That is, to argue that being Romanian is or is not an inner disposition is to accept the premise that humans *have* inner dispositions, which may or may not prove to be the seat of ethnic character. The creation of subjectivities, recognized as such, entails the prior creation and recognition of interior spaces; only thereafter can appeals to inner sentiment be efficacious. To the extent that specifically national subjectivities became a politically significant means of mobilizing the sentiments of the masses of Romanians, I submit, this required first the development of a sense of Romanianness as a subjectivity among the elite who made such mobilizing its task. Discussions about the national essence contributed to this part of the ideological process.

If I am correct in seeing here the production of a national subjectivity, then its vehicle is the idea of "spirituality" that was seen as associated particularly with the Orient or with Romanians' non-western qualities, distinguishing them from the material civilization of the West. I have suggested elsewhere that western representations of the East were basic to the formation of western personality structures, in which the reasoned and disciplined ego (represented as masculine and western) sought to moderate the impulse-gratifying irrational and childish desires of the id (represented as female and eastern) (see Verdery n.d.). In their concern with spirituality, certain Romanian intellectuals made a similar use of representations of the East in relation to their people, promoting a subjective ("spiritual") national disposition by means of orientalist imagery. They intended, however, that it would *resist* rather than *serve* the imposition of western reason and discipline. Indigenists and pro-orientalists were putting orientalist imagery to potentially counterhegemonic purposes, in their quest to reappropriate the space within which their people had been represented (as oriental) by the more powerful West. In other words, the same Orient that was helping to constitute disciplined western subjects was entering into the constitution of a Romanian resistance to westernization.

Nevertheless, the pro-orientals and indigenists would not have the last word, for the national subjectivities they helped to create could be tapped not only by persons opposing the values of capitalism and the West but also by would-be nation-state builders *promoting* these values. The subjectivities that were implied in the debates over the national essence, therefore, enter into the contradictory relation between nation-building and state-building already discussed; with them, the Nation that has been produced can be defended by all aspirants in even more internally compelling ways.

Conflict and Alliance within the Elite: The Role of the Peasantry in Images of the Nation

Besides revealing alternative possible relations to capital and furthering the internalization of Romanian identity as a subjective condition, the debates on the national essence served as an important locus for representing changed class and intraclass relations and for struggle among agents of religious and secular institutions, each claiming preeminence in defending the Nation. These latter two processes are especially visible in how participants defined the relationship of the Nation to the peasantry.[13] The "peasant problem" was a major concern of the period, and it had several roots, relating to changes in the country's class structure. Three of the most important were the rising tide of populism throughout the whole region (the Narodniks in Russia became prominent at this same time), the devastation wrought by a massive rebellion of Romanian peasants in 1907, and—with the enactment of universal male suffrage—the new imperative of incorporating into party platforms and public appeals a peasantry that had been largely ignored in most parts of the country.[14]

The peasantry provided fertile ground, first, for conflicts among groups within the elite, as different parties defended their programs by identifying them with the peasants and the Nation. People accused one another of betraying the Nation, its national mission, and/or its peasant masses (for example, Dobridor 1935; Madgearu 1921), invoking the three elements interchangeably. Such wording for intraelite contests was visible as early as the first decade of the 20th century, in a series of acrid debates ostensibly about the place of populist values in literature. Among the most widely known of them was a fierce attack launched by one Transylvanian leader against another under the guise of a discussion of literary values (see, for example, Popovici 1908a, 1908b; Tăslăuanu 1908a, 1908b). The instigator argued that so-called national leaders (his opponent) have sold out Romanian identity, adopting foreign culture and imitating foreign models alien to the culture of the masses. Charging that this adopted international culture was detrimental to the national culture, he drew the moral that claims to defend Romanian unity are sometimes deceitful. He set himself up as representing those whose organic connection to the peasantry will make them seek to obtain from the state what the "unconscious masses" desire. His opponent countercharged that the instigator was promoting socialism and anarchy, dividing the Nation by class war, and therefore detracting from its unity and progress. This and related arguments show the peasantry being put to use by different elite groups arguing over the definition of the Nation and the right to speak for it.[15]

The effort to strengthen parties and constituencies through defining the national essence in relation to peasants is evident in a second way as well: the connection between those parties or politicians who advocated the idea of a "peasant state," free of industrial artifice, and those writers who insisted that the national essence was to be found in the purity of peasant souls. Particularly prone to see the essence of Romanianness as residing in the peasants were the indigenists. This fit with their rejection of western-style industrialization and urbanism, as seen in the following:

> What state politics do we now propose? . . . A wholly revolutionary politics, . . . [which] recommends: decoupling us from world politics; closing us up in our own borders as completely as possible; taking into consideration what is realistic for Romania; provisionally reducing our standard of living to a realistic level; and laying the foundations for a Romanian State of peasant structure, the only form in which we can truly live according to the indications of our nature and the only one we can implant that will enable the powers of our race truly and completely to bear fruit. [Ionescu 1937:286–287]

For people who held such views, an important concomitant was to deny the peasants "coevalness" with the persons writing about them (see Fabian 1983). Here, for example, are two indigenist partisans of the peasantry who saw it as inhabiting a space untouched by time:

> The village has not let itself be tempted and drawn into the "history" made by others over our heads. It has preserved itself chastely, untouched in the autonomy with which poverty and mythology have endowed it, and awaits the time when it will serve as the sure foundation of an authentically Romanian history. [Blaga 1980 [1937]:258]

> [The peasant remains] on the same patch of soil, generation after generation, confined in the immobility of the same destiny, while outside his radius everything is in perpetual change. . . . Peasant life has no history. It absorbs itself in nature. But like the seeds that lie in nature's breast, like the minerals hidden in the folds of the earth, the embers of possibility smoulder in this primitive life. [Crainic 1936:89]

Even those who took westernizing positions and did not see peasants as the heart of the nation manifested concern with the peasantry. For example, in distinguishing his views from some of the "peasantist" writings, one quasi-westernizer wrote:

> They criticize new forms, regret the old order, and admire the patriarchal peasants as a remnant of the times of [princes] Michael and Stephen. And they idealize this peasant precisely because he was so backward and removed from the civilized life of Europe. We see something else in the peasantry: a peasant who is a social being, who is poor, who needs reforms and raising up. Transforming him presupposes the complete occidentalization of the country, the complete destruction of old forms. Thus, in opposition to the conservatives and literary peasantists we must defend new forms and push for universal suffrage, . . . [so as to make peasants] into *citizens*. Our ideal has not been the picturesque, illiterate peasant with long hair and a wide belt who sits in his poetic hut all day playing his pan-pipe. Our ideal has been the peasant dressed in European clothes . . . with a brick house and barn, who can read . . . the peasant who lives in a village with electricity and plows his field with improved machinery or works in factories nearby. [Ibrăileanu 1925:143–144]

It is clear, however, that unlike the two writers quoted above, this scholar does not see the peasants as irrevocably outside time, just as needing a forward push within it.[16]

The discursive interest of intellectuals in the peasantry accomplished several things, I suggest, akin to discursive interests in women, in other times and places (see, for example, Poovey 1986; Scott 1987): it distanced and silenced them, and it rendered them an open field for intellectuals and the state to colonize. The distancing and silencing are eminently visible in those quotations that remove peasants from time, as well as in a sociologist's angry accusation that one of the most eloquent proponents of the peasantry's "boycott" of history (philosopher Lucian Blaga) had never set foot in a village to find out what real peasants actually thought about anything.[17] Scholars who excluded peasants from time colonized them by calling upon the state to preserve their blessed innocence (see the first of the four extracts above). Other scholars, while admitting the peasantry into history, colonized it in a different way by calling upon the state and other social groups to *raise it up* (see the fourth extract above). While both invocations strengthened the state by inviting it in and giving it work to do, the first of the two entailed less penetration for purposes of control and surveillance than did the second: the reformers, when they at length won out, would overrun the villages with research teams, domesticating peasants to the purposes of science and furthering their acquaintance with state-run education.[18]

Both groups, however, used a language impressive above all for its paternalism and condescension. This widened the chasm between the peasants and those who claimed to speak in their defense. Behind the celebrations of peasant innocence and the many proposals for reform of the countryside lies a celebration of the peasantry's elite patrons, set firmly apart on the far side of a class barrier. Particularly clear illustration of how defense of the peasantry and the Nation celebrated specific elite statuses is to be found in one of the vehicles intellectuals used in striving to capture and defend the Nation: the exaltation of Reason. This vehicle enabled thinkers of present themselves as superior to the church, which they accused to fostering the people's ignorance through mystical and irrational practices. Exalting Reason and science went well beyond arguments against the church, however: reformers argued fervently that the church was merely the most important of several breeding grounds of ignorance and superstition, which anyone having the interests of the peasants and the Nation truly at heart should strive to extirpate. Intellectuals, the builders of science and knowledge, were to become teachers of the Nation. Among the enthusiasts of such arguments were not only the westernizers, but many indigenists. An example is philosopher-psychologist Constantin Rădulescu-Motru, one of Romania's most influential intellectuals between 1900 and 1945, who tried to develop a national ideology resting on Reason as against the mysticism of both religion and other national ideologies (Rădulescu-Motru 1936). Through these and many similar appeals, persons involved in producing the Romanian Nation and claiming its defense also produced the grounds of their own legitimation: acceptance of the central value of knowledge (see also Bauman 1987:18).

The purveyors of this knowledge might work hand in hand with the builders of the state, and then again, they might not. Historically, intellectuals have sometimes served to strengthen the state by calling for it to intervene to solve social problems (see Rabinbach 1986; Scott 1988), while in other cases they have set themselves at a distance from it (Engelstein 1986). Some Romanian intellectuals, such as sociologist Dimitrie Gusti, invoked the state and worked with it, offering it their services so that it could govern the people in a reasoned way (Gheorghiu 1990:11). Historian Nicolae Iorga rendered a variant of this notion vividly in a speech for the semicentenary of the Romanian Academy: he observed that just as paintings of churches showed them supported on the right side by the king and on the left by the bishop, the state should be shown as supported on the right side by the king and on the left by the man of science. Others placed themselves above state-makers, and thus in potential opposition to them, arguing that politicians should be mere executors of the plans that intellectuals arrived at scientifically (Gheorghiu 1990:11).

Still others encouraged open defection from state purposes. For example, one contributor to the leftist newspaper, *The Society of Tomorrow*, wrote an urgent appeal entitled "The Defense of the Nation" to argue for the vital matter of strengthening "the spiritual resistance of our people, which should be the daily preoccupation of our leaders" (Ghiulea 1926:509). Ordinarily, he said, the moral and social education basic to such strengthening is the obligation of the state. But the Romanian state seemed lately to have forgotten its responsibility to the nation, having become a vehicle for exploiting the people rather than a truly ethnic organization. Its leaders do not care whether the people are satisfied or not, whether the national treasure is wasted or used to good effect. The Romanian state cares only to build up its unlimited power; it is not an ethical entity and does not work to raise up the Nation but, rather, strives to plunder it and to serve the interests of our enemies (Ghiulea 1926:509). If, as this writer claims, the state has abdicated its responsibility to the Nation, who then remains to defend the people's interests? Those who serve its moral and social education, of course, and have created a peasant people in need of supervision and reform.

Beneath arguments about the peasantry and the national essence was a further dispute, concerning whether the Nation is a phenomenon of *nature* or of *culture*. The same contest underlay the different views on recruitment, discussed earlier. For those who saw the Nation as a phenomenon of nature, recruited through "natural" genetic processes, it was logical to find the Nation's epitome in the peasant as a child of nature. Those who saw the Nation in less genetic terms were likely to represent peasants as *social* objects warranting attention and control, and as merely a part of the Nation rather than its epitome. This dispute over nature and culture can be seen, following Poovey, as part of a more general struggle among various institutions and groups for pride of place in speaking for the Nation. Poovey suggests that proponents of a "nature" position in Victorian debates over the use of chloroform in childbirth were giving pride of place to God and his earthly representative, the church, while those arguing for "culture" were supporting secular institutions (in her case, the medical profession) (Poovey 1986:139). The strength of the Romanian Orthodox Church as an institution, the long-standing authority of its spokesmen, and its great nationalist role make it plausible to pursue this possibility, enabling us to see in the debates about the national essence not just a contest between intellectuals and the state but a three-way competition involving the church as well. The competition often invoked the peasantry (as in the following examples) but also spread far beyond them.

A number of participants in the debates on the national essence upheld the church as a vital preserver of the Nation; those favoring this connection invariably opposed modernity and westernization.[19] For example, one of the most vociferous defenders of the Nation, philosopher-theologian Nichifor Crainic, defined Romanian identity as inextricably tied and defined by Orthodoxy. His argument infuriated a host of other writers, who rejoined that because Orthodoxy was not restricted to Romanians, it could not define their national identity; some even went so far as to claim that the actions of the church had impoverished the people and impeded its mission (for example, Ghibu 1924). Directly attacking the claims of churchmen and others that religious institutions had preserved the existence of Romanians through centuries of deculturating foreign rule, such writers sought to capture the Nation from the grip of the church. For example:

> The Orthodox Church is and has been perpetuated as foreign. Faith manifests itself in acts; the Orthodox faith is not represented by a single Romanian Orthodox act in a single domain of religious application: miracles, proselytism, oratory, writing, propaganda, sacrifices. Not a single initiative begun under the sign of a religious sentiment [has been Romanian in its character]. [Arghezi 1928]

The dispute was not simply among those speaking for the church and those speaking for secular reason (although this too was a major dimension) but involved redefining the relationship between religion and the state. Since the end of automatic state funding for the church, in the 1860s, coupled with the state's invasion into spheres hitherto reserved for the church, such as village schooling, the church had found itself on the run before an increasingly greedy state. We can see these issues neatly combined with the defense of a peasant Romanian essence in the question of calendrical reform, which was finally effected in 1924 with the official change from the Julian to the Gregorian calendar. The changed calendar evoked a fascinating "defense" of the peasantry on the part of some intellectuals, who condemned the change as an assault on national identity because it undermined old religious traditions on which identity rested. Peasants, it was said, were upset that the new calendar separated them from their ancestors: "we are losing our identity, we're taking after the Germans" (see Băncilă 1924–1925). One commentator observed that the change affected work discipline, inasmuch as the religious calendar determined the agricultural cycle of labor (ibid.). With this, he came close to revealing the true significance of the reform: that by seizing time, the state had captured from the church the definition of the laboring world. The calendar change therefore diminished the power of religion to define both persons and the world, to the extent that these are based in labor and in its relation to time.

The chief contenders for defense of the Nation, then, were the church, the state, and various groups of intellectuals, siding now with one and now with the other of the first two. The peasantry was a major actor in those contests, sometimes providing the vehicle by which alternative programs for the Nation were articulated. Sometimes, the challenge posed by the peasant masses united elites in the urgent political task of imposing discipline and order on the dangerous rabble (Bauman 1987:78), in the name of serving the Nation's larger interests. In discussions among these contenders, persons acting from within state and church had an institutional position on which to base their defense. In the following section I will ask how the third group, the intellectuals, achieved something comparable, by means of the national discourse, enabling them to voice their ongoing concerns for the Nation whether or not individuals among them entered the halls of power.

Intellectuals and the Disciplines

To the extent that intellectuals retained some critical autonomy from the state, we might ask how they constructed that autonomy and what role the debates on the national essence played in the process. I argue that the debates themselves helped to produce the structures within which intellectuals might continue to defend the Nation against those who claimed to serve its interests through state politics. That is, the debates actively created part of the material infrastructure that would sustain the defense of the Nation, at the same time that they further solidified the Romanian national ideology.

When the Romanian state was formed, between 1859 and 1881, there grew up with it those institutional structures associated with the consolidation of any state of the "modern" type: educational institutions such as universities, with a growing number of departments and chairs; a national academy on the French model; a variety of cultural organizations and multitudinous publications, some of them with state subventions; a State Archive; national museums; and so on. Intellectuals unwittingly entrenched themselves within these newly given institutional settings through arguments about the Nation and its "essence." In part by means of these arguments, academic disciplines were consolidated and differentiated, university chairs and publication subventions and other resources competed for, and institutional personalities strengthened and sharpened in ways that would not always suit the governing political party. The very material of the discourse on nationality therefore provided a means for disciplinary proliferation. I do not argue that the national discourse *caused* this proliferation, for disciplines were being established in all western countries during this period and not always through nationalism.[20] I argue only that the medium within which this larger process was occurring in the Romanian context was the language of nationalism (rather than a language invoking science or social progress, for example), and this fact had consequences for the relation of scholarly activity to defense of the Nation.

The process of disciplinary growth and differentiation in Romania included claims and counterclaims that one or another discipline had superior capacity to treat aspects of the national identity. Typical of such claims is the following rationale one writer offered to promote a discipline of ethnopsychology distinct from ethnology: "Ethnology has to do only with *externalities:* distributions, kinship, migrations, customs; it does not occupy itself with the residues all these changes leave in the spirit of the people, with the psychological substrate" (important matters that a discipline of ethnopsychology would treat) (Eminescu, cited in Babu-Buznea 1979:105n). In making claims of this sort, I must emphasize, scholars were not consciously and intentionally manipulating the national idea in the interests of expanding their turf. If their turf did nonetheless expand, this was most probably unintended and shows the material consequences of the national ideology Romanian intellectuals were producing. Lacking the space to illustrate this process extensively, I will give only a few examples from sociology in relation to other disciplines (see Verdery 1987).

The Nation and debates about it could figure, to begin with, in the definitional struggles within any given discipline. One observer divides the interwar sociological field into three camps: the national reformist, the national cultural, and the extreme right, their leaders arguing among themselves from different cities on both scientific and political grounds.

> Romanian sociology . . . was the terrain of an implicit and explicit ideological battle centering on the problem not so much of the nation in general as of the Romanian nation confronted with internal social contradictions, tested by the plague of fascism, and threatened by external perils. [Mihu 1984:518]

The exponent of the first camp and interwar Romania's most famous sociologist, D. Gusti, defined his agenda thus:

> [Sociology as] a positive science, that is, oriented to facts, cannot fail to consider the hierarchy of problems posed by reality itself. From the moment that the nation reveals itself to us as the most significant form of modern social life, the science of society—sociology—must constitute itself as the science of the nation. . . . The science of the nation will determine for it the ethics and politics through which the people will find its true road to self-realization. . . . This science will make it possible to establish, at last, the true national ideal, which will not mean an estrangement, a departure from the historical path of the people but a maximum development toward the fulfillment of all its natural capacities. [Gusti 1968 [1937]:493, 506]

In the name of discovering the exact character of Romanian social reality so as to determine the people's true path and then to press for appropriate social reforms, he developed a complex theoretical and methodological system and set the landscape crawling with sociological researchers.

His definition of sociology did not go unchallenged, however. His former student P. Andrei, among others, argued that the science of sociology should be more than simply a descriptive and methodologically narrow sociography, built upon innumerable village monographs and aimed at social reform (Mihu 1984:528). Departing somewhat from Gusti's insistence that the nation was the *raison d'etre* of sociology, he instead saw it as only one of several objects, another of which should be the study of society's spiritual life. This said, however, he regarded the Nation as the most powerful form of spiritual human community and pressed for the development of the national culture as a major goal of sociological work (1984:530). Thus, even for Andrei the discipline was to be defined in large part by its relation to the Nation, as object of both study and social action.

The national essence and its proper treatment could become the basis for claims and struggles over turf not simply within the discipline itself but also across the border between sociology and other disciplines (across *any* such borders). Against Gusti's definition of sociology, consider a statement by a partisan of psychology:

> If our sociology is relatively far advanced because, thanks to [our best researchers] we know aspects of the formation and functioning of some of our classes—the nobility, the gentry, the peasantry, and the bourgeoisie—Romanian psychology contains not one single chapter, has gathered material for not one single problem, because no one has yet posed a problem for it. And yet no one would disagree that Romanian psychology is every bit as necessary as Romanian sociology. [Ralea 1943:81]

He then makes clear that the proper object for this sorry discipline is the study of ethnic psychology. In this scholar's reading, sociology really has little to do with the ethnic essence as such: rather, its proper object is the social structure of the national society. For him, a better claim to treating the national essence adequately is offered by psychology.

Arguing from within sociology and in opposition to ethnography, another scholar noted that the rise of national consciousness brought an interest in folklore, which was expected to "enlighten our understanding of the nature and destiny of the Romanian people" but has produced nothing of scientific importance (Herseni 1941:5). He explains this by the inadequacy of folklore as a discipline, both methodologically (it is too unsystematic) and scientifically (it lacks rigor). "Collections made at random, by persons full of zeal but lacking scientific training, deepen the national sentiment more than the knowledge of ethnic reality and therefore have more an educational and political than a scientific value" (1941). Earlier studies of the Romanian people will have to be taken up again, with deepened and broadened methods, work techniques, and conceptualization. Sociology, he claims, is vastly preferable to ethnography and folklore for this: rather than being a science of *things,* as ethnography often is, it rests on assumptions that are functionalist, integralist, and vitalist, making it a better tool than other disciplines for researching the Romanian people. "Only in collaboration with sociology can ethnography and folklore satisfactorily fulfill their task" (1941:6–13).

An especially lively dispute concerned the border that separated sociology/ethnography and philosophy; its protagonists were sociologist Henri Stahl and philosopher Lucian Blaga. Blaga offered a philosophical theory of the national essence that purported to link it with village life and folklore. In response, Stahl published several papers in the late 1930s flatly rejecting Blaga's proposals and contending that ethnographers and folklorists had offered far more plausible accounts of the elements of folk life that Blaga claimed to interpret. Stahl took particular offense at Blaga's speculating upon the Romanian village without actually studying it by any other than armchair means, and at his arrogant assumption that because the "Romanian phenomenon" has nothing to do with real historical time or sociological space, philosophy is the only way to study it. Objecting to the implicit sociology in Blaga's philosophy of culture, Stahl comments sarcastically:

> Modern sociology affirms that any fact of social life takes a certain form on account of a series of factors [the natural environment, biological, psychological, etc.] that determine one another reciprocally . . . Mr. Blaga, on the other hand, finds that social phenomena have only a single law:

style, which springs from a single series of factors: the unconscious. . . . But we find criticism of Mr. Blaga's sociology not only justified but imperative, for in the present day we have embarked upon systematic research into the history and forms of Romanian popular culture. We have barely crossed the threshold of the most abject ignorance and behold! right in our path is an unforeseen obstacle, put there by the enticing formulas of the philosophy of culture . . . [which wants to make] any further study of the Romanian phenomenon superfluous. Mr. Blaga has given us the key to the problem: the stylistic matrix explains to us the style of any Romanian creation. . . . The thoughtless ease . . . [with which] he brushes aside scientific research and all other domains but the philosophy of culture irritates those of us who do scientific field research, and we will fight against it. [Stahl 1937:491; emphasis in original]

In more recent essays, even less polite in tone than those of the 1930s, Stahl objects in so many words to Blaga's claim to "monopolize knowledge of the Romanian cultural phenomenon" (1983:78).

A final complaint, this one from ethnography rather than sociology, shows how the Nation, its defense, and a discipline might be linked with expansionary processes furthered by study of the national essence:

It is amazing how all the disciplines that study the people—history, philology, geography, etc.—have created special institutes in all the universities; only ethnography has nothing but a university department . . . [He lists some causes of this dismal state of affairs.] Thus postwar *arrivisme* has led to the perversion of ethnicist sentiment and to ignoring the treasures that lie buried in village life. . . . When the spiritual equilibrium of intellectuals will be reestablished, when the state will consider it a capital obligation to promote ethnographic research, then . . . ethnography will be able to stand with greater success in the service of one of the loveliest missions of all: knowledge of the nation. [Pavelescu 1939:462]

This complaint indicates what I see as a major consequence of the debates on the national essence: their role in producing an institutional environment, a material infrastructure, that would help persons not in power to sustain their defense of the Nation.

As is by now apparent, part of the self-perceived task of the intellectuals who "produced" the Romanian Nation was to defend it against the abusive practices of politicians, whose policies often departed from what at least some formulations of the national essence said they ought to do. In particular, those thinkers who identified the Romanian essence as antithetical to western bourgeois ways regarded with horror or distaste the industrial development promoted by most of the interwar Romanian parties; they raised a loud defense of the Romanian people against this threat to the national mission. They were enabled to raise this defense, however, because—like the politicians who defended their own version of the Nation's interests from the ramparts of the state—they had secured in university departments and institutes a stable vantage point for their critique. The means for securing this vantage point were, in part, claims that one or another discipline's superior treatment of the Nation entitled it to more institutional resources.

The effect of all this carving up of disciplinary turf on the basis of the Nation was not only to bring into existence a more substantial material grounding for the Nation's defense, but also to embed the Nation permanently in intellectual discourse, which came to be shot through with it in every sphere of inquiry and creation. "The nation" and "the people" had become the unquestioned basis for every statement made in the debate: nowhere was anyone asking the question, "Is there such a thing as 'the Romanian people'?" Despite sometimes fierce disagreement on the particulars, these notions had become the ground for interaction across the whole spectrum of political and cultural life. In this sense, the national discourse can be said to have become a basic ideological premise of all argumentation in Romania, the language of political argument both among intellectuals and between them and others actively engaged in politics.

This essay has examined some debates about Romanian identity, illuminating means whereby a national ideology was constructed that became and has remained hegemonic. I have suggested that if we inspect the terms used in arguments concerning Romanians' essence, we see the production of cultural notions simultaneous with the production of politics. Asserting an "eastern" or "western" character for Romanians entailed political programs relating to capitalist industrialization; discussions about "spirituality" and inner essence posited interior subjective spaces relevant to creating political subjection; linking national character with peasants involved representations and projects for reform that forwarded this subjection by setting the masses squarely in another camp from those who spoke for them; and groups settled themselves more firmly within institutional structures, through claims about their capacity to research, represent, and defend the Nation.

These processes involved both discord and harmony among those engaged in them. Indeed, I claim that the construction of Romanian national ideology rests precisely on a combination of discord and harmony that obscured fundamental shared premises by suppressing them in argument. I also claim, however, that the vitality of the national discourse (a vitality rooted partially in its vigorous development *prior* to the formation of the Romanian state in the late 1800s) gave it an ambivalent relationship to the process of state-building. That is, the hegemonic ideology that developed through the processes I have outlined has not uniformly supported the further consolidation of the Romanian state, as state-makers and others claiming to speak for the Nation only sometimes work in concert with one another. During the debates, the Nation became an object of protection, every participant arguing how it might best be defined so that its needs might best be served. Some claimed to serve these interests from positions of government. But through the idea that politicians might well implement paths of development fundamentally unsuited to the national character, the groundwork was laid for others to defend the Nation against a deculturated state leadership accused of having defected from it.

Thus, the legitimacy of those holding power in Romania is always subject to challenge in the name of defending the Nation. This pattern holds good into the present, despite massive changes in the class and political structure since 1945. Because the debates embedded the Nation deeply not just in intellectual and political discourse but also in institutions supporting intellectual and political life, continued action within these ideologically saturated institutions reproduces Romanian nationalism further, complicating the attempt of alternative ideologies (such as Marxism-Leninism) to secure an institutional foothold.

Notes

Acknowledgments. I wish to thank Andrew Abbott, Richard Fox, Richard Handler, and a large number of Romanian historians and sociologists for their helpful comments on versions of this essay. Keith Hitchins, Paul Michelson, and Anna Watkins gave generous bibliographic assistance.

1. The words used in these discussions varied. The word for "people" *(popor)* means both the ethnic "people" and people in the sense of "masses." The former is usually the sense intended, but it is shadowed (usually helpfully) by the latter. The words for "nation" are usually either *națiune*, whose sense is clear, or *neam*, the most common *(neamul românesc)*. *Neam* comes from a Finno-Ugrian (and possibly Turkic) root *nem-* having the multiple meanings of kinship group, tribe, and people or nation. It has no good English translation. My discussion reduces these meanings to the word "nation."

2. The area Romanians call *Țara Românească*, the southern of the two Principalities that were joined in 1859 into a single polity, is known in English publications only as "Wallachia." The roots of this term are foreign and Romanians do not like it. "Muntenia" was the largest part of this entity (the remainder was "Oltenia"), and some Romanian and other writers therefore use the term "Muntenia" to refer to the whole area. I follow their usage.

3. To avoid the cumbersome placement of quotation marks around the word "nation" at each use, but to keep its particular meaning consistently in the mind of American readers likely to forget it, I will write Nation with a capital N. The particular meaning I wish to signal thereby is that the Nation is not simply a *"country,"* as in the League of Nations and the usage of "nation" common to Americans; it refers to the ethnic idea of *people*, who may or may not in fact *have* a "country."

4. See note 3 above.

5. I offer an analysis of Romanian national ideology in the contemporary period in Verdery 1990b.

6. "National essence" is an approximate translation of the Romanian *specificul național*. Romanian translations of works on the theme often render the term as "national specificity," indicating emphasis not on the *essence* but on the *particularism*. "National specificity" does not work as well in English as "national essence," however, and since it is only philosophers who will care about the difference between a particular and an essence, I prefer the second.

7. This definition is adapted from Anderson (1983).

8. In the present essay I do not have the space to locate this problem, as should be done, within the literature on the sociology of knowledge. Theorists such as Marx, Mannheim, Foucault, and Gramsci have offered very different arguments about the situation of intellectuals in society and their role in producing ideology. This essay takes a mixed Foucault/Gramscian approach, concerning itself, as Gramsci would, with the construction of hegemonies that may differ between "civil society" and the state, but not assuming that the intellectuals engaged in this are necessarily "organic" to the lower classes— rather, that they produce and serve power despite appearing to oppose it, as Foucault might suggest.

9. To cite a few examples from among the influential intellectuals (several of them cited below): Constantin Rădulescu-Motru came from a family of medium wealth, based in both land-ownership and the professions; Lucian Blaga was the son of a village priest; Nichifor Crainic was unusual in being of poor peasant origin; Nicolae Iorga's father was a lawyer; Eugen Lovinescu's a schoolteacher; Constantin Stere's a well-to-do landowner; Garabet Ibrăileanu's a merchant. (The likelihood of peasant origins was somewhat greater among intellectuals from Transylvania, owing to the difficulties Romanians encountered there in obtaining higher education under Hungary's assimilative policies.) Among the most important leaders of political parties, the Brătianus and Sturdzas, for example, had been major landowning families.

10. For example, "intellectual" Nicolae Iorga (a historian) was briefly prime minister; philosopher and literary critic Titu Maiorescu was Minister of Education, as was sociologist Petre Andrei; economist Virgil Madgearu was Minister of Commerce and Industry; and a number of well-known figures from cultural life were members of parliament.

11. The two views also have different implications for the role of intellectuals. A "malleable essence" makes it more possible for Romanians to *lose* identity, while a "fixed essence" makes Romanianness something that can be neither won nor lost—one is born Romanian or not, in or out. The former view

therefore implies cultural action to renew and strengthen ethnic boundaries and shore up national identity, the job of an intellectual elite. The latter view makes such cultural action superfluous.

12. This question was raised for me by my experience of interviewing peasants about Romanian history; on two or three occasions, I was amazed to see the elderly men with whom I was discussing one or another 17th-century prince begin to weep as they told of the prince's exploits. This sort of emotional identification with national symbols struck me as requiring its own account. I have not made much progress yet toward providing one; literature in psychological anthropology and the psychological analysis of symbolic systems (e.g., Obeyesekere 1982) will lead us further toward that goal.

13. The Romanian example is to be contrasted with that in Smith's paper (this volume), where peasants were not brought into the definition of national identity directly but were pushed into the hinterlands or compelled to assimilate to a new national identity.

14. In Transylvania, where the peasantry formed the sole base of support for aspiring Romanian delegates to the Hungarian parliament, the elite had accorded some attention to the peasantry well before World War I; elsewhere in Romania this was not the case.

15. The Romanian sociologist Mihai Dinu Gheorghiu (1985, 1990) is currently developing an ingenious argument about other ways in which the intellectuals put the peasantry to use toward glorifying intellectual values. He sees the debates about populism and the national essence in literature as forming and seeking to monopolize an internal market for symbolic capital via protectionist measures, just as protectionist politicians were forming an internal market for financial capital and material goods. Different groups of writers sought to eliminate their opponents from the field by insisting that their own creations better represented the national or peasant essence, while others were betraying the Nation by importing foreign values. Gheorghiu applies this argument to both literati and other fields of intellectual endeavor, most notably sociology.

16. Behind these proposals, and motivated in part by the silence to which the peasantry had been reduced, was concern about the spread of socialism within impoverished peasant ranks. The validity of this concern was clearly revealed by the reaction of peasants mobilized in the Romanian army on the eastern front, after the Russian revolution was proclaimed: peasant demands for land were among the factors that led the king himself to visit the front and to promise a land reform, so as to enspirit the troops and keep them fighting.

17. This point is discussed in further detail later in the paper.

18. The reference here is to Dimitrie Gusti's famed Romanian School of Sociological Research, which conducted extensive investigations into the condition of the peasantry all across Romania during the interwar years. It is revealing of Romania's complicated sociopolitical life that Gusti prevailed over competing schools of sociology in large part because his wife's sister was Magda Lupescu, mistress of Romania's King Carol; the coffers of the Gusti School were continually replenished with public funds, while other sociological enterprises had to compete for smaller shares.

19. Not all opponents of modernity accepted the Orthodoxist argument: indeed, many of the most renowned "traditionalists" rejected it (see Ornea 1980).

20. I am indebted to Andrew Abbott for this observation.

References Cited

Alexandrescu, Sorin
    1983 "Junimea": discours politique et discours culturel. In Libra: études roumaines offertes à Willem Noomen. J. P. Culiana, ed. Pp. 47–79. Groningen: Presses de l'Université.

Anderson, Benedict
    1983 Imagined Communities: Reflections on the Origin and Spread of Nationalism. London: Verso.

Arghezi, Tudor
    1928 Epistola Dlui Sabin Drăgoi [Letter to Mr. Sabin Drăgoi]. Bilete de papagal (21 xi 28).

Babu-Buznea, Ovidia
    1979 Dacii în conştiinţa romanticilor noştri: schiţă la o istorie a dacismului [The Dacians in the Consciousness of Our Romantics: Sketch for a History of Dacianism]. Bucureşti: Ed. Minerva.

Băncilă, Vasile
    1924–1925 Reforma calendarului [The Reform of the Calendar]. Ideea europeană 6 (159):1–2; (160):2–3; (161):2–3; (165):3.

Bauman, Zygmunt
    1987 Legislators and Interpreters: On Modernity, Post-Modernity, and Intellectuals. Ithaca: Cornell University Press.

Blaga, Lucian
    1921 Revolta fondului nostru nelatin [The Revolt of Our Non-Latin Essence]. Gândirea 1:181–182.
    1980 [1937] Elogiul satului românesc [In Praise of the Romanian Village]. In Discursuri de recepţie la Academic Română. Pp. 250–262. Bucureşti: Ed. Albatros.

Comarnescu, Petru
    1985 Kalokagathon. Bucureşti: Ed. Eminescu.

Crainic, Nichifor
    1929 Sensul tradiţiei [The Meaning of Tradition]. Gândirea 9:1–11.
    1936 Puncte cardinale în haos [Cardinal Points in Chaos]. Bucureşti: Ed. Cugetarea.

Dobridor, Ilarie
    1935 Tradarea intelectualilor [Betrayal by the Intellectuals]. Gând românesc 3:216–223.

Engelstein, Laura
    1986 Morality and the Wooden Spoon: Russian Doctors View Syphilis, Social Class, and Sexual Behavior, 1890–1905. Representations 14:169–208.

Fabian, Johannes
    1983 Time and the Other: How Anthropology Makes Its Object. New York: Columbia University Press.

Filotti, Eugen
   1924   Gândul nostru [Our Intention]. Cuvântul liber (series II) 1:2–4.
Gheorghiu, Mihai Dinu
   1985   La stratégie critique de la revue "Viaţa românească" (1906–1916). *In* Culture and Society. Al. Zub, ed. Pp. 127–136. Bucureşti: Ed. Academiei RSR.
   1990   Specificul naţional în sociologia românească (MS) [The National Essence in Romanian Sociology]. *In* Cultură şi societate. Al. Zub, ed. Bucureşti: Ed. Ştiinţifică şi Enciclopedică (in press).
Ghibu, Onisifor
   1924   Rostul politic al vizitei patriarhului dela Ierusalim în România [The Political Meaning of the Visit of the Patriarch from Jerusalem to Romania]. Societatea de mâine 1:555–557; 579–580.
Ghiulea, N.
   1926   Apărarea naţiunii [The Defense of the Nation]. Societatea de mâine 3:509–510.
Gusti, Dimitrie
   1968 [1937]   Ştiinţa naţiunii [The Science of the Nation]. *In* D. Gusti: Opere, vol. I. Pp. 492–507. Bucureşti: Ed. Academiei RSR.
Herseni, Traian
   1941   Probleme de sociologie pastorală [Problems of the Sociology of Pastoralism]. Bucureşti: Institutul de Ştiinţe Sociale.
Ibrăileanu, Garabet
   1909   Spiritul critic în cultura românească [The Critical Spirit in Romanian Culture]. Iaşi: Ed. Viaţa Românească.
   1925   Ce este poporanismul? [What is Populism?] Viaţa românească 17:135–149.
Ionescu, Nae
   1937   Roza vânturilor [The Wind Rose]. Bucureşti: Cultura Naţională.
Livezeanu, Irina
   1984   Pages from a Troubled Book: an Episode in Romanian Literature. Cross Currents 3:297–319.
Madgearu, Virgil N.
   1921   Intelectualii şi ţărănismul [The Intellectuals and Peasantism]. Ideea europeană 3(75):1–2.
Mihu, Achim
   1984   Problematica naţiunii române în sociologia interbelică. (Trei sociologi, trei concepţii despre naţiunea) [The Problem of the Romanian Nation in Interwar Sociology. (Three Sociologists, Three Conceptions of the Nation)]. *In* Naţiunea română. Ş. Ştefănescu, ed. Pp. 518–546. Bucureşti: Ed. Ştiinţifică şi Enciclopedică.
Obeyesekere, Gananath
   1982   Psychoanalytic Anthropology and Some Problems of Interpretation. Lewis Henry Morgan Lectures, Rochester, NY. Manuscript.
Ornea, Z.
   1980   Tradiţionalism şi modernitate în deceniul al treilea [Traditionalism and Modernity in the Third Decade]. Bucureşti: Ed. Eminescu.
Pavelescu, Gh.
   1939   Etnografia românească din Ardeal în ultimii douăzeci de ani (1919–1939) [Romanian Ethnography in Transylvania in the Last Twenty Years]. Gând românesc 7:449–462.

Poovey, Mary
  1986 "Scenes of an Indelicate Character": The Medical "Treatment" of Victorian Women. Representations 14:137–168.
Popovici, Aurel
  1908a Demagogie criminală [Criminal Demagogy]. Convorbiri literare 42:296–307.
  1908b Idei anarhice [Anarchic Ideas]. Lupta 2 (86):1–2; (87):1–2.
Rabinbach, Anson
  1986 The European Science of Work: The Economy of the Body at the End of the Nineteenth Century. In Work in France: Representations, Meaning, Organization, and Practice. Steven Laurence Kaplan and Cynthia J. Koepp, eds. Pp. 475–513. Ithaca: Cornell University Press.
Rădulescu-Motru, Constantin
  1936 Românismul: catehismul unei noi spiritualități [Romanianism: Catechism of a New Spirituality]. București: Fundația Regală.
Ralea, Mihai
  1943 Între două lumi [Between Two Worlds]. București: Cartea Românescâ.
Said, Edward W.
  1978 Orientalism. New York: Random House.
Scott, Joan
  1988 "Ouvrière, Mot Impie, Sordide:" Women Workers in the Discourse of French Political Economy, 1840–1860. In Gender and the Politics of History. Pp. 139–163. New York: Columbia University Press.
Stahl, Henri H.
  1937 Satul românesc: o discuție de filozofie și sociologia culturii [The Romanian Village: a Discussion of Philosophy and the Sociology of Culture]. Sociologia românească 2 (11–12):489–502.
  1983 Eseuri critice despre cultura populară românească [Critical Essays on Romanian Popular Culture]. București: Ed. Minerva.
Tăslăuanu, Octavian
  1908a Două culturi [Two Cultures]. Luceafărul 7:59–64.
  1908b O lămurire [An Explanation]. Luceafărul 7:305–306.
Therborn, Goran
  1980 The Ideology of Power and the Power of Ideology. London: Verso.
Verdery, Katherine
  1983 Transylvanian Villagers: Three Centuries of Political, Economic, and Ethnic Change. Berkeley: University of California Press.
  1987 The Rise of the Discourse about Romanian Identity: Early 1900s to World War II. In Românii în istoria universală, vol. II-1. I. Agrigoroaiei, Gh. Buzatu, and V. Christian, eds. Pp. 89–138. Iași: Ed. Junimea.
  1990a Intellectuals Construct the Nation. Berkeley: University of California Press (in press).
  1990b National Ideology under Socialism: Romanian Identity, Intellectuals, and the Politics of Culture in Romania. Berkeley: University of California Press (in press).
  n.d. Images of East: "Orientalism," "Communism," and the Toll at the Border. Author's files.

6

Nationalism, Traditionalism, and the Problem of Cultural Inauthenticity

Brackette F. Williams
Queens College of
The City University of New York

Among human beings new cultural forms are continually created out of anything available and suitable to the material and intellectual problems confronted by members of the population. All members of a population take part, albeit not the same part, in ordering, reordering, and supplementing the elements (for example, materials, actions, ideas, and interpretations) necessary to create new cultural forms or to maintain old ones. Some of their creations are categorized as mere adaptive strategies, everyday practices, superstitions, and deviant behavior, or otherwise labeled to indicate that they are not "real culture." In nation-states, within the category real culture, some are marked as subordinate or "subcultural" forms, while still others are elevated as high culture or hallowed traditions.

For the most part the categories remain stable, but the content changes. The hallowed traditions of one historical period may become the backward superstitions or the folk customs of another period. The high culture of a period may be recategorized as something "less than real culture" if, for example, members of the lower classes make innovations as they adopt its elements. In contrast, cultural forms previously identified as folk or as part of lower-class traditions when adopted by the upper classes may ultimately enter the category real or even high culture.

These are difficult and dangerous processes that develop in all human populations, but which become all the more treacherous when the population is composed of so-called distinctive races and their "ethnic" cultures. How these processes and the changes they instigate are connected to the international power structure and its impact on postcolonial national cultural production and authentication become all the more difficult to fully specify. In both pre- and postcolonial situations we often think that the most powerful members of a society always have the ability to select, categorize, and authenticate those aspects of the existing heterogeneity. In this view we fail to recognize that although the most powerful members of any particular nation are likely to have greater control than others in the society over the determination of which types of cultural forms are recognized as authentic culture, their designations are subject to further evaluation in the arena of international competition. In this arena what one nation deems authentic culture, another labels folk practices. One nation's hallowed traditions are to another nation pretentious, gaudy nonsense. Moreover, in conjunction with previous or continuing colonial ties, nations sharing similar positions in the international arena may judge one another's cultural productions to be vernacular imitations or lower-class misinterpretations of cultural traditions borrowed during the colonial era. Hence, we come to recognize that the position of a national elite in the international arena is part of what structures and delimits its ability to authenticate cultural forms in its national arena. An elite's effort to select and authenticate culture within limits resulting from its position in the international arena also influences how non-elite citizens respond to the elite's authenticating effort. Moreover, where the material ideas and actions that give body and form to eliteness are not uniform within the nation, how the culturally fractured elite can link its national culture to the international arena is fraught with further difficulties. These difficulties also have counterparts in the processes that structure relations among the fractures of the elite, their often competing international goals, and the ethnically identified local populations they must aim to make partners in their task.

We also tend to assume that the citizens of the most powerful nations have the greatest impact on all evaluations in the international arena, only to discover that this issue is also more complex. Often the citizens, upper and lower classes, of the so-called First-World nations do label the less powerful, recently independent, or developing nations, "banana republics," with mongrel, imitation or, the no less damning labels, quaint, colorful cultures. Nonetheless, within the category of First-World nations, the age of the particular nation and its historical linkages to other nations in that category of the international order, the ebb and flow of its economic and political fortunes and interdependencies all influence international (and intranational) responses to its citizens' assessments of the authenticity of competing national cultures.

Battles over cultural ascendancy and authenticity long waged in the territories of Europe, China, and the Indian subcontinent were transported along with people to the settlements in the Americas and the Caribbean. To try to determine when, how, and by whom charges of imitation, aping, illegitimate innovation, and other evaluations of cultural inauthencity will be leveled at the producers of a national culture is to try to disentagle a complex of historical continuities in patterns of everyday interactions, discourses, and staged performances of all kinds. Locating "tradition" is locating the politics of meaning in the production of a putative homogeneity.

Thus, when we consider the problem of cultural authentication as part of our interest in the connections among nationalism, traditionalism and their roles in identity formation and cultural change,[1] we must always devote attention to historical and ethnographic particulars. How old is the nation in question? What are its historical, political, economic, and cultural links to other nations in the international order? How do these links vary when viewed in relation to the internal diversity (that is, culturally constructed distinctions of race, ethnicity, and religion) of that nation? How have these internal and external connections, in combination with changing political and economic circumstances, influenced the development of the ideological precepts that shape the tenets of a nation's or preindependence movement's nationalist ideology? At any given point in these developments, which social groups have played which roles in the processes of categorization, homogenization, and authentication, and what have been the responses of other social groups to their actions? How do the features of these processes serve to structure the interaction of persons belonging to different social grouping (ethnic, religious, racial) as they construct and evaluate new cultural forms?

To explore some of these issues in ethnographic context, I will turn first to a description of the ideological field (that is, a set of interrelated, sometimes contradictory, sometimes complementary precepts for the interpretation and evaluation of the acts, ideas and beliefs of everyday life) on which Guyanese in colonial British Guiana created cultural forms and attempted to authenticate them. Next I will examine one cultural form, the Tadjah festival, as it was performed between 1835 and 1935, focusing on the ways the racially, ethnically, and religiously diverse residents of a particular community experienced and understood the Tadjah's development and demise.[2] Although this cultural form was moribund over 30 years before Guyana gained independence, the ways it was created, the distribution of roles in it, and the reasons for its demise are traceable to contradictions and limitations inherent to the ideological field on which it was created. A field that I have argued elsewhere still shapes Guyanese efforts to produce and authenticate a national culture (Williams 1983). Thus, the Tadjah's development and demise are here taken to foreshadow contemporary problems in Guyanese cultural production and authentication as one example of the postcolonial ideological predicaments facing many new nations.

The Historical Development of an Ideological Field

British Guiana developed as a plantation economy heavily dependent on sugar cane cultivation by African slaves. After emancipation in 1834 the African labor force was augmented by the importation of indentured laborers from China, Portuguese Madiera, India, and the West Indian islands. The British maintained control until 26 May 1966, when the colony gained its independence.

Throughout the colonial era, the dominating power bloc—primarily Anglo-European planters and merchants—justified its economic and political domination on grounds of racial and cultural superiority (Robinson 1970; Smith 1962). Thus, Englishmen and English cultural elements were considered superior to persons and cultural elements associated with the other ethnic groups. Yet, while Europeans' rationalizations linking economic and political domination to English superiority placed Europeans and things English at the top of a sociocultural status hierarchy, they never formally specified the ranking of the non-European segments relative to one another (Williams 1983). Instead, the relative ranking of other racial and ethnic segments shifted with changes in stereotypes emanating primarily from the planters' actions as they made decisions about and tried to differentially allocate economic roles along ethnic lines (Bartels 1977). Colonial administrators, especially those who were also planters, tended to justify these allocations in terms of alleged differences in the innate capabilities and cultural propensities of the different ethnic and racial groups.

During this period ethnically identified persons adopted the more positive aspects of stereotypes of their group as criteria to justify claims to certain economic roles (Bartels 1977). At the same time they pointed to the negative aspects of other ethnic stereotypes in efforts to exclude competing ethnic groups from desirable economic roles and positions of power. All groups used aspects of "established" ethnic stereotypes and generated new features that could serve as criteria to claim for their group the second-ranking status position in the colonial sociocultural hierarchy.

These subordinated groups developed a view of the social status hierarchy as composed of "givers" and "takers," based on contribution to the development of the Colony. Their view inverted the European dominated social status hierarchy. The Europeans were seen as those who always took more than they contributed, thus falling on the lowest rung of the inverted social hierarchy. Members of the other ethnic groups, using a range of cultural and economic criteria, could then argue that their group contributed most to the Colony's development and ought, therefore, to have the greatest say in the allocation of political positions and economic roles. Members of any given ethnic group manipulated such criteria to define their group as the paramount giver and to promote a view of other ethnic groups as takers, unfairly benefiting from the contributions of the paramount giver group while making few or no worthwhile contributions.

Criteria used to identify a particular ethnic group as givers or takers relative to another were linked to stereotypical views of the innate abilities and cultural propensities of the target ethnic group. For example, Africans could argue that it was their ancestors, the strongest and most physically suited to the tropical climate, who labored as slaves to build the Colony and whose communal values following emancipation led to the formation of peasant villages. East Indians could counter that while African slaves built the Colony, following emancipation the lazy, spendthrift, individualistic behavior of their descendants led to its decline; only capital produced from the labor of the "naturally" industrious indentured Indians saved the colony from absolute ruin. Members of both these groups dismissed Amerindian, Portuguese, and Chinese claims to ethnic dominance on still other grounds. Within the broader ethnic segments—African and East Indian, for example—religious differences and the forms and practices associated with them were subject to similar patterns of evaluation. Muslims could claim that Islam, lacking many of the practices that colonial administrators and missionaries considered backward, provided a better source of criteria that East Indians as an ethnic group could use to compete effectively with Africans and others claiming superiority as Christians.

Nonetheless, while each group generated slightly different specific criteria, they produced all the criteria within the constraints of a debate that linked contribution to political-economic dominance through a rationalization of cultural superiority, and they all lacked the combined economic and political power to alter these limits. The structure and limits of this debate remained consistent with those established by the ways dominant power-bloc rationalizations used stereotypic conceptions of innate abilities and cultural propensities of ethnic groups to explain the "naturalness" of practices through which they allocated economic roles and political positions. Members of all the groups could symbolize their accomplishments by adopting Anglo-European modes of conduct, but they could not elevate their own cultural productions to a position of equality with the Anglo-European forms.

The latter failure was, however, more a problem for assessments of ethnic group status and ranking than for everyday assessment of interpersonal status claims. Although an individual was expected to behave in certain stereotypic ways based on ethnic identity (or religious categorizations within an ethnic group) in daily interactions in local communities, evaluations of personal status claims also included careful attention to personal and family reputation—"face" and "name" (Hickerson 1954; Skinner 1955; Williams 1983). That is to say, in impoverished rural communities a person's greatest assets were his good face and name,[3] and his ability to use these to get his kin, neighbors, and friends to help and cooperate with him when necessary. In turn, this ability was based on recognizing *mati* interdependence. While the concept of *mati* may have been at one time most applicable in intraethnic interactions (cf. Jayawardena 1963), its major features—cooperation, reciprocity, respect for others as human beings, and self-respect (Guyanese English: shame) subsumed in the expression "living well with people"—ultimately transcended ethnic boundaries to identify a category of ideologically defined equals (Skinner 1955; Williams 1983). It was as *mati* among *mati* that status claims were presented and ultimately judged.

Just as the economic interdependence of everyday life in local communities weighed against assessments of status claims based solely on group identity and the struggle to rank ethnic groups, the patterns of everyday interaction weighed against the maintenance of cultural distinctiveness within the religious categories of an ethnic group and across ethnic boundaries. These patterns of interaction favored the production of syncretic and ultimately creolized cultural forms and practices. Creolizations and other forms of innovation, however, raised questions about the "ethnic ownership" of new cultural forms. Where ownership could be called into question, the range of contributions associated with an ethnic identity was potentially deceased. In the long run this possiblity threatened the structure of competition but did not alter or provide a substitute for the ideological justifications on which it was based.

To authenticate cultural forms and practices presumed to belong to all because they belonged to no particular group required a change in the ideological conceptions of links between non-Anglo-European identity/culture and the symbols of class status. Without such changes each group expected the others to try to gain a position of dominance, though all lacked the combined economic and political control necessary to assume such a position. Thus it behooved each group, and even segments within groups, to aim for ethnic distinctiveness as the proof of their contribution and, hence, as potential justification for their group status claims.

With this background in mind we will turn to the Tadjah festival to explore its syncretic development between 1835 and 1935. Our focus will be on (1) how notions of ethnic ownership and ethnic stereotypes affected the structure of ethnic participation in the festival; and (2) how residents' and others' ideologically defined ideas about the rights of different ethnically identified groups to participate in, and to innovate on, a tradition—in this case a religious tradition—that they could not equally claim to own affected their assessments of the festival's cultural authenticity.

Ethnic Ownership, Innovation, and the Death of "Rum Tadjah"

The Guyanese Tadjah (from Tazzia, bier or tomb) festival had its roots in the Shi'ite festival of Muharram traditionally held on the tenth day of the month of Muharram, the first month of the Islamic lunar year. The festival culminated ten days of mourning for the deaths of Hosein and Hassan, grandsons of the Prophet Mohammad, slain during the 7th-century conflict over succession to the caliphate in which the brothers aligned with their father Ali and his followers. The Ali faction lost the struggle but refused to accept the leadership of Umayyad caliphs, establishing instead the Shi'ite sect (Bisnauth 1979). Annually, the festival of Muharram commemorated the deaths of the brothers and reinforced their followers' allegiance to the Shi'ite sect.

The festival was brought to the Caribbean region by Shia, a small minority encapsulated by a slightly larger Muslim minority in what was a predominantly Hindu indentured labor population. Under the particular pattern of Anglo-European colonial domination, these religious differences, especially among those who became the elite of that population, could be pragmatically subordinated to a cultural construction of East Indianness. The rise of the festival was part of this construction, though it ultimately produced messages inconsistent with the Muslim quest for prestige within the East Indian ethnic group. During the 19th and early 20th centuries, in Guyana and other parts of the Caribbean, the festival occurred annually on estates and in villages where Shia Muslims were part of the population. The festival centered on the construction and display of a tadjah—a 50-foot, pyramid-shaped bamboo structure covered with brightly colored tinsel paper and decorated with ornaments such as paper butterflies and life-sized replicas of peacocks. In Shia interpretations the tadjah symbolized the tomb of, or a temple for, the slain brothers.

According to ethnohistorical accounts collected during the field period, in the four days of activities that followed the completion of the tadjah, there were prayer services and several processions in which participants carried the tadjah, often first to the manager's house, then through the community and, finally, on the third day, to the public road, displaying it in competition with tadjahs from other communities. In these processions, wailing females, drumming males and other males engaging in mock combat and other gymnastic exercises followed the tadjah (Bronkhurst 1883). On the fourth and final day, the tadjah participants stripped and threw it into a body of water, thus concluding the festival.

Tadjah processions were occasionally accompanied by religious conflicts and acts of violence between Muslims and Hindus or Muslims and other nonbelievers creating, according to Bronkhurst (a clergyman who objected to all forms of non-Christian ritual) "no little disturbance" (1883:306). Acts of violence were also committed against members of the plantocracy as the processions sometimes took the opportunity provided by procession to attack those estate managers against whom they may have had specific grievances (Jayawardena 1968). These attacks may have been encouraged by the general disturbance, but it seems they may also have been inadvertently encouraged by the Court, which did not always punish those persons who committed such acts. Instead, such cases were often dismissed with the argument that the Government sanctioned the festival and such acts were typical of the festival (Bronkhurst 1883:360–361).

However, Ordinance Sixteen of 1869 provided more stringent regulations for the festival activities by requiring that for every tadjah procession, the participants had to select several—but not more than six—headmen, who would be held responsible for breaches of the public peace by any member of the procession. It also required that organizers submit their names and the date of the intended festival 15 days in advance to the magistrate, who then provided written authority for the festival and who reserved for himself the right to define the route of the procession. Estates wishing to hold a joint procession had to submit a joint list of headmen and gain written permission from the magistrate. No procession was to enter the city of Georgetown or the town of New Amsterdam. When on the public road, the procession was to keep to the left side of the road and not unduly obstruct the flow of traffic. The procession was not to linger on the side of the public road or form groups there.

The headmen, responsible for seeing that all these regulations were followed, also had to silence the participants when the procession came within 50 yards of any vehicle drawn by a horse or other animal, any person on a horse or mule, or any led or driven animal. And, according to Section Five of the Ordinance, any headman or participant convicted of willfully disregarding these regulations was subject to imprisonment with or without hard labor for any term not exceeding six months, or a fine not to exceed 96 dollars. A notice drafted 19 January 1871 by Government Secretary H. M. Grant reiterated these regulations. Despite these stringent regulations, Tadjah festivals were still held in the countryside.

Its roots in Islamic sectarianism defined neither who participated nor the range of activities included. In the 1870s and 1880s Chinese were often employed to construct the tadjahs and African Christians participated in the festival. In addition, on 19 April 1873 and 27 February 1877 the *Royal Gazette* reported that African Christians built tadjahs and held processions of their own. Fines levied against African Christians who organized or participated in the festival were insufficient deterrents as Bronkhurst states: "The black people in certain districts have followed the example of the Coolies, and have a Tazzia procession every year" (1883:365). Observers also reported the presence of Hindus among the East Indian participants.

The diverse participants brought with them a range of influences and changes. Bronkhurst, comparing the Guyanese Tadjah festival to Muharram festivals he had apparently observed in India, believed the practice of destroying the tadjah in water at the end of the Guyanese festival was a direct mimicry of the Hindu practice of destroying the Durga idol at the end of the Desserah. Responses to these changes were neither uniform nor entirely positive. By the early 20th century, while McNeill and Lal, in a report to the Government of India on the conditions of Indian immigrants in four British colonies, declared the festival of Muharram one of the three most popular festivals in Guyana, they also noted that it was becoming "less attractive to better Musalmans [Muslims] and Hindus, the colonial-born Indian and the youthful black being more prominent, which in the present holiday making has lost almost all religious significance" (1915:20).

Although informants were not familiar with this report, their historical constructions of the rise and demise of the Tadjah festival coincide with the period of this report, and its sentiment on the lost religious significance was consistent with the premises that informed their ultimate evaluation of participants' rights and final judgments of authenticity. Considering that in colonial India and colonial Guyana, Islam stood in a similar ideological position to Christianity, this is not surprising. In both situations it was a competing world religion deemed inferior to Christianity but superior to the idolatry of Hinduism.

In the research community this creolization process continued until about 1935, when informants believe the last festival occurred. When the festival was still held, preparations began several weeks before. At that time a man, called the chief builder or simply the builder, circulated through the community requesting donations for a fund to purchase materials to build the tadjah structure. There was only one tadjah built for the entire community, and anyone, regardless of racial or religious background, interested in the Tadjah festival contributed to the fund.

After collecting sufficient funds, the builder enlisted the aid of others to help with the actual construction. Informants believe this work crew was composed solely of East Indians, but they did not think all the East Indians were Muslim. An elderly East Indian Muslim, who took over when his father, who long had been the builder, died, said he could recall only one time when an African helped with the construction. He said this African man and his father had always "moved well" together (were good friends) and his father therefore asked the man to help.

Once the work crew was chosen, the builder selected a location on which to construct the tadjah. Five Muslim religious leaders *(majis)* came to bless the location and to say prayers for a successful celebration. According to informants, anyone could come to observe, but only Islamic religious leaders could perform this service.

After this service, construction workers began building a wooden stage (platform) on which to build the previously described tadjah structure. At the corners of the stage, they mounted on springs small replicas of the larger structure. Next to these replicas, they placed life-sized pigeons(?), also mounted on springs and constructed of bamboo and tinsel paper. They topped the main structure with a life-sized replica of a peacock constructed of the same material and similarly mounted.

Workers completed the final work on the Tadjah Friday morning, and Friday evening the builder held a thanksgiving service to mark the successful completion of the task. Informants could not remember all the details of this service, but referred to it as a *puja* (a Hindu religious service). Some thought that this and the entire festival were "Hindu t'ing." They said that although the builder was always a Muslim, during this service his actions were those of a Hindu. They say these participants performed the *Sanatan Dharma* Hindu fire ritual *(Havan Koon)*, after which the builder circumambulated the structure seven times carrying a *tarray* (a flat metal pan) in which he lit a camphor flame (acts similar to features of *Sanatan* wedding and mortuary rites). Following these activities, he distributed *mithai* (sweetmeats) and fruit to those in attendance (also typical of *Sanatan Dharma* Hindu rituals).

There was no activity around the tadjah structure on Saturday morning. Hindu East Indian and Christian African women spent this time preparing food to sell to the crowd that would gather Saturday evening.

The Saturday evening activities began when the *majis* and other Muslims returned to the tadjah to bless it as a memorial to Hosein and Hassan. No one could remember anything specific about the *majis'* actions. They simply said the *majis* prayed and, again, that they were the only ones who could say these prayers. When they finished praying, others came to pray for blessings and to give thanks for prayers answered since the last festival. Persons most likely to take part in this service were those who believed their previous prayers had been answered. They were also the participants who contributed most to the construction fund.

Although anyone who believed in the effectiveness of praying to the tadjah could take part in this prayer service, informants believed young Hindu women predominated. Childless women came to pray for the birth of a child in the coming year. Others who had no sons came to pray for the birth of a son. Anyone else who wished to pray for, or give thanks for, good health and good fortune joined these women.

African informants were the least certain about this part of the Saturday activities. They say few Africans participated in the prayer service because it was considered an "Indian t'ing." However, if an African chose to participate, no one objected to his involvement. Nonetheless, it was after this service that, informants say, the organizers turned the Tadjah over to Africans and Hindus and it became "Rum Tadjah."

The prayer service concluded just before midnight. At that time young African males, stereotyped as the strongest members of the community, removed the tadjah from the construction site and carried it throughout the community. They were accompanied by drummers, most of whom, informants believe, were male East Indian Hindus. Any residents wishing to pray before the tadjah or simply to admire its beauty, could ask the procession to pause briefly in front of their house. They usually paid a token fee for this privilege, which went toward the following year's construction costs.

After carrying it through the community, the bearers placed the tadjah near one of the local rum shops. Before they removed it from the construction site, rum shop proprietors (all were Portuguese) pulled straws to decide nearest which shop it would be located. Informants described this phase of the celebration as a night of "sport," in which young men and women enjoyed themselves. They also described it as a business night when African and Hindu women earned money from the sale of food, and Portuguese rum shop proprietors did a brisk business selling rum and beer as residents crowded around the tadjah to listen to the drummers, to eat, drink, and gamble.

A day of sport and competition followed this night of sport. The African bearers carried the tadjah to the public road, displaying it along the roadside with tadjahs built by other communities. In the research community, wailing Muslim women, Muslim and Hindu men drumming or engaging in mock combat with *godca* sticks (wooden weapons), and a throng of local residents followed the tadjah and its African bearers. Informants say the wailing, combat, and drumming were "Indian t'ing" in which Africans and Portuguese took no part. Although it was a Muslim thing, reportedly most of the drummers were Hindu because Hindus were believed to be better drummers than Muslims.

Sunday was a time for *mati* to meet *mati*. The people from nearby villages and estates mixed and mingled around the tadjahs. The tadjah builders greeted one another and exchanged compliments on the quality of one another's craftmanship. The people admired the beauty of the tadjah and enjoyed the acrobatics of the combatants. But the central focus of Sunday's activity was the impromptu drumming contest that took place between drummers from different communities. Villagers placed bets on the local drummer they considered to be most likely to carry home the title, best drummer. Although informants were uncertain about who judged these contests, they agreed that, even where there was a clear winner, those who bet on the loser were more likely to start a fight than to graciously accept defeat. Thus, while it was a time for *mati* to meet *mati*, it was also a time for one locality to pit its talent against other localities.

It was, however, in recalling these drumming contests, that informants mentioned one instance when an African man drummed in the Tadjah festival. The residents of a nearby estate circulated a rumor that they had the best drummer in East Coast Demerara. Several East Indian Hindus who had heard this drummer play believed that a local young African man was the only person with a chance of beating the other drummer. They encouraged him to join the local drummers so they could bet on him. Here they subordinated race to the triumph of locality and to the personal interest of winning a bet, just as friendship had overriden race when the tadjah builder's father included an African in his work crew. Yet, like friendship, here also the subordination of race is accomplished by stressing the unusual background of this African drummer. They say he grew up as an East Indian because after his African mother died, the East Indian woman his father took as a common-law wife raised him. Although he was especially talented, they say, it was equally important that he had acquired discipline from his socialization and he had perfected his drumming technique by beating the drum at Hindu rituals.

Sunday evening the drumming, sporting, and commercial activities continued. Informants say Muslims, especially devout Muslims, withdrew from this part of the celebration. They also took no active part in the final day of the celebration when, on Monday, Africans and Hindus carried the tadjah to a small pond where they stripped and dumped it. Informants associated no religious service with the final destruction of the tadjah.

In summary, then, all ethnic segments participated in the celebration, however, the form of their participation refracted local conceptions of the ethnic/religious ownership of rituals and stereotypes about the physical capabilities and talents of the different ethnic segments. The sacred aspects of the ritual, though not limited to Muslim participation, had to be conducted by Muslims. Other sacred actions not consistent with Islamic practices, though conducted by a Muslim, were seen as Hindu contributions which, for some informants, raised questions about the ownership of the ritual (a Hindu versus an Islamic thing). Nonetheless, these suggest refractions rather than reflections (mirror images) of ethnic/racial stereotypes because personal interests, locality, friendship, and the evaluation of particular individual talents influenced the actual distribution of roles on the ground.

Previous economic role differentiations and their ideological justifications, reified in ethnic and racial stereotypes, were more nearly direct reflections in the role assigned to and accepted by the Portuguese rum shop proprietors. Portuguese particiation, though not entirely limited to the commercial aspects of the celebration, was shaped by the broader politicoeconomic constraints that had resulted in the Portuguese retail trade monopoly as much as it was shaped by local stereotyping of the role to which they were, during the life of the festival, assumed to be best suited.

That their roles were either reflections or refractions of previous concrete relations and their stereotypical overdetermination did not alter participants' conclusions about the ownership of the religious tradition on which the festival was based and, hence, of the festival itself. Only Muslims knew the religious significance of the Tadjah because the Tadjah "belonged" to their religious tradition. They say the Muslims saw the celebration as a sacred memorial to the slain heroes, Hosein and Hassan, while others saw it as the Rum Tadjah, a time for secular enjoyment and economic gain. As one 75-year-old Hindu woman put it:

> In India the tadjah had great meanin' . . . but the creole [local born members of all ethnic segments] people ah wicked people. Dem love too much ah rum so dey drunk rum and spoil de t'ing. [Author's fieldnotes, 25 January, 1980]

She went on to say that she too was a "wicked wench" who went to Tadjah only "fo' de sport." Yet, following her references to sport, and her acceptance that real meaning had been lost through secularization of the celebration, she added comments that suggested that Rum Tadjah and the practices it included had gained great local meaning focused on concerns about solidarity and living well with *mati*. In her view, the Muslims built tadjah because Hosein and Hassan were their Cain and Abel. Although she could not be specific, she believed Hosein and Hassan had somehow "destroyed *mati*" and the community held the festival to remind people of the brothers' evil deed.

Other informants' guesses echoed her explanation. Some believed Hassan, jealous of Hosein, plotted his death under cover of battle. After his fellow conspirators slew Hosein, he regretted his part in the act and was himself killed as he attempted to avenge his brother against those with whom he had originally conspired. Others believed it was the older brother Hosein who, after a personal conflict with Hassan, slew him under cover of battle and was then himself slain in the same battle. Nowhere, however, was this secularization of the origin and meaning more worked out than in a myth told to me by a 62-year-old Ahmadi (follower of Mirza Ghulam Ahmad, an Islamic reformer who declared himself a prophet in the early part of this century), whom I interviewed after being repeatedly referred to him by others who believed he would know the religious significance of Tadjah.

As with other guesses, his emphasis was on the commission of an ill deed and the battle is only a background factor. In his explanation the two brothers expose their father to the wrath of the more powerful personified Earth—a wrath their father incurred only because he did a good deed for a poor woman. They selfishly committed the deed to satisfy their curiosity about a coffin magically lodged high in a tree. They committed this ill deed although they had information that suggested that they should not do so. In exposing their father, whose corpse had been safely resting in the magic coffin, they damaged their faces and the celebration became a mockery of them rather than a commemoration of their heroic deaths in battle. The call to arms became a call to remember that the exposure of others is a simultaneously face-damaging exposure of self. This myth, like the other guesses, unorthodox though they are, suggests that residents may well have come to understand the celebration in terms that were consistent with local values and ideas that transcend ethnic and religious boundaries. That is to say, they came to understand the characters and their actions in terms of local ideas about *mati*, living well with people, and the importance of maintaining a good face and name.

Nevertheless, the ritual belonged to the Muslims and their understanding of ownership, contribution, and the giver/taker discourse for rank ordering ethnicity underlay their conclusion about why the secularization offended the more devout and wealthy Muslim. In their conception their national rank was tied to international religious authenticity. Hence, they specifically objected to the gambling and drinking and to Hindu and African women selling what was, to them, unclean food. These objections, combined with the fights associated with the drumming contests, resulted in these Muslims' viewing the celebration as an embarrassment to the entire Muslim community. It was not only sacrilegious, in its creolized form it had questionable links to its international origin. Questions raised about the authenticity of these links were also potentially questions about the usefulness of criteria associated with Islam in disagreements between Hindu and Muslim on the issues of how to most positively represent East Indianness against other racial-religious cultural conflations. The price of the new culture was, from an elite Muslim point of view, withdrawn from their symbolic capital by those who had made no worthwhile contribution to it.

They moved to have the festival banned. Although they did not succeed in having it banned, they did succeed in getting additional restrictions passed, which had the same result. I was unable to find a specific ordinance; however, informants say, several wealthy Muslims convinced the legislators to pass an ordinance requiring that five Muslim religious leaders sign a petition before a Tadjah celebration could take place. Informants say it was impossible to obtain the requisite number of signatures because the religious leaders, fearing ostracism, did not want to be responsible for allowing the celebrations to continue. As the last chief builder told me over an old, dusty box of tinsel paper he still kept and cherished, that spelled the death of Tadjah, "T'ing dead out, gaan!"

Conclusion

Interactions structured under particular circumstances and residents' creative interpretations of these interactions permitted, perhaps even made necessary, the production of a new cultural form—Rum Tadjah. However, the authenticity of its foundation was in the past, a past outside of Guyana but linked to its historical development: a past claimed and subject to authentication only by a particular type of Muslim. The possible authenticity of innovations on that foundation was in the future, a future to be claimed by Guyanese subjects who, in a land still ideologically—then as now—peopled by Africans, East Indians, Portuguese, Chinese, and Amerindians, were not available to come forth to claim and authenticate the product of their creativity.

Under the hegemonic dominance of Anglo-European cultural forms (their prestige drawn from an international arena and buttressed by local control), elite and non-elite members of the subordinated colonial population created and attempted to categorize the heterogeneous elements of their creativity. They did so in accordance with the limitations of the colonial ideological field. As they did so they recognized different possibilities for linking their evaluations to the international power structure and the additional ideological constraints it imposed. Consequently, participants, including non-elite Muslims and a racially diversified, class-stratified range of others, lacking the economic and political power necessary to redefine the ideological basis of ownership, identified it as a "true Guyanese t'ing," and mourned its passing while simultaneously recognizing the legitimacy of the elite Muslim's role in its demise. Under those ideological conditions they were deemed to have the need, the right and the *obligation* to act to protect their property. Moreover, to recognize their claim was to protect one's own group claims, accomplishments, and future position. Until everyone and everything was simply Guyanese it was too risky for anyone to claim simply to be Guyanese. In an international arena where the prestige of colonial Guyanese products was suspect, what meaning was to be attributed to such an identity? This was one problem, among others, that the death of Rum Tadjah foreshadowed in the cultural universe of independent Guyana.

When culture is objectified as tradition, social emphasis shifts from pragmatic meaningful interpretations of human biogenetic capabilities and the ecological constraints under which they are exercised to a struggle to control the way the diverse meanings generated out of such interactions are to be interrelated and what their implications are for the distribution of the material bases of human existence. Where the objectified tradition is not unitary but composed of several historically distinguishable traditions, these traditions are further selectively objectified. They become competing sources of criteria around which persons with different claims to these selected features can construct the coordinates of their struggle to control the total system of meanings or to defend themselves against others who would do so.

Notes

1. For purposes of this discussion, nationalism is defined as a set of ideological precepts partially focused on ordering, evaluating, and homogenizing internal heterogeneity, and partially on situating a politically defined territory (the state), its people (the nation) and its culture (the nation-state) in an international arena (an order of nation-states). Process of authentication refers to the contestation and resolution, however partial, which take place among the strata of the nation over the legitimacy of a particular distribution of the elements of heterogeneity across the aforementioned categories ranging from not real to real culture. It also refers to the efforts of a segment of the population to press, in the international arena, not only for recognition of the distinctiveness of whatever it views as the homogenized elements of a national culture, but also for a positive evaluation of this culture, the nation, and its people. Traditionalism, as an effort to return to either presumed precolonial traditions or to authenticate creolized or syncretized elements of the heterogeneity created during the colonial era, is taken here to be one among many strategies used to link the aforementioned roles of nationalism to the two dimensions of the process of cultural authentication.

2. The data for this exercise were collected between 1979 and 1980 in a small community in the East Coast Demerara region of the People's Cooperative Republic of Guyana (formerly British Guiana). Located about 25 miles east of Georgetown, the capital city, the community which serves as the ethnographic setting is composed of the descendants of African slaves and the indentured Indians (referred to throughout the Caribbean as East Indians to distinguish them from indigenous peoples, referred to locally as Amerindians) introduced to British Guiana to augment the plantation labor force after the emancipation of African slaves in 1834.

Like many rural coastal settlements in this region, its population of approximately 5,000 is about equally divided among East Indians (51%) and Africans (45%). The balance is made up of persons of full or partial Portuguese descent (Portuguese from Madeira were also initially introduced as indentured laborers, along with a few other Europeans and some Chinese) and persons of mixed African-Indian parentage, most commonly referred to as "*doogla*" or "no nation." There are a couple of Amerindian women married to or cohabiting with Africans and some individuals who claim partial Chinese ancestry, but there are no Chinese or Amerindian households per se.

3. Face is primarily concerned with a moral evaluation of individuals' behavior, in particular whether there are inconsistencies in their pattern of interaction with other community members. A person's face is the reputation he or she develops among peers as one who respects and adheres to local values and norms. Name, in contrast, is the overall or composite reputation of families—persons who share a surname through geneological connections to a common ancestor.

The face of an individual contributes to the overall reputation of a family (name), while a family's reputation influences the evaluation of an individual's face apart from his own actions. Both face and name develop from the adjudged moral quality of an individual's strategic interactions with others as he competes to improve his status.

References Cited

Bartels, Dennis
    1977   Class Conflict and Racist Ideology in the Formation of Modern Guyanese Society. Canadian Review of Sociology and Anthropology 14(4):396–405.
Bisnauth, Dwarka
    1979   Islam Moves across the Atlantic. Georgetown: Guyana Extension Seminary MSS.
Bronkhurst, Henry V. P.
    1883   The Colony of British Guyana and Its Labouring Population. London: T. Woolmer.
Hickerson, Harold
    1954   Social and Economic Organization of a Guiana Village. Ph.D. dissertation, University of Indiana.
Jayawardena, Chandra
    1963   Conflict and Solidarity in a Guianese Plantation. London: University of London Press.
    1968   Ideology and Conflict in Lower Class Communities. Comparative Studies in Society and History 10(4):416–446.
McNeill, James, and Chimman Lal
    1915   Report to the Government of India on the Conditions of Indian Immigrants in Four British Colonies and Surinam, part I. London: His Majesty's Stationary Office.
Robinson, Pat
    1970   The Social Structure of Guyana. In The Cooperative Republic of Guyana. L. Searwar, ed. Pp. 51, 76. Georgetown: Government of Guyana.
Skinner, Elliot
    1955   Group Dynamics in British Guiana. Annals of the New York Academy of Sciences, 83.
Smith, Raymond
    1962   British Guiana. London: Oxford University Press.
Williams, Brackette F.
    1983   Cockalorums in Search of Cockaigne: Status Competition, Ritual and Social Interaction in a Rural Guyanese Community. Ph.D. dissertation, Department of Anthropology, The Johns Hopkins University.

7

The Politics of Heritage in Contemporary Israel

Virginia R. Dominguez
Duke University

In the spring of 1981, Israeli television aired a multipart series on the history of Zionism entitled *Amud HaEsh*—Pillar of Fire. Documentary filmmakers, researchers, producers, and writers collaborated in producing what many critics and viewers alike regarded as the most comprehensive representation of the history of Zionism yet produced on the screen (cf. Rosenthal 1982). Not surprisingly, it failed to mention most of the Jewish communities of North Africa, the Middle East, and India. When public and private Sephardic/Oriental Jews in Israel called attention to that omission, the researchers, writers, and producers replied by calling attention to the absence of "any real indigenous Zionist movement" in those communities and to their low level of participation in the *world* Zionist movement. The appeal to *factuality* and authority moved the locus of the discourse to the hallowed halls of Israel's academic institutions. Politicized Sephardic/Oriental historians dug deeper into their own research into North African and Middle Eastern Jewish communities increasingly to assert that only a particular representation of contemporary Jewish history—Eurocentric and Orientalist at its core—would deny the various, and sometimes alternative, ways in which a number of North African and Middle Eastern Jewish communities had participated in the 20th-century movement that led to the establishment of the modern state of Israel.

Disagreements are more the norm than the exception in Israeli society, but what made this a noticeable incident was that it was about the *history* of Zionism—that history was subjected to scrutiny as a politicized representation and not just as fact, and that it was Zionism itself, for so long Israel's version of the sacred cow, that had become fair game in the battle between Ashkenazim and Sephardim. The Ashkenazim involved in the series' production looked either arrogant/defiant or politically naïve. As far as they were concerned, facts were facts and credit should be given where credit was due—to the Ashkenazi, mostly Eastern and Central European, Jews whose political consciousness and agitation led to the migration of hundreds of thousands of Jews to Palestine before independence in 1948, and to Israel after independence, and who created the institutional infrastructure that made the internal governmental transition to independence smoother.

But why air such a series with its particular representation of modern Jewish historicity in 1981? By then over half of the Jewish population of Israel was Sephardic/Oriental, not Ashkenazi, and had, throughout the 1970s, become increasingly vocal about having been systematically discriminated against by the Ashkenazi population on almost all political, social, cultural and economic fronts at all periods of Israeli history. Various sectors of that non-Ashkenazi Jewish population had also already won several political battles—not the least of which was ousting the Labor party from power in 1977 and bringing in people, like Begin, who though Polish (and therefore also Ashkenazi), had long been unempowered in Israel and, therefore, were not seen as responsible for the attitudes and policies that discriminated against the Sephardic/Oriental population. Airing *Amud HaEsh* in 1981 *had* to be politically naïve *or* condescendingly defiant.

And yet there was little in what was included in the series, or even in its representation of history, that was itself new or different. The television production was an audiovisual representation that reiterated the long-dominant textual, pedagogic, governmental, and oral representation of the creation of the state of Israel and of its founding fathers. It was defiant, however, to flaunt it once more in front of the Sephardim—as if saying you may have ousted us from power (temporarily) but you will never be able to change "the facts of history."

An Ideology of Nationhood in Search of Content

Indeed, power and participation are critical issues in the Sephardic-Ashkenazi struggle in Israel today. It is different from conflicts with people seen as Other because this one is regarded as internal, and yet it is equally about empowering, reempowering, and disempowering. It is about whether a numerical minority can legitimately rule over the demographic majority even when that majority, too, is Jewish, and about whether the long un- and underempowered want a proportional share of power or their turn to rule.

But it would be a serious mistake to think that it is all about form and the exercise of power, and not about content. In fact, producing an ideology of *nationhood* has never been as problematic an issue in Israel as producing and perpetuating a national *ideology*—of what is and is not a good society, what its customs and practices should be, or how it should even view itself. Unlike most African and many Asian states, which were granted their independence and their "national" territories by European colonial governments even in the absence of an already existing sense of a national *peoplehood* within their borders, Israel came into being at least in part because of a widespread assumption among Jews about the national peoplehood of the Jews. A survey done by Liebman and Don-Yehiya published in 1981 revealed how this shows up in contemporary Israel. Ninety-four percent of Israeli Jews, they reported, affirm "the attachment of Israel with Jewish peoplehood, culture, and history" (Liebman and Don-Yehiya 1983). Few Israelis today question the peoplehood of the Jews or the right of the Jewish people to a state of their own.

The problem is that affirming the peoplehood of the Jews paradoxically complicates the task of determining its cultural and historical content. Jewish peoplehood has long been determined genealogically through the successive application of a rule of matrilineality and the periodic creation of "fictive kin ties" in rituals of conversion. Neither beliefs nor practices technically make or break a Jew. This has enabled enormous cultural, ideological, and practical differences to develop among Jews, and it has meant that after 2000 years of life in the Diaspora, the differences among Jews and Jewish communities around the world may be far greater than their similarities. This includes the experiences and representations of at least 2000 years of separate, even divergent, histories. Hence the issue of the cultural content of the Jewish state—what it is, what it could have been, and why it wasn't—is always alive, even when it does not appear to be foregrounded.

Put in this light, Zionism is arguably a movement or project that in seeking a solution to one Jewish problem—that is, perpetual vulnerability, lack of autonomy, and geographic dispersal—created another from which it is not likely to recover, at least not in the near future. The explicit and implicit mechanisms of domination by which primarily secular European Jews imposed their version of European culture on the rest of the population have created an embittered and alienated Jewish majority now assimilated and acculturated enough to know how to work the system successfully.

To illustrate this form of domination I will stray deliberately from the more usual presentations of areas of discrimination, not because they are irrelevant but because they are better documented. Israeli journalists and social scientists have done a creditable job, especially since the 1970s, uncovering and reporting some of the more explicit discriminatory policies and practices for which the Labor Zionists were responsible in the first two decades since independence and which seemingly find a way of being quite recalcitrant (cf., for example, Ben-Rafael 1982; Eisenstadt 1985; Elazar 1986; Peres 1977; Segev 1984; Smooha 1978; Swirski 1981; Weingrod 1985).

At the heart of the system they all describe was a form of socialist paternalism, which saw the centralized state as the agent of and for social transformation and, thus, as the ultimate teacher. Its self-perceived mandate was wide-ranging, if not perhaps all-encompassing. It affected housing, language, health, technology, production, dress, and even childrearing—not to mention electoral politics or patterns of consumption. Two clear examples of how far this attitude went concern kindergarten education and the attempt to dictate to the Israeli public an appropriate content for Israel's Independence Day—arguably, or at least apparently, two less than central arenas in the life of a nation-state.

But consider the case of early-childhood education, especially in the first decade of independence. The Law of Obligatory Education, promulgated in 1953, made kindergarten mandatory for children at age 5, and placed the supervision of kindergartens under the aegis and control of the national Ministry of Education (Shamgar-Handelman and Handelman 1986:75). This was not just for bureaucratic efficiency. As Shamgar-Handelman and Handelman point out (1986:75–76), "the kindergarten was conceived of as an instrument of national purpose: one that would help to transform the child into an Israeli person different from that of his parents," one that would "inculcate the meaning of Zionist existence, and to teach somewhat vague notions of Israeli 'culture,' not only to children but also to their parents." They quote educators extensively. Katerbursky (1962:56), a veteran educator writing of the Mandatory period before the establishment of the State, unabashedly and without hint of doubt wrote: "The obligation of the kindergarten is to uproot bad habit that the children bring from home. . . . We understand that the parents, especially the mothers, are still very distant from understanding many of the educational . . . [and] social problems of education; and we will have to educate them as well." The text goes on to say that, whenever the occasion allowed, "mothers were given instructions on how to behave towards their children, on correct attitudes towards the development of the child, on how leisure time with children should be spent, and on the kind of cooking that children would enjoy eating at home" (Shamgar-Handelman and Handelman 1986:76). Quoting another teacher, Shamgar-

Handelman and Handelman illustrate what they perceive to be the intensification of these themes of inculcation after the establishment of the State. Zanbank-Wilf wrote in 1958, "Our influence on the surrounding can be great with the help of our faithful partners, the children, if only we will know how to inject into the home one common version of customs. . . . It is not the first time in the history of this country that the child fulfills an important role in educating the nation. . . . That is why we can hope that in the new assignment of the 'ingathering of the exiles' *(kibbutz galuyot)* . . . the child will fulfill his mission and will not disappoint us."

The same paternalistic view of the state and its citizens runs through early as well as more recent governmental discussions surrounding the celebration of Yom HaAtzma'ut, Israel's Independence Day.[1] In a detailed analysis of government designs for the celebration of Yom HaAtzma'ut in the first few years of the state, Eliezer Don-Yehiya (1984) refers with regularity to "the collective values that [the holiday] represents" and to "national and state objectives" it carries out. The view sounds functionalistic, but isn't. He goes on to show that the political discussion and activities initiated by the "state" reflected the governing elite's view of the collective values of the state. The symbolism was instrumental; the goal, the affirmation and strengthening of the collective values of the "state."

This meant much more than may readily meet the eye. It would be easy to list the many issues that have provoked government arguments surrounding Yom HaAtzma'ut, for they have concerned many of Israel's unresolved issues—about just how secular this holiday should be, just how peaceful or militaristic its main message would be, and just how much accommodation there would be to the "psychological" and political needs of Israel's minority of Arab citizens (cf. Dominguez 1989). But I don't even have to refer to these hot issues of policy to illustrate the extent of the paternalism. In 1972, the Israeli Government Information Office commissioned a study to help in the planning of the 25th anniversary celebration of Yom HaAtzma'ut. The Israel Institute of Applied Social Research obliged by sampling 1,892 adult Jewish residents in the four major urban areas—Tel Aviv, Jerusalem, Haifa and Beer Sheva. Questions probed both attitudes toward, and participation in, the celebration of Yom HaAtzma'ut. Charles Kamen, then on the staff of the Israel Institute of Applied Social Research, reported five years later that one of the explicit reasons for commissioning the study was "the fear that people were not enjoying the holiday" (Kamen 1977:19).

Two years earlier another study conducted by the Israel Institute of Applied Social Research on "culture and leisure" in Israel had determined that to 63% of those surveyed Yom HaAtzma'ut primarily meant the enhancement of a feeling of belonging to the nation and to the state, whereas to 30% it was primarily an opportunity to be happy (Katz et al. 1972:50). Government officials in most new nation-states, concerned with instilling or promoting feelings of national identity in their populations, would be envious of those survey results (cf. Bocock 1974). But to Israeli public officials in charge of the planning of Yom HaAtzma'ut each year, they were cause for worry. According to Kamen, degree of popular enjoyment had become "the unofficial measure of the 'success' of any year's Independence celebrations" (Kamen 1977:7).

This image is not a transient one. Year after year the newspapers, the radio and the television news broadcasts anticipate the ceremonial passage from the *solemnity* of Remembrance Day to the *happiness* of Yom HaAtzma'ut. The former is billed as a day of remembrance for Israel's war dead; the latter, as a day of festivities, celebrations, entertainment. The two form a neat contrast set conceptually. The pathos of a day to remember the dead contrasts with the joy of a day to remember the establishment and survival of the state.

The juxtaposition is not accidental. Yom HaAtzma'ut is celebrated on a certain day each year because it was on that day in 1948 that the leaders of the Yishuv (the Jewish community in Palestine before Israeli independence) proclaimed the establishment of the state. Remembrance Day is commemorated the day before Yom HaAtzma'ut by design—signaling that Israel's survival is ensured from generation to generation by the ultimate sacrifice made by those who die fighting to preserve its independence.

The juxtaposition is, however, also forced. The design is to lead Israelis to mourn before they rejoice, to make it difficult, if not impossible, for citizens to swing into a festive mood without first putting it all in a particular perspective, and to remind the bereaved that their loved ones did not die in vain. The combination signals a striving for equilibrium, perspective, respect, and a sense of achievement. But it also signals an attempt on the part of state institutions to channel citizens' emotions by clockwork. Children attend school on Remembrance Day, because the government fears that it might acquire a festive atmosphere if children looked forward to a holiday from school. But the government worries if the public does not sufficiently enjoy itself on Yom HaAtzma'ut.

These examples speak for themselves as explicit practices of domination—a peculiarly Jewish form of domination based on the assumption, rather than the denial, of shared peoplehood. What made them work was not the state's ability to enforce its policies, but rather its continued appeal to the problem of cultural content unleashed by the Zionist movement. The reason *that* worked was that it could, and did, mean different things to different people.

The primarily secular, Ashkenazi Labor Zionists, usually credited with creating Israel's infrastructure and shepherding the transition to independence, had both an explicit and an implicit agenda. Many, if not most, of the early Zionists—socialist and Eastern European in origin—had sought in Zionism a way to be Jewish without having to have Judaism provide the content of their Jewishness. In that sense, though it is rarely a definition of Zionism, I would say that Zionism *to the majority of the Zionists* in the Yishuv was the *practice* of calling attention to the problematic *content* of Jewishness, while paradoxically invoking history, descent, and heritage as the bases of its legitimacy. Explicitly they wanted a society/homeland/state where Jews were autonomous and in charge. Explicitly they wanted a democratic, secular state with a communal socialist infrastructure. Explicitly they wanted a society in which they would feel no need to participate in religious rituals in order to assert their Jewishness. Implicitly, however, and partly without consciousness of its anti-egalitarian implications, they were deeply Orientalist and anti-egalitarian in their view of culture. They wanted a "civilized" society, and meant a European one. Religion would be privatized, as they perceived it to be in Europe; worthwhile music, art, and literature would be those canonized by the Europeans.

But to Jews migrating to Israel in the late 1940s and 1950s, the polyglot and multicultural characteristics of the emerging society were salient enough to allow them to sympathize with the "state" when it appealed to them to cooperate in the project of resolving Israel's problem of cultural content. It *was* true that there were serious cultural differences and serious problems communicating with each other. It took a long time for Sephardic/Oriental immigrants to realize the impact of what the "state" meant, and mount a working opposition. Only the orthodox and ultra-orthodox religious communities were organized enough and aware enough of the struggle for content to mount a steady opposition to both secularization and westernization.

The Paradoxes of Cultural Domination

The irony of secular Ashkenazi domination for so long is that, in choosing a non-Judaic content for Israel's cultural life, it enhanced the probability that opposition to Ashkenazi cultural domination would increasingly see in Judaism an *alternative* source of cultural content.

Here is where the most implicit mechanism of domination—the discursive practice of distinguishing between culture *(tarbut)* and heritage *(moreshet)*, and "finding" them the historical product of different, hierarchically evaluated sectors of the Israeli Jewish population—creates, or at least helps create, an alliance between religious Ashkenazim and the majority of the Sephardic/Oriental Jewish population that undermines the original Labor Zionist project of finding (at times creating) content outside Judaism.

Tarbut and *moreshet* are loaded terms. They are also found everywhere—especially in Israel's institutional life and media. A systematic study I conducted of references to culture *(tarbut)* in the first 100 issues (1982–1984) of *Koteret Rashit*—a weekly and "liberal" news-analysis and feature-story magazine—clearly showed how references to *tarbut* (even in this self-perceived liberal circle) carry with them an implicit hierarchy of the content of different people's lives and reveal attempts to affirm, change, or create a hierarchical order by which individuals would, then, be judged (cf. Dominguez 1989).

The Israel Museum, for its part, institutionalizes the semantic differentiation. In addition to it having an archeological wing, a youth wing, a sculpture garden, and a special structure for housing the Dead Sea Scrolls, the Museum is organized into a series of departments and sections together known as the Bezalel National Museum. These include the departments of Jewish Ceremonial Objects, Contemporary Art, Far Eastern Art, Ethnic Art (with material objects from around the world), Prints and Drawings, Design and Israeli Art, and Jewish Ethnography. Of special interest here is the work of the Department of Jewish Ethnography. The fact that the departments of Jewish Ceremonial Objects (heritage in the Judaic sense?) and Jewish Ethnography (heritage in the pre-Diaspora sense) are structurally separate has long bothered the curators of Jewish Ethnography, but in four years of following the staff and their work I never heard any complaints about overlaps with other departments.

Both curators it had during this period frequently refer to the need to collect and preserve "material culture of disappearing Jewish cultures." Neither could possibly be faulted for selectively applying the term culture only to Ashkenazim. But the department's overwhelming tendency has long been to exhibit material from non-Ashkenazi Jewish communities before they migrated to Israel—material and communities not exhibited elsewhere in the Museum, except if they are identified as ceremonial objects.[2] Though the permanent exhibition, which opened in the spring of 1985, does include a reconstruction of a sample room of the home of an "average" German Jewish family in the 1930s, the fact that the majority of the exhibits labeled ethnography display material items associated with non-Ashkenazim promotes the impression that they and their past are proper and worthy *ethnographic* subjects, with all the typical popular assumptions about ethnographic work applying to them—that their culture is traditional (if not altogether backwards), that it represents an earlier stage of cultural development, and that the tangible items they produced are noteworthy as representative of the life of a group of people, not as beautiful or valuable objects on their own.

These structural patterns foster an image of Sephardic/Oriental culture that the more politicized Sephardim increasingly regard as its folklorization. Shimon Shitrit made it explicit in a piece published 13 April 1982, in *Ma'ariv*, which he entitled "Between Political Folklore and Cultural Depth." Andre Elbaz was quoted in *Ha'aretz* early in the spring of 1983 making the same point. "When people speak about the Ashkenazim," he argued, "they use the word culture while when they speak about the Sepharadim they use only [the term] heritage" (Galibi 1983:15). The distinction shows up frequently, though often without much awareness, in the discourse of many Ashkenazi intellectuals and government officials. A typical example of how it enters discussion came through in an interview on "Israeli culture" 12 August 1984, with S. N. Eisenstadt, the long-time "dean" of Israeli sociology, which the Israeli press considered newsworthy enough to print two days later. When asked about the Sephardim, he replied that "the so-called Oriental communities do not want to establish an Oriental culture here . . . [but that] they want to be integrated into Israeli culture and society and *to bring with them some of their traditional symbols*" (emphasis added). Perhaps the most blatant example is the fact that the office in Israel's Ministry of Education and *Culture* created in the late 1970s upon growing demands from Sephardim for content recognition was named the Center for the Integration for the *Heritage* of Oriental Jewry (Merkaz leShiluv Moreshet Yahadut HaMizrach).

But what is noteworthy about this mode of domination is how, in a sense, it has structured its own opposition. Heritage *(moreshet)* connotes the Judaic tradition—a history, a set of rituals, a particular historicity essential to the religious Jew's sense of his/her Jewishness. By appropriating a "western" secular content for Israeli society *and* contrasting it with the heritage of the Jews, Ashkenazi Labor Zionists have probably enhanced the appeal of a far less secular and much more Judaic content among Israel's many Sephardic/Oriental Jews.

How this can and does work became evident in reactions to a talk I gave at Bar Ilan, Israel's most religious university in 1985, which I entitled "The Concept of Culture in Popular Usage."[3] In it I attempted to work out the complementary distribution of the use of *tarbut* (culture) and *moreshet* (heritage) in Israeli popular discourse. I had a hard time anticipating feedback. I expected my colleagues there to pay careful attention to the mode of analysis, premises, and theoretical framework in which I presented the argument. That they were also overwhelmingly Ashkenazi led me to expect them to react at least in part as "informants" listening to an outsider's rendition of some phenomenon they take for granted. That many, though not all, were observant Jews led me to wonder if and how Judaism would enter their exegesis of my material. But I was not aware of any other preconceptions.

What interested me in the aftermath of the discussion was the way in which what several of my colleagues said in that forum pointed to a counterstream or theme that seemed almost deliberately, if not consciously, to seek to balance the hierarchy and differentiation that surrounds the concept of *tarbut* (culture) in Israel. The atmosphere at the seminar was scholarly, intellectual, polite, even warm. There was little debate about my claim that the difference between *tarbut* and *moreshet* is substantial in Israel today, but there was, nonetheless, some agitation about my lack of emphasis on Jewishness as a unifying factor.

An advanced middle-aged man volunteered the opinion that the key to the differences between *tarbut* and *moreshet* lies in the Diaspora experience of the Jews. *Moreshet*, he argued, for years referred to the lives of Jews, while *tarbut* appeared in conversations between Jews that referred to non-Jewish life. All Jews had a Jewish heritage whose common core was the basis of their Jewishness. Differences in customs were considered secondary and, therefore, inconsequential. But Jews, he continued, because of the Diaspora lived among a host of different peoples whose strength, value, aesthetic, moral, and technological production could be compared. Some Jews, thus, lived in societies with more advanced cultures than others, and it is to that difference that Israeli Jews refer when they speak of culture. There is, he concluded, no hierarchical evaluation of the heritages of Jews from different Diaspora communities, but there is justifiably—he maintained—a hierarchical evaluation of the cultures of different non-Jewish peoples.

A middle-aged, religious woman known to be a supporter of Jewish settlements on the West Bank complained that *Koteret Rashit* gave a distorted picture of the ordinary language meaning of *tarbut* because it was so secular and so antireligious. The Jewish concept of *tarbut*, she insisted, implied no internal hierarchy within the Jewish people. All I had to do, she suggested, was to look in the newspapers and weeklies put out by religious Jews for a religious leadership—*HaTzofe* (the organ of the National Religious Party), *HaModia* (the organ of the ultra-Orthodox communities in Israel), *HaNekuda* (a paper published by

Jewish residents of the West Bank for the Jewish population of the West Bank), even, she added, the newspaper put out by the students at Bar Ilan. A third established member of the faculty politely but firmly suggested that I not forget that *moreshet* "usually refers to *hamorasha hayehudit*" (the Jewish heritage).

Self-avowed secular friends back in Jerusalem offhandedly dismissed the Jewish theme I reported to them as feedback to my talk. That, they remarked with a smile, is Bar Ilan. The university is Jewish and religious by design. All students, regardless of degree of observance or field of study, are required to take courses in Judaica, and the faculty members of at least some departments—including the department of sociology and anthropology—have ongoing Talmudic study groups whose sessions take place in the departments themselves. Judaism and Jewishness are at least as important there as each department's academic discipline.

But if my female colleague at Bar Ilan seemed to live in a world of her own that denied the legitimacy of nonreligious voices, so my secular Jerusalem friends likewise closed themselves off to much of Israel's public discourse by dismissing the legitimacy of religious voices. The longer I digested the comments I got at Bar Ilan the more I realized that they indexed a common and persistent theme of public discourse intent on affirming and reaffirming the unity of the collectivity it presupposes. Too much emphasis on, or acknowledgment of, fragmentation among Jews threatened the presupposition of the existence of a collectivity known as the Jewish people. Interpreting references to *moreshet* as references to Jewishness, they thereby implied, would show what keeps Jews together even when so much prejudice and differentiation persists between them.

The point is not that more religious Jews stress unity and more secular ones stress difference and inequality. Rather, it is that a positive evaluation of heritage in Judaic terms, nonetheless, coexists with a condescending one, and that the condescension may, in fact, ironically propel those who feel victimized by it to seek to reappropriate the very notion of heritage—not surprisingly turning to the alternative highlighted by religious sections of the population.

But is this, in fact, really happening? Whenever Israel goes through a period of marked tensions with Palestinians (or even non-Palestinian Arabs), media commentators, government officials, and social scientists return to a periodic theme of public discourse: Are Sephardic/Oriental Jews in Israel more militantly nationalistic than Ashkenazi Jews? Could it be that their experience over many generations living among Muslims has made them less tolerant of Arabs? Or, perhaps, that they just come from more *traditional* sociocultural environments that make them vulnerable to the rhetoric of Ashkenazi *religious* nationalism arguing for Israeli Jewish control over the "whole of the Biblical Land of Israel?" To many secular Ashkenazim, especially Labor Party supporters, any Sephardic/Oriental support for religious movements or parties feels like a thorn in their side. Many derided Begin's periodic use of religious symbols during his years in power (1977–1983), and looked down on his Sephardic/Oriental supporters who fell, in their eyes, for his "demagoguery." Was it deliberate affront to the Labor Ashkenazi establishment, or just their "unthinking adherence to religion and tradition?" Whenever tensions are high, the questions reappear openly in public discourse.

While much of this discourse rests on stereotyping, some of those stereotypes work well enough to persist because there are periodic events, polls and elections that lend them some air of reality. A particularly interesting recent example was the creation of a political party generally referred to as Shas just before the 1984 Knesset elections. While some might assume that its emergence on the Israeli political scene raises questions about the alliance I am suggesting between religious Ashkenazim and Sephardic/Oriental Jews in Israel, I think it ultimately reinforces my argument.

Sephardic/Oriental in leadership, self-definition, and appeal, Shas was created out of the ranks of Agudat Israel (the most established ultra-Orthodox political party in Israel) in order to give direct voice and representation to the thousands of Sephardic/Oriental Israelis who had for years been a mainstay of Agudat Israel, whose leadership remained, nonetheless, consistently Ashkenazi. While the break-off signaled the perception of discrimination and inequality among the ranks of the religious, it also made it possible to see very clearly that a large percentage of the electoral support for Agudat Israel and its very Orthodox rabbis had long come from Sephardic/Oriental quarters. In fact, it has never been the Ashkenazi traditions in Judaism per se that attracted its non-Ashkenazi supporters but, rather, the opportunity to combine a vote for a nondominant political party with an affirmation of a positive valorization of heritage in which, at least theoretically, they felt included by definition as Jews.

The Ideological Objectification of Zionism

Most of us know that a great deal has been written about "Zionism" over the years—its rise as a political movement, a philosophical movement, a social movement, a nationalist movement; its practically convergent but ideologically competing streams; its relationship to other movements of "national liberation"; and its awkward, often dependent, often antagonistic, relationship with various forms of Judaism (for example, Avineri 1981; Cleeman 1945; Halpern 1969; Isaac 1976; Kimmerling 1983; Laqueur 1972; Rubinstein 1980; Sachar 1982). Many will also know that a fair amount, too, was written especially in the 1950s and 1960s about Israel's "problems of nation-building," how this required an institutional infrastructure characteristic of a "modern" society, the "absorption" of hundreds of thousands of immigrants in a very short period of time, and the then-perceived need to get these immigrants—especially those from non-European backgrounds—to abandon their "traditional" cultures and become acculturated, responsible citizens in their new "modern" society (for example, Eisenstadt 1954, 1967; Matras 1965; Shokeid 1971; Shuval 1962; Weingrod 1965; Willner 1969).

I have already mentioned the increasing number of politicians, journalists, and academics who have, in addition, over the past ten to fifteen years begun to expose the institutional discursive and nondiscursive practices that discriminated against Sephardic/Oriental immigrants throughout much of the history of independent Israel and frequently led to the perpetuation of significant socioeconomic and political gaps between Ashkenazim and Sephardim. Most recently, in the news (when not talking about the Palestinian intifada) are the increasing number of reports by academics and media commentators, especially since the start of the 1980s, concerning groups and events that suggest a rising popularity of religiosity in circles otherwise described as secular (Avruch 1979; Deshen 1978; Goldberg 1987; Goldscheider and Friedlander 1983; Kotler 1985; Newman 1981; Segal 1987).[4]

These are all relevant and rich pieces of work. Their authors show great concern for Israel's past, present, and future, and express praise and criticism for what has, in their eyes, gone right and what has gone wrong so far. Their concerns clearly form part of the lively debates about, and strategies for, creating the kind of society Israelis want to live in; that is, they participate in the processes of shaping the content of Israeli society in ways that could easily be seen as ideological. Yet they signal something else as well—that so much attention has been paid both in Israel and abroad to Zionism as Israel's ideology that most people assume that it is, or at least should be, everyone's analytic starting point. The result is that any discussion of the production of national ideology in Israel almost automatically looks strange, perhaps even misguided, if it is not explicitly and primarily a history and epistemology of Zionism as an ideology (or at least a related set of ideologies) and the practices that are believed to follow from it.

And yet it is precisely in the privileging of Zionism as the objectified national ideology of Israel that we find the preeminent mechanism of discursive, ideological domination of Israel. There is no doubt a great deal of talk about ideology in Israel (cf. Dominguez 1984), but most of it, if not all of it, is about known "isms" and how they relate to Zionism—socialism, revisionism, capitalism, nationalism. In the process, much that is not directly identified as ideological—such as the concepts of *tarbut* and *moreshet*, or the ways in which people celebrate Yom HaAtzma'ut—rarely become the object of prolonged or heated public debate but work, nonetheless, both to exert domination and to be contested by those who see themselves as victims of domination. Ironically, then, it is the special concern with Zionism that keeps the project of producing a national ideology in and for Israel open to contestation. And in the end, it is the representation of an objectified Zionism that may be subject to reappropriation.

Notes

Acknowledgments. This essay is the product of long-term research I have conducted in and on Israel since the summer of 1980. It is work that has been made possible by generous grants from several foundations and the cooperation and support from several academic institutions. The Trent Foundation funded two months of preliminary research in the summer of 1980. The U.S. Social Science Research Council, the Mellon Foundation, and the Duke University Research Council funded the period of intense fieldwork in Israel from May 1981 through August 1982. A Fulbright teaching award allowed me to spend another 14 months in Israel from June 1984 through August 1985, while teaching in the Department of Sociology and Social Anthropology at the Hebrew University. To all of them my sincerest thanks.

In addition, I owe a special gratitude to the Jersualem Institute for Israel Studies, the Department of Sociology and Social Anthropology at the Hebrew University, the Jerusalem Anthropology Circle, the Israel Anthropological Association, and the Jerusalem Semiotics Study Group for their general hospitality and the interest they showed in my work. My thanks go to the Duke administration as well for giving me leaves of absence when these wonderful opportunities arose.

But above all I feel indebted to my friends, acquaintances, colleagues, "informants," neighbors, students, research assistants, and even those I did not get along with so well in Israel for forcing me to examine questions and assumptions I had never before thought to question and always showing me greater and greater complexity. This is especially true of my now deceased friend and colleague Eileen Basker, and my research assistants over the years, Malka Porges and Shoshana Halper. In the macropolitical climate in which Israel is an active participant, the very act of research in Israel is political, though the assumption (often made outside Israel) that one knows a person's politics when one hears that they live and do research in Israel is as misguided as thinking that all North Americans are wealthy.

1. A lengthier exposition of this material appears in my recently published book (Dominguez 1989).

2. The main exhibitions mounted by the Department of Jewish Ethnography since the founding of the Museum and before the opening of the "permanent exhibition" in 1985 were on Bukharan Jewry (1967–1968), Moroccan Jewry (1973) and Kurdish Jewry (1981). The latest large-scale "temporary exhibition," which opened May 1989, is on Sephardic (primarily Ladino-speaking) Jews of the Ottoman Empire.

3. This discussion is taken from a much longer exposition, which appears in Chapter 5 of *People as Subject, People as Object* (Dominguez 1989), entitled "The Object of Heritage."

4. These are some of the major works, but there is quite a large bibliography on Israel and Zionism in addition to these cited items. Useful references include the bibliographies in Deshen and Shokeid (1984), Eisenstadt (1985), Handelman and Deshen (1977), Kimmerling (1983), Krausz (1980 and 1985), Swirski (1981), and Weingrod (1985).

References Cited

Avineri, Shlomo
    1981   The Making of Modern Zionism: The Intellectual Origins of the Jewish State. London: Weidenfeld and Nicolson.
Avruch, Kevin
    1979   Traditionalizing Israeli Nationalism: The Development of Gush Emunim. Political Psychology 1 (spring):47–57.
Ben-Rafael, Eliezer
    1982   The Emergence of Ethnicity: Cultural Groups and Social Conflict in Israel. Westport: Greenwood Press.
Bocock, Robert
    1974   Ritual in Industrial Society: A Sociological Analysis of Ritualism in Modern England. London: Allen & Unwin.
Cleeman, M.
    1945   The General Zionists. Jerusalem: Institute for Zionist Education.
Deshen, Shlomo
    1978   Israeli Judaism: Introduction to the Major Patterns. International Journal of Middle Eastern Studies 9 (2):141–169.
Deshen, Shlomo, and Moshe Shokeid, eds.
    1984   Yehudei HaMizrach: 'Iyunim Antropologiyim al HaAvar veHaHove. [Jews of the Middle East: Anthropological Perspectives on Past and Present.] Tel Aviv: Schocken. [in Hebrew]
Dominguez, Virginia R.
    1984   The Language of Left and Right in Israeli Politics. Political Anthropology 4:89–109.
    1989   People as Subject, People as Object: Selfhood and Peoplehood in Contemporary Israel. Madison: The University of Wisconsin Press.

Don-Yehiya, Eliezer
  1984 Khag vetarbut Politit: Khagigot Yom HaAtz ma'ut beIsrael baShanim HaRíshonot lekiyum HaMedina. [Holiday and Political Culture: Independence Day Celebrations in Israel during the First Few Years since the Establishment of the State.] Medina, Memshal, ve Yakhasim Benleumiyim 23 (summer):5–28. [in Hebrew]
Eisenstadt, S. N.
  1954 The Absorption of Immigrants. London: Routledge & Kegan Paul.
  1967 Israeli Society. London: Weidenfeld and Nicolson.
  1985 The Transformation of Israeli Society. Boulder: Westview Press.
Elazar, Daniel
  1986 Israel: Building a New Society, Bloomington: Indiana University Press.
Galibi, Lili
  1983 Tarbut mul Moreshet. [Culture vs. Heritage.] Ha'aretz, 1 April, p. 15. [in Hebrew]
Goldberg, Harvey, ed.
  1987 Judaism Viewed from Within and from Without. Albany: State University of New York Press.
Goldscheider, Calvin, and Dov Friedlander
  1983 Religiosity Patterns in Israel. *In* American Jewish Year Book. Pp. 3–40. New York: Jewish Publication Society.
Halpern, Bernard
  1969 The Idea of the Jewish State. Cambridge: Harvard University Press.
Handelman, Don, and Shlomo Deshen
  1975 The Social Anthropology of Israel: A Bibliographical Essay. Tel Aviv: Tel Aviv University Institute for Social Research.
Isaac, Rael J.
  1976 Israel Divided: Ideological Politics in the Jewish State. Baltimore: The Johns Hopkins University Press.
Kamen, Charles S.
  1977 Affirmation or Enjoyment? The Commemoration of Independence in Israel. Jewish Journal of Sociology 29 (1):5–20.
Katerbursky, Zivya
  1962 B'netivot Hagan. [The Ways of the Garden.] Tel Aviv: Otsar HaMoreh. [in Hebrew]
Katz, Elihu, et al.
  1972 Tarbut Israel 1970. [Israel Culture 1970.] March, Pp. 41–52. Jerusalem: Israel Institute of Applied Social Research. [in Hebrew]
Kimmerling, Baruch
  1983 Zionism and Territory: The Socio-Territorial Dimensions of Zionist Politics. Berkeley: Institute of International Studies.
Kotler, Yair
  1985 Heil Kahana [in Hebrew]. Tel Aviv: Modan.
Krausz, Ernest, ed.
  1980 Migration, Ethnicity, and Community. Studies of Israeli Society, vol. 1. New Brunswick: Transaction Books.
  1985 Politics and Society in Israel. Studies of Israeli Society, vol. 3. New Brunswick: Transaction Books.
Laqueur, W.
  1972 A History of Zionism. London: Weidenfeld and Nicolson.

Liebman, Charles, and Eliezer Don-Yehiya
 1983 The Dilemma of Reconciling Traditional Cultural and Political Needs: Civil Religion in Israel. Comparative Politics 16(1):53–66.
Matras, Judah
 1965 Social Change in Israel. Chicago: Aldine.
Newman, D.
 1981 The Role of Gush Emunim and the Yishuv Kehilati in the West Bank, 1974–1980. Durham: The University of Durham Press.
Peres, Yochanan
 1977 Yakhasei Edot b'Israel. [Ethnic Relations in Israel.] Tel Aviv: Tel Aviv University and Sifriyat Poalim. [in Hebrew]
Rosenthal, Alan
 1982 Israeli Television Documentary and "Pillar of Fire." Studies in Visual Communication 8 (1):71–83.
Rubinstein, Amnon
 1980 From Herzl to Gush Emunim. Tel Aviv: Schocken.
Sachar, Howard
 1982 A History of Israel: From the Rise of Zionism to Our Time. New York: Alfred A. Knopf.
Segal, Haggai
 1987 Akhim Yekarim. [Dear Brothers.] Jerusalem: Keter Publishing House. [in Hebrew]
Segev, Tom
 1984 1949: HaIsraelim HaRishonim. [1949: The First Israelis.] Jerusalem: The Domino Press. [in Hebrew]
Shamgar-Handelman, Lea, and Don Handelman
 1986 Holiday Celebrations in Israeli Kindergartens: Relationships between Representations of Collectivity and Family in the Nation-State. Political Anthropology 5:71–103.
Shitrit, Shimon
 1982 Between Political Folklore and Cultural Depth. Ma'ariv, April 13.
Shokeid, Moshe
 1971 The Dual Heritage: Immigrants from the Atlas Mountains in an Israeli Village. Manchester: Manchester University Press.
Shuval, Judith
 1962 Emerging Patterns of Ethnic Strain in Israel. Social Forces 40 (4):323–330.
Smooha, Sammy
 1978 Israel: Pluralism and Conflict. London: Routledge & Kegan Paul.
Swirski, Shlomo
 1981 Lo Nekhshalim ela Menukhshalim. [Orientals and Ashkenazim in Israel: The Ethnic Division of Labor.] Haifa: Makhberot le Mekhkar ule-Bikoret [Notebooks for Research and Criticism]. [in Hebrew]
Weingrod, Alex
 1965 Israel: Group Relations in a New Society. London: Pall Mall.
Weingrod, Alex, ed.
 1985 Studies in Israeli Ethnicity: After the Ingathering. New York: Gordon and Breech.
Willner, Dorothy
 1969 Nation-Building and Community in Israel. Princeton: Princeton University Press.

Zanbank-Wilf, Aliza
   1958   Hagan K'markiv B'yetzirat Avirat Khag Babayit. [The Kindergarten as a Component in Creating a Holiday Atmosphere at Home.] *In* Khagim U'moadim Bakhimukh. [Holidays and Times in Education]. Esther Rabinowitz, ed. Pp. 57–59. Tel Aviv: Urim. [in Hebrew]

8
Failed Nationalist Movements in 19th-Century Guatemala: A Parable for the Third World

Carol A. Smith
Duke University

In early modern Europe, nationalist ideologies emerged together with capitalist relations of production and the modern form of the state. This correspondence in time, together with certain of its consequences for Europe, have led scholars who otherwise agree on little else about the modern world to see nationalism as an inevitable, indeed necessary, accompaniment of modernity. Though they use distinctive sets of terms, both modernization theorists and Marxists see nationalism as a populist or corporatist ideology which, by creating a sense of cultural unity based on shared traditions or history, effectively neutralizes class struggle such that state-building and capitalist development can proceed (Gellner 1983; Nairn 1977; Tilly 1975). Popular belief in a unified nation whose government represents the interests of the whole allows the state to substitute hegemonic for coercive forms of rule. Since scholars assume that a state governs more effectively through the exercise of persuasion rather than of force, they also assume that all modernizing states will be compelled to develop a nationalist ideology in order to compete effectively in an inter-state system in which some states already have a nationalist tradition.

This particular view of nationalism, clearly Eurocentric, assumes a universalism to the relationship between capitalism, the modern state, and nationalism about which scholars of the Third World might well harbor some doubts. At the same time one must acknowledge that Third World nations are attempting to build nationalist ideologies and modern state apparatuses as supports to their own programs for capitalist development. As Anthony Smith puts it:

> "nation-building" describes succinctly what Third World elites are trying to do. If anything "nation-building" is *the* basic Third World ideology and

project.... The question then becomes one of discovering the forces that make such a quest for nationhood universal in the Third World. [1983:232; emphasis in original]

Smith answers the question he poses with views very similar to those cited above, viz: "in the modern era, an era of nationalism, statehood can only be legitimized in terms of the 'nation' and nationalism, and states must therefore be seen to be 'nation-building' " (1983:263). Smith, however, observes that the situation for nation-building is quite different in the Third World than in the First.

Challenging the view that First World nations invented nationalist traditions after the emergence of the modern state, Smith argues that ethnic (national) consciousness developed before the state in the West and provided the foundation upon which the modern state could be created. Rather than the state creating the nation, nationality created the state. Smith concedes that ethnic identities are social constructs rather than primordial essences, but he argues that ethnic identities are not easily or quickly created; on these grounds he is pessimistic about the possibilities open to "pluralistic" Third World states. The contradiction he identifies in them is that the exercise of state power, which is now a prerequisite of existence in the modern world, is necessarily coercive in the absence of national unity. This stirs up ethnic competition and antagonisms, which work against the possibility of creating a unified nationalist project.

While Smith is virtually alone in recognizing that state-building and nation-building can be contradictory processes, he nonetheless affirms that nationalism is functionally necessary for state-building. That is, ultimately he agrees with Gellner (1983), Tilly (1975), and Nairn (1977) that if the nation does not exist prior to the state, it must be created shortly thereafter if the state is to pursue its development aims successfully. I want to take Smith's views of contradiction further to argue that the pursuit of nationalist development in the Third World with the First World experience as model is often that which stirs up the ethnic antagonisms so evident in Third World states, which in turn leads to coercive state responses and continued national disunity. On this basis I will question the functional fit between state-building and nation-building in the modern era, at least for the Third World.[1]

As evidence for my case I will examine two points in Guatemala's 19th-century history, during which efforts at development (both political and economic) took very different forms. At the beginning of the period I examine, 1800, Guatemala was neither a state nor a nation.[2] Its social relations were identical to those in the rest of the Central American colony (which included Chiapas, El Salvador, Honduras,

Nicaragua, and Costa Rica, as well as Guatemala). At the end of the period, 1900, Guatemala was a coercive state divided into two nations, well into the type of capitalist development process common to the Third World. And its social and ethnic relations were entirely different from those existing in the rest of Central America.[3] The events that took place in that period were critical for creating the class and ethnic divisions that shape Guatemalan politics today.

Guatemala is presently about half Indian, which is to say that half of Guatemala's population refuses incorporation into any general concept of Guatemalan nationhood. One hundred and fifty years ago, when the Spanish empire controlling the province of Guatemala crumbled, Guatemala had more Indians than it has today (perhaps 75%), but what some Guatemalans today call the national/ethnic contradiction (the division between Indians and Ladinos) was not the same kind of problem it is today. I will argue that the Indian/Ladino contradiction was created by the way in which Guatemalan elites tried to create a Guatemalan nation. Because Guatemalan elites experimented with different ways of creating a Guatemalan nation in the 19th century, and these different experiments created different ethnic outcomes, we cannot argue that Guatemala's ethnic divisions were the inevitable result of its colonial experience. What we will see instead is that ethnic division and a coercive state regime resulted from a particular historical experience.

The Historical Background

Guatemala was one of five provinces in the Audiencia of Guatemala, an administrative entity that stretched from what is now southern Mexico to Costa Rica. The administrative center and largest city of the Spanish colony was located in Guatemala. Because power was so highly centralized within the colonial system, Guatemala attracted and held more Spanish bureaucrats and their elite descendants than other provinces of the isthmus. At the same time, Guatemala had a denser surviving Indian population than other provinces, and Indian communities rather than individual Indian workers provided the main source of wealth in the colony. These two factors contributed to the special character of social relations in colonial Guatemala. Because the colonial apparatus was located in Guatemala, state control mechanisms for protecting Indian communities and extracting revenue from them were more effective than they were in outlying provinces; and because there were few mines or major exports from which to extract wealth in Guatemala, these control mechanisms were also more necessary.

State protection of Indian communities had a two-sided character. On the one hand, no one but the Church or Crown had easy access to Indian labor or products in Guatemala. But on the other hand, the Church and Crown directly exploited Indians in Guatemala rather than acting as mediators between them and Spanish settlers. Thus while few Guatemalan Indians worked in mines, Spanish workshops, or on large export-producing estates, they were often drafted as laborers for various Church and state projects and were heavily taxed and tithed. This kept Guatemalan Indians more isolated from non-Indian settlers than Indians in other parts of the New World. It also prevented the rise of a powerful landed oligarchy in the province, independent of the state.[4]

These special conditions, together with the spatial separation of Indians and non-Indians (the former mostly rural, the latter mostly urban), saved Guatemalan Indians from the fate of most Indians in the rest of the colony—that is, the wholesale destruction of their communities and separate social identities. These conditions did not, however, maintain Indian culture in a pristine form. Indians retained some of their rituals and their separate languages, mainly through the active intervention of the Church, which could better maintain its exclusive access to Indian souls and resources through these means (van Oss 1986). But in most other respects, Indians were as highly assimilated in Guatemala as elsewhere. Elements of culture that today distinguish Indians from non-Indians—their religious practices, dress, and community forms of political rule, such as the *cargo* system—were not surviving pre-Hispanic forms but resulted from the fusion of native and Spanish traditions (Martínez Paláez 1971). What maintained Indians as Indians was their separate legal and economic status in the colony: wards of the state and payers of tribute. By various mechanisms, class distinctions among Indians were gradually eradicated (Carmack 1979).

By the end of the colonial period, Indian communities remained strong only in western Guatemala, Chiapas, and southwestern El Salvador. Elsewhere, slave running, forced migration, expropriation, miscegenation, and the like created a different social category, known throughout Central America in the period as the *castas*.[5] The *castas* were not necessarily mestizos or people of mixed descent—though people of mixed descent usually joined the *castas*. They were people who had lost ties to particular Indian or Spanish communities through a variety of processes. Neither subject to regular tribute nor owners of resources, most of the *castas* worked as artisans and petty merchants in the towns and cities, farmed unclaimed land (mainly in eastern

Guatemala), or became personal retainers of one sort or another for the Spanish ruling class (which included the clergy).

Throughout the colonial and postcolonial period, Indians who left their communities, for whatever reason, "became" non-Indians. Few Indians, at least in the western highlands, appear to have chosen this status voluntarily because it meant separation from the main form of property not monopolized by the white elites—the lands held by corporate Indian communities.[6] Such people were known as "Ladinos" because in the colonial period, the term Ladino meant someone of Indian descent who spoke Spanish and presumably took on other cultural characteristics of the non-Indian minority. Later, the term meant anyone who was neither Indian (in cultural terms) nor white, and thus came to subsume all members of the *castas*. Later still (in the modern period, beginning around 1945, which is not treated here), the term Ladino came to mean anyone who was not culturally Indian, and thus came to subsume even whites. Most Guatemalans with a clearly white or *creole* genealogy, however, do not use the term Ladino to refer to themselves (see Lutz 1982:433–434). One reason is that the term, as it shifted referentially through time, maintained the suggestion of racially "impure" origins. In certain parts of the country, moreover, Ladino was a term of opprobrium. More cannot be said about the meaning of these ethnic terms in Guatemala without the historic context because the meanings were, of course, historically constructed.

Non-Indians who were not Spanish fitted uneasily into the colonial governance system that had room for only conquered and conquerors but, lacking resources, they were more a social anomaly than a political threat to the operation of the colonial system. By the end of the colonial period, *castas* constituted the majority of the population everywhere except in Guatemala and El Salvador, where they constituted between one-third and one-fourth of the population (MacLeod 1983). In the colonial period, however, the status of these people was no higher than that of Indians (MacLeod 1973). Nor were they highly differentiated from Indians, except in legal terms.[7]

The two dominant classes in the colony *(peninsulares* and *creoles)* were more divided by privilege and interest than the two lower orders. *Peninsulares* were people of Spanish descent (born in Spain) who held positions in the system of imperial governance and thus ruled the colony. And *creoles* were people of Spanish descent (mostly born in the Americas) who lacked positions in the imperial system but who held local power through a variety of mechanisms (Woodward 1985). United mainly by race and racial ideology and their shared rights to Indian labor, *creoles* and *peninsulares* were divided by the fact that the latter held ultimate authority in the colony. Guatemalan *creoles,* unlike their counterparts in other parts of the New World, rarely held positions of power that were not granted to them by the state and thus controlled by *peninsulares* (Wortman 1982). The growing divorce of power between *peninsulares* and *creoles* ultimately undermined the Spanish colonial system. The collision did not begin in Guatemala (which was all of Central America in the colonial period), because of the dependent position of the *creoles*, but Guatemalan *creoles* were sufficiently resentful of their weak political position to jump into the opening that shouts for independence sparked elsewhere.

The gradual disappearance of Indian communities throughout the Spanish empire and the development of the new and anomalous social category of *castas* also played a role in the disintegration of the colonial system. Without Indians, the system simply did not function properly. Yet the disenfranchised *castas*, who had fewer rights than Indians, were not the leading social actors in the independence movements. The white *creoles* led these movements with the aim of taking power rather than of transforming its unequal distribution. Five Central American states eventually emerged from the independence movements, but insofar as they lacked a popular base these movements were simply anticolonial rather than "nationalist" in character. In fact Benedict Anderson suggests (1980:50) that the drive for independence throughout Latin America was spurred more by fear of popular mobilization against elite privilege than by anger at colonial restrictions on elite privilege.

Anderson, however, considers the creole revolts of the 19th century to have been true "nationalist" movements, in the sense that they were inspired by attempts to distinguish "American" culture from Hispanic culture. It is nonetheless notable that the American culture aspired to was pan-Latin American, that is, the culture of the white *creoles*; since *creoles* in each country were concerned above all to distinguish themselves from the lower orders in their countries, they clung to external sources of identity (whether European or North American) and thus did not develop any sense of local cultural identity. A sense of local or national culture among Latin American elites, in the sense of being rooted in particular traditions and histories (and thus necessarily involving the masses) is still largely absent in much of Latin America.

As elsewhere in Latin America, the Central American nations that emerged were defined by colonial boundaries (Woodward 1987). That is, the identity of each nation was given to it by its past administrative structure rather than by any shared sense of distinct cultural identity. The *creole* elites in each of the six colonial provinces of Central America had much more in common with each other (and with the Spanish rulers) than they had with their local peoples. But cultural commonality did not override local-level political and economic interests. The *creole* elites of each chartered city wanted to control their local resources without interference from higher authority, whether that authority be Spain or Guatemala (Woodward 1985; Wortman 1982). Hence most of the independence wars were fought with other national contenders rather than with the imperial center. Eventually the forces for separation prevailed. By 1840 five of the former provinces had become sovereign entities, while Chiapas joined Mexico. Internal wars continued in most countries other than Guatemala for many more years, ending in most cases in economic exhaustion or the imposition of a despotic regime in one of the competing provincial cities (often a compromise city) capable of eradicating its competitors. In this process, states were formed by default and modern nations were formed nowhere in Central America. Nationhood was a 20th-century phenomenon, brought on by new economic wars fought with foreign powers.

Surprisingly, Guatemala was the most nationally integrated Central American state in the early 19th century, though later it became the most divided. What made Guatemala's situation different was the way in which Guatemala's aspirations to become an isthmian power created the conditions that would exacerbate ethnic division. When it still seemed plausible that Guatemala might rule the entire isthmus, elite Liberals overcame Conservative inertia to make a brief attempt (1831–1838) to incorporate Indians and other members of the "lower orders" as equal citizens in what would be a Central American nation. The attempt, unique in Central America, was brief, quickly reversed, and never again attempted until 1944. What was accomplished in this period was less important than the reaction it provoked. In 1839 a populist movement uniting Indians and the *castas* gained sufficient momentum that its leader, Rafael Carrera, was able to seize the state and to govern in the interests of his followers for 30 years. Carrera's state, neither Liberal nor Conservative,[8] established the conditions by which Indian communities survived in Guatemala—when similar communities in the rest of Central America were destroyed as such (though people known as Indians survived for varying lengths of time). It also established a political regime in which Indians and *castas* cooperated politically in order that each retain their local political and economic autonomy. While the populist government did not destroy the economic power of the *creole* elite, it did thwart *creole* attempts to dispossess peasants in that era.

A new group of Liberals took over the state in 1871, strengthened by their ties to external capital. It was clear to them that they could expand their political control over peasants only by dividing peasants into two separate categories: Indians and Ladinos. Out of Guatemala's unique 19th-century experience of revolutionary politics, then, ethnic difference crystallized and a new social category emerged, the non-Indian Ladino. Ladinos did not share in *creole* power then (or even now), but their own exploitation was lessened as they assisted in the process of creating a semi-proletarianized Indian workforce for Guatemala's path to capitalist development.[9]

With the creation of the non-Indian Ladino, the ethnic division that most Guatemalans describe as the "Indian problem" came into existence and continues to haunt Guatemalan politics today. This division was created by a relatively powerful national state in its effort to develop coercive mechanisms that would prevent popular resistance from sabotaging the state's economic development projects. The relationship of ethnic divisions to state- and nation-building in Guatemala was thus quite the opposite of Anthony Smith's. Rather than concluding that Guatemala's coercive state resulted from irremediable ethnic divisions based in a colonial past, as Smith would have it, I conclude that Guatemala's ethnic divisions resulted from the actions of the coercive state, which could pursue its development goals only by dividing rather than uniting its working populations (see C. Smith 1990).

Elite Nationalism: Guatemala's Early Liberal Period

Literate Latin Americans in the 19th century identified strongly with European civilization. For many, the end of colonial rule opened the possibility of universalizing European values in America: "Latin Americans believed Europe to be the focal point of history, regarding their own histories as extensions of European history. . . . The question was not whether to Europeanize but how" (Burns 1980:45, 46). Embracing the Liberal ideology of the period, progressive Guatemalans wanted to both "enlighten" and "whiten" their nation. The first goal would be achieved through a vast overhaul of national institutions in imitation of western (especially U.S.) models, the second would be achieved by encouraging European migration, also following the U.S. model.[10] White Guatemalan progressives blamed Spanish colonialism for Guatemala's backwardness, they had no program for development other than a dependent, imitative one. As they saw it, development required all of Guatemala to become as Europeanized as the *creole* elite.

> Independence in 1821 elevated to power a segment of the elite that had imbibed the heady wine of Enlightenment thought and, judging the In-

dians to be backward terminated the benign neglect of the Crown.. . . .
[it was assumed] that Guatemala would mature to adulthood nurtured
on a European diet. In short, if Guatemala were to progress, then the
Indians had to be Europeanized. [Burns 1980:96]

According to John Lanning, "the lag of American learning behind European, far from being 300 years, was probably never great and in the second half of the eighteenth century the gap closed so rapidly that only the time needed to cross the ocean remained" (1956:347). Four interconnected institutions, centered in Guatemala City, actively promoted the Liberal credo: the University of San Carlos, the weekly newspaper *La Gazeta*, the Economic Society of Guatemala, and the Royal Consulado (merchant guild), created in the last decade of the 18th century. Liberal ideas spread widely throughout Central America, but only in Guatemala did Liberals succeed in quashing internal conflicts to legislate sweeping reforms of a Liberal (and nationalist) character in the early 19th century.

The utopian flavor of the early Liberal ideology is captured in a manifesto prepared in 1821 by Jose del Valle.[11] Frequently alluding to the "natural rights of man," and citing Montesquieu, Buffon, Rousseau, and Adam Smith, among others, del Valle envisions a Central America freed of Spanish tyranny. In his vision, Guatemala would flourish in arts and letters as well as progress economically, the Guatemalan population would become homogeneous, and the Indian would discard his unintelligible languages, to become "a noble being who, with eyes raised up, will make known his worth." The new society would bring the greatest good to the greatest number, not for its own sake but so that all of the Americas would experience unprecedented development:

America will not walk a century behind Europe: at first she will march alongside her: later it will surpass her; and finally it will be the place most illuminated by the sciences as it is the most illuminated by the sun. [cited in Braiterman 1986:26]

To achieve these aims, Indians had to be actively integrated into the Guatemalan nation as equal citizens rather than as special wards of the Church and Crown. The assumption was that Indians would become "useful farmers" if the feudal barriers standing in their way were removed. And at that point in time, it should be emphasized, the development model was the United States, whose growth was thought to be rooted in its small property-holding system and free market economy, both based in equal citizenship. The propellant to this whole utopian vision of freedom, it should be noted, was a dream of economic growth that would place Guatemala among the leading nations of the world.

Guatemala had never been an especially wealthy colony and its major export product of the late colonial period, indigo, was suffering a severe slump at the time of Independence. Indigo required relatively little labor, which in Guatemala was supplied mainly by the *castas*. Indians were protected from working in indigo production and the few dragooned into it inevitably lost touch with their Indian communities such that they too became *castas*. Thus at the end of the colonial period the native peoples of the indigo-growing areas (in and around San Salvador) were mostly non-Indian (MacLeod 1983). The most promising export of the early Independence period was cochineal, a dyestuff extracted from insects, the production and processing of which was almost entirely in Indian hands. As MacLeod puts it, "Indians possessed a skill, a knowledge monopoly or 'trade secret' that made Spanish attempts to interfere [in its production] ineffective" (1983:200). The dominance of cochineal production in the early Independence period (as opposed to indigo or coffee, which had very different production possibilities) is probably relevant to the way in which the Guatemalan elite envisioned how they would develop in the 1820s and 1830s. Guatemala's first constitution,[12] written in 1824, established the equality of all Guatemalan citizens, at the same stroke eradicating the protections given by the Crown to special groups such as Indians communities and the Church. It took nearly a decade for the constitution to have any effect because of uncertainties over the Central American Union, fiscal problems, divisions among the elites, and strong Church resistance. The implementation period was 1831 to 1838, under the presidency of Mariano Gálvez. Gálvez's reform program, which was rapidly if unevenly implemented, had four major planks: to restrict the power of the Catholic Church by creating a secular state; to institute a new and more viable taxing system; to rationalize property-holding by eradicating most communal forms of tenure; to encourage European migration by offering colonists favorable terms in the acquisition of land; and to break down Indian insularity by using educational and political means to draw them into the Guatemalan nation.

The Church was the first target of Guatemalan Liberals, even before Gálvez came to office. At the time, the Church appeared to embody Conservative opposition to Liberal reform. (Popular opposition to liberal reform, it should be noted, had not yet figured into the power equation.) The Church was also the biggest challenge to state power in Guatemala, inasmuch as the Church collectively owned more property than did the rest of the *creole* elite—and the most profitable properties at that (van Oss 1986). It also earned more income than the newly formed state, through its various capitalized enterprises and the Indian tithe, to which it was legally entitled (Ingersoll 1972:86). Thus, shortly after Independence, most members of the Spanish religious orders were expelled. The state confiscated the property held by these orders and later distributed it among its Liberal supporters. With Church institutions eradicated or seriously weakened, the new state, under Gálvez, was able to implement the reform program drawn up at Independence.

Gálvez's religious reforms continued along the lines already established. In 1832 a federal decree established freedom of religion. In the same year the Church tithe was abolished. In 1834 Church holidays were limited, and in 1837 marriage and divorce became civil contracts. Popular reaction to the anticlerical legislation was uneven. Most were indifferent to the confiscation of Church property and delighted by the end of the Church tithe. The later reforms, however, were much less popular and added to the rural restiveness at the end of the Gálvez period.

Tax reform was the greatest failing of the Gálvez administration. The colonial authorities had briefly stopped collecting tribute in 1811 and then tried to reimpose it a few years later.[13] Indians rebelled against the reimposition and in many areas never paid tribute again. Gálvez substituted a land tax for the Church tithe and a head tax (equivalent in value) to the tribute, but was never very successful in implementing these new taxes. As the fiscal crisis of the state deepened, dozens of new taxes were imposed, none accepted as legitimate by the peasantry, who protested them all. In desperation, Gálvez reimplemented forced labor laws to meet some of the more crying construction needs of the new state, but that enraged peasants all the more. By the end of 1837 Gálvez was essentially unable to collect taxes in most of the rural areas (Ingersoll 1972:57).

The most radical of Gálvez's reforms were those designed to rationalize the use of land and labor in the former colony. Laws had already been passed eliminating all forms of communal property except for a small portion of village *ejido*. These laws had largely been ignored until Gálvez attempted to implement them with a universal census of people and land, accompanied by surveys of village lands—to be paid through communal (municipal) funds. Peasant reaction to the surveys in both Indian and non-Indian areas was immediate and direct, though it did not take a collective form. In most cases, peasants simply did not allow the land assessors into their communities. Rioting broke out where land assessors were brought in by wealthier individuals hoping to claim some of the communal land. And everywhere peasants went to court, bringing ancient land titles and insisting that they be respected. By the end of the Gálvez period, less than half of the national territory had been surveyed and titled. And in this period peasants lost much less land than the Church lost.[14]

Land reform was more successful in areas of low population density where peasants had no communal property traditions. One of the Liberal government's first laws was that encouraging foreign immigration and permitting immigrants to obtain title to "unoccupied" lands. Gálvez implemented these laws with abandon, such that at the end of his presidency he had ceded to three foreign companies land amounting to about three-fourths of Guatemala's national territory. None of these projects brought more than a handful of colonists. And while most projects were located in sparsely populated areas, one project was located close to several "Indian" towns in Chiquimula, the area where the Carrera reaction began. While many people criticized Gálvez's colonization schemes, again there was no collective action against them until other reform programs were put in place. Indians in the western highlands had relatively little interest in the colonization schemes or other parts of the economic program that did not affect them directly. Since communities in the western highlands were quite effective at passive resistance to the new reform, they were relatively quiescent until their community institutions came under direct attack.

The Gálvez attempt to undermine Indian culture through educational reform also had relatively little direct impact. The basic idea was to draw Indians into national culture by forcing Indians to ape the manners of non-Indians. Thus, "the government ordered every department of the state to create [schools] for Indians boys between seven and fourteen years of age, designed to teach them Spanish, mathematics, vocational skills, the arts, values and manners. These [schools] would civilize their students by obliging them to wear western clothing, to eat food at a table, and to sleep in a bed" (Braiterman 1986:33). To find sufficient students, a protector system was established wherein Indian orphans and the children of parents who refused to send their children to school were put into the custody of whites for seven years. Indians officials were required to wear western clothing. And to combat what was seen as the chief Indian "problem" the legislative assembly limited the production of alcohol and limited the number of religious festivals that Indians could celebrate (Braiterman 1986:33–34). Again, Indians resisted rather than rebelled against these reforms. But Indians began to associate cultural assimilation programs with much more dangerous attacks on their rights, while the Guatemalan elite, who embodied the Guatemalan state at that point, came to see Indian cultural backwardness as the source of the political rebellions brought on by the final and most "progressive" part of the Liberal program.

What brought resistance to a head and created the conditions for a broad rebellion that included both Indian and non-Indian peasants was Gálvez's attempt to create modern judicial forms in the rural areas through the Livingston Codes.[15] While this code was meant to make all citizens equal before the law, in practice it meant curtailment of the political autonomy already enjoyed in peasant communities. Few Indians or *castas* were likely to become literate under the limited and fumbling educational programs of the period, especially with most Church schools closed. The new legal code required literacy because it was based on new laws rather than old traditions. Its effect, then, was to make illiterate peasants more rather than less prey to those who would represent them. And those who would represent them, no longer the Church, had even fewer interests in common with peasants than the clergy.

The "equal citizenship" provision of the 1824 constitution had removed barriers to Indian physical and social mobility. But removal of these barriers also allowed, theoretically, non-Indians to move into Indian communities, which colonial law kept isolated. How "mixed" communities were to be governed under the new political system was not entirely clear at first. But with the implementation of the Livingston Codes it became clear that peasant communities were to be governed by state codes as interpreted by literate urbanites and lawyers rather than by traditional native elders, who had previously handled all local political and legal matters. The Livingston Codes required the use of Spanish (which few Indians spoke fluently), lawyers (which few Indians could afford), and jails (which Indian labor had to build). They also brought state power down to the local level. Peasants were accustomed to handling local conflicts by an entirely different (restitutive) system, which maintained the power and authority of local leaders. Thus for peasants, the Livingston Codes, usually introduced to them as a tax on their community chest and a forced-labor, jail-building project, were anathema. As they interpreted them, these codes would end the autonomy of the peasant community, making it much more vulnerable to all the threatening legislation of the period—which the relatively autonomous peasant communities had rather successfully resisted to this point. Thus, as Gálvez attempted to impose the Livingston Codes on peasant communities in 1837, peasant revolts occurred throughout rural Guatemala. When a cholera epidemic broke out later that year, peasant revolts coalesced, with the assistance of an embittered native clergy, into a collective movement against the Liberal state under the leadership of a mestizo peasant, Rafael Carrera.

The Gálvez period was clearly a "progressive" period in Guatemalan history, and has been enshrined as such in Guatemalan histories. But it provoked the most unified political reaction among Guatemala's masses, Indians and *castas* alike, yet seen in Guatemalan history. The "reaction" was once attributed to Church machinations. A revisionist trend, mostly among North American students of Guatemala (Burns 1980; Ingersoll 1972; Miceli 1974; Woodward 1971), now attributes the reaction to well-grounded fears of capitalist incursion on precapitalist forms of property. Attention to the details of the reaction, however, suggests that peasants were much more concerned about losing their political autonomy than their property. As long as their community institutions were intact, peasants seemed capable of staving off attacks on their property. The greatest threat to the community was the "nationalist" program of the Gálvez period, the attempt to create equal, free, individual citizens within a homogeneous nation. Because the nationalism of this period was an imposition of elite culture on the masses and because it had no respect for local cultural forms, it provoked a popular, cultural reaction. The new nation under Carrera, which protected the distinctive cultural forms of the peasants, became a much stronger and more homogeneous state than the preceding Liberal state. It also created the basis for nationalist unity, in that Guatemalans of many different backgrounds held political power, formed an integrated national army, and interacted much more intensively than ever before with relatively little conflict. This "nationalist" state, however, could not withstand the development pressure that was to build as cochineal exports, based on peasant production, declined.

Nationalism in a Weak State: The Carrera Period

Rafael Carrera, who came to be known as "the protector of the people" was born a *casta*[16] in Guatemala City, held jobs variously as a servant, an irregular member of the army, and a pig merchant, before settling as a small farmer in the Mita district of eastern Guatemala, where he came to lead the popular resistance against the Gálvez reforms at the tender age of twenty-two. Nineteenth-century sources provide more information about Carrera (down to the percentage of black and Indian "blood" in his veins) than about the people he led in the uprising. They tell us even less about the particular issues galvanizing the masses. What the sources do make clear is that between 1837 and 1839 Carrera led a popular uprising in eastern Guatemala that included as supporters both *castas* and Indians. Carrera also had the strong support of the local clergy, though the Church elite (mostly white and resident in the capital) were less enthusiastic about him (Ingersoll 1972:79).

The ostensible cause of the popular rising in eastern Guatemala was an outbreak of a cholera epidemic and actions taken by the government to contain it. But as Hazel Ingersoll, the major chronicler of Carrera, points out, the rallying cry of the time was not just "the government is poisoning our waters," it also included "so that they can steal our land" (Ingersoll 1972:46). Ingersoll convincingly argues that the underlying causes of the 1837 revolt were the economic and political threats to peasant autonomy discussed above.

Though Carrera rose to power on the basis of leading the 1837–39 peasant revolt in eastern Guatemala, most of whose active followers appear to have been mestizos or *castas*, it is important to see his movement in the context of several major popular revolts of the period that involved Indians. Between 1811 and 1831 there had been almost continuous revolt by Indian villagers in the western highlands, mainly over issues of tribute (Martínez Peláez 1973). From that time on, government control over the area was extremely shaky in that many communities refused to pay tribute from that point on, others refused admittance to government officials doing land surveys or censuses, and yet others hounded unpopular priests or officials from office (Ingersoll 1972:45–76). While Carrera did not appeal to the Indian communities of the western highlands until after his first national victory (in 1839), he appears to have had their support (as well as Indian support in eastern Guatemala) from the beginning. Carrera did not actually take formal power until 1844, abdicated in the face of new uprisings in eastern Guatemala among his former followers (the Lucíos) in 1848, and then took power "for life" again in 1851. Upon taking power for a second time, with the strong backing of the Indians from western Guatemala, Carrera put down the Lucíos revolt, even though that revolt was in his home territory and led by his original *(mestizo)* followers who were disappointed in the rewards they received for supporting Carrera earlier on (Ingersoll 1972:285–331). It would be entirely wrong, therefore, to see Carrera's movement as one representing the *castas* or Ladinos; it represented the interests of both Indians and *castas* as they existed in that period.[17]

In June 1837 Carrera outlined the demands of the forces he led: (1) abolition of the Livingston Codes; (2) abolition of the head tax; (3) the return of the Archbishop, the religious orders, and political exiles; and (4) protection of life and property and respect for Carrera's orders as law under pain of death to violators (Woodward 1971:56). Later that year he added two additional demands: (5) repeal of the civil marriage and divorce laws; and (6) termination of the English colonization contracts (Braiterman 1986:64). Given the concern with Church issues (demands 3 and 5, and to some extent 1), one might interpret Carrera, as many Guatemalan historians have, as a simple conservative supporter of the Church. But Carrera's relation to the Church was not simple. He did not support the reinstatement of the Church tithe, he did not want clergy to hold office, and he did not return the Church property confiscated by the earlier Liberal governments. Ingersoll's interpretation of Carrera's church position (1972:77–113) is probably the most reasonable: Carrera supported the local clergy who had usually acted in the interests of the peasants, but he did not support the power of the Church hierarchy, which was every bit as exploitative of peasants as others of the white *creole* elite were.

Because of Carrera's overwhelming popular support (as well as continued divisions among the *creole* elite, each faction of which tried to woo Carrera to their cause), he was able to enforce most of his demands by 1840, even though he did not take formal power until 1844. In response to his demands, Guatemala's 1839 constitution reflects a changed attitude toward Guatemala's Indians:

> Although nature has given all men equal rights their condition in society is not the same. . . . To establish and maintain social equilibrium, the laws must protect the weak against the strong. . . . Thus, the Indian being in this [weak] group, the laws must protect them and better their education, to avoid their being defrauded of what belongs to them in common or as individuals, and so that they will not be molested in the usages and customs learned from their ancestors. [quoted in Ingersoll 1972:260]

With this justification, the National Assembly decreed a return to the colonial Laws of the Indies concerning the Indian, establishing a permanent commission for their protection and development. They also recreated the office of Indian interpreters, provided for the special handling of Indian cases in the court system, provided for the reestablishment of the office of the *corregidor* (Indian governor) as well as the traditional offices of the Indian villagers. A further law in 1841 provided for separate municipal elections for Indian and non-Indian officials (Ingersoll 1972:274).

A U.S. traveler during the Carrera years had this to say of the period:

> Heretofore, in all the wars and revolutions the whites had the controlling influence, but at this time the Indians were the dominant power . . . Carrera was the pivot on which this turned. He was talked of as El Rey de los Indios, the King of the Indians. He had relieved them

from all taxes. . . . His power by a word to cause the massacre of every white inhabitant no one doubted. [Stephens 1969 [1841], vol. 2:111–112]

To a student of Guatemala's modern period, the most striking aspect of the documents that describe Carrera and his regime is their failure to make clear distinctions between Indians and people who are now known as Ladinos. Carrera himself was a mestizo who led an uprising in the Mita district, a district that is now almost entirely Ladino but which was described as mainly Indian in the 19th century by Guatemalan sources.[18] A major North American historian of the period, Murdo MacLeod (1983) argues that by the end of the colonial period the Mita district consisted of mixed communities, some Indian, but more made up of *castas* from a variety of backgrounds. Few communities in the area, whether Indian or not, held the protected status of Indian communities common to the western highlands. Yet the literature of the 19th century suggests that Guatemalan *creoles* considered the entire population of the district to be effectively "Indian." White *creoles* invariably referred to Carrera himself as "the Indian." Descriptions of the Carrera rebellion, which began in eastern Guatemala and only later spread into the western highlands, portray it as an Indian rebellion (Ingersoll 1972:160–203). Gálvez himself warned that Guatemala faced in the Mita district a "race war." The conclusion one must reach is that Guatemalans did not then distinguish among Indians and Ladinos the way they do today. All "colored" people were Indians, none of them civilized.

It is also clear that Carrera received as much popular support from western Guatemala as he did from his own eastern district. And when in power he did as much to protect the Indian peasants in western Guatemala from the Liberal reforms as he did the *casta* and Indian peasants of eastern Guatemala (Miceli 1974). Carrera overturned the entire Liberal program, including much (but not all) of the anticlerical legislation, the new taxing system, the hated Livingston Codes, and much of the agrarian legislation. He also restored various protections to Indian communities and allowed them to use traditional forms of political organization. Guatemalan historians, who note that Carrera dropped the attempt to impose universal citizenship on Guatemalans, describe him as a despot. But the record of the period, even as presented by a champion of Liberal reform (for example, Ingersoll), indicates that Carrera responded primarily to popular demands and treated the different groups within Guatemala, including the *creole* elite, even-handedly throughout his long period of rule. Ingersoll summarizes the effect of popular government on Guatemala as follows:

> Rafael Carrera was the first non-white to come to total political power in Guatemala and he used this power to bring the Indians and the mixed bloods into political life. . . . [His] government, which came to power in 1839, addressed itself seriously to the problem of the Indian masses. Unlike the Liberal government of Dr. Gálvez, which had sought to force the Indian into modern life, the legislation of the Carrera period was a return to many of the laws of the colonial period in which the indian, if he lacked freedom, at least was protected by the government. [1972:273]

Ingersoll, like most Guatemalan interpreters of the period, sees the Carrera years as reactionary rather than progressive. Yet her own account indicates that the increasing political autonomy of the peasant community was coupled with increasing peasant involvement in commodity production, as the cochineal boom, encouraged by Carrera, spread its effects throughout the country. Guatemala did not sink into self-sufficiency and economic decline during the Carrera years, but actually experienced sufficient financial prosperity that the government and army could expand without imposing additional taxes or labor levies on the peasants. One of the unintended results of the Carrera years, in fact, is that Indians, who retained freedom of movement and trade from the Liberal reform era, became more fully integrated into the national economy than ever before. While they continued to maintain tradition (language, dress, religion, and the like), they did not do so as marginalized "precapitalist" remnants. They did so as the mainstay and primary producers of Guatemala's growing market economy (C. Smith 1984). Carrera did not end the private titling of land, but saw to it, often personally, that peasants had first claim on the land they held traditionally. Land litigation was fierce during the Carrera period, but the legal procedures gave no undue advantages to foreign settlers or to the *creole* elite. Carrera's "modern" nationalist sentiments can also be seen in his legislation against foreign imports, and his suspicion of external capitalists.

Considering the achievements of Carrera's era: peace, order, prosperity, and a certain degree of national unity, we have to wonder why the national direction was so abruptly reversed with Carrera's death. One important factor is that the Carrera experiment was virtually unique in Latin American history. Elsewhere Liberal programs waxed and waned in response to political jousting and the strength of popular resistance. But only in Guatemala did a non-white populist leader take power to actually reverse Liberal political-economic policy. In this sense, then, we can see that Carrera was fighting against the main social and political current of the period, in which capitalist development was the primary goal in all of Latin America and in which capitalist development was associated with foreign colonists, foreign capital, and European notions of civilization and progress.

In addition, Carrera was indeed a populist figure, who never institutionalized his policies through developing new or stronger state apparatuses. Carrera'a bureaucracy was made up of the traditional elite, as well as his own military bodyguard. And Carrera (as opposed to his successors in the new Liberal state) is properly depicted as the traditional Latin American *caudillo*, who ruled by strength of arms and wily strategems: a sign of weak state institutions. The state erected upon Carrera's death was, in contrast, a much stronger state in terms of both infrastructural and despotic powers (see McCreery 1990; C. Smith 1990).[19] Populist governments are often thought to thrive on ethnic divisions. But the most unusual feature of the Carrera period is the degree to which ethnic division seemed muted. The main social division was that between the white *creole* elite and the colored masses. Carrera promoted a unified national identity in class rather than in ethnic terms, an extremely radical position for the era. But inasmuch as Carrera's reforms did not confiscate elite property or prevent *creoles* from holding government office, they did not institutionalize a revolutionary state. Carrera merely halted capitalist development in Guatemala for some thirty years.

Carrera's ability to galvanize popular discontent with the Gálvez government proves that an imported elite nationalist ideology could not easily build a nation. The Liberal conquest of Guatemala six years after Carrera's death suggests that nationalist integration based on a populist ideology cannot be maintained without a strong state. The actions of the powerful Liberal state that did establish capitalism in Guatemala also suggest that, where appropriate, the goal of capitalist growth could be met more easily by creating disunity rather than unity with respect to ethnic relations and the myth of a single national will. Indians and Ladinos were not opposed to one another in the Carrera interlude. But they became opposed groups in the following era because Carrera's success showed Carrera's successor, Justo Rufino Barrios, that Guatemala's masses could not be dispossessed as long as they remained politically unified. Thus Guatemala's "strong" state, which began in 1871 and continues into the present, was built upon ethnic division rather than on an ideology of national integration.

Conclusion

Those who question the legitimacy of the modern Guatemalan state are less inclined to lionize its creator, Justo Rufino Barrios, than to seek a less oppressive vision of its past in Rafael Carrera. The history outlined above has not been told as such by Guatemalan historians, who still portray Carrera as a savage despot and Barrios as the "father" of the Guatemalan nation. North American historians rescued Rafael Carrera from the obscurity to which he had been consigned and also began chipping away at the pedestal on which Barrios had been placed by literate (white) Guatemalans. North Americans took on this revision of Guatemalan history for their own reasons—partly to show that the latter-day development of Guatemala's military state, which not only represses but annihilates resistant Indians, was not entirely the result of U.S. intervention. Yet the degree to which social relations in Guatemala were restructured in the 19th century has been underplayed by all historians. Histories exist to find the seeds of the present in the past and thus tend to a linear vision of how the present came to be. Historical guidance makes it easy to believe that the present oppression of Indians in Guatemala is a remnant of colonial relations constructed in the aftermath of conquest and then intensified by the capitalist relations of production introduced with Barrios (cf. Martínez Peláez 1971). I want to suggest a different way of reading Guatemalan history. I also want to suggest a different basis for Guatemala's present ethnic divisions.

It is clear that Guatemala's second Liberal state built on the social possibilities already extant in Guatemala. It is also clear that the opportunities provided by the world coffee market in the latter third of the 19th century allowed for the growth of a stronger state than had been possible earlier. But it was not preordained that the division between Indians and Ladinos, which today plagues any attempt to build other than a coercive state in Guatemala, was an inevitable outcome of building capitalism on the social relations bequeathed by Spanish colonialism. The examples of other Central American countries prove that Guatemala could have taken advantage of world market conditions for coffee in several different ways—by creating a small rather than large estate system, for example, or by completely proletarianizing its peasants.

Ultimately, the path chosen in Guatemala did not just build on past social relations, but created new ones: relations that put the elite, together with their foreign backers, in an unchallengeable position of power; that elevated Ladinos into a new power position in the coffee zone as plantation agents; and that virtually enslaved those who remained categorized as Indians—at the same time preserving them as a separate and resistant culture. The Carrera years had opened up quite a different alternative. It is true that following through on that alternative would have fully disempowered the white colonizers of the New World who, in the long run, were disempowered nowhere. It is also true that the 19th century saw few anticolonial revolutions of such a radical nature. But alternative possibilities *did* exist. Burns (1980) describes Paraguay of 1810 to 1870 as one such alternative possibility.[20] The fact that these exceptions remain a silent space in general western (and Latin American) thought helps "naturalize" the belief that economic development cannot take place in a context of cultural plurality and that colonized people are forever doomed to failed development and coercive states—except possibly with western intervention. These ideologies of development have been as important as the different material conditions for development in producing the kind of development we see throughout the Third World.

If we consider Guatemala's nonlinear history in the theoretical terms that opened this paper, we gain a rather different vision of the relationship between capitalism, state-building, and nation-building in ex-colonies from that posited by Anthony Smith. Smith arrives at his conclusions by comparing present-day realities rather than the different histories of developed and underdeveloped capitalist states. It is true that ex-colonies are often ethnically divided nations held together by coercive states. But without history, we cannot tell what is cause and what is effect. Smith posits that ethnic divisions create coercive states that are unable to achieve capitalist growth because of that unlucky combination. But Guatemala's history suggests that capitalist growth created the coercive state, which reified ethnic divisions.

But this, too, is an incomplete history. World conditions for development and for state-building also have to be considered. We should not forget that those (western) states that achieved national identities through the creation of mythic traditions also pursued a mission of conquering the rest of the "unlucky" world. They could "invite their masses into history" (if not power) mainly because of the space opened by world conquest, which lowered the costs of incorporation to western elites—much as Ladinos were brought into Guatemalan history, if not power, by a similar logic. Further, European states were compelled to unify as nations because competition among them over imperialist spoils led to World War.

There are other problems with European formulations of the national question for ex-colonies. Ethnic divisions are not the inevitable result of colonialism, as attested to by the varied experiences of Central America. Indians were gradually assimilated in colonial Nicaragua and Honduras, for example, and simply eradicated in colonial Costa Rica (Newson 1986, 1987). In El Salvador, Indians were as numerous as in Guatemala at the end of the colonial period, their later assimilation brought on by the social relations of coffee production.[21] In Guatemala, by contrast, it was the social relations associated with coffee production that ended the easy assimilation (or parallel development) of Indians. Nor is there a clear correlation of coercive states with the continued existence of ethnic divisions. Only Guatemala had a populist state in the 19th century. While it developed a coercive state with its coffee plantation economy, so too did the ethnically homogeneous nations of Central America. Throughout Latin America, in fact, capitalist relations of production were created by coercive states, whether or not they began the process with ethnically divided populations.

The Central American cases refute other European views of nation-building. First, development efforts in the context of underdevelopment do not necessarily bring on attempts at nation-building, as Nairn (1977) has argued. Throughout Central America development efforts were everywhere the exclusive concern of white *creole* elites, anxious to keep their masses separate rather than conjoined with them, by even token myths of national unity. Moreover, coercive states seem to have had no difficulty in constructing capitalist economies in quick order, regardless of ethnic division. A comparison of El Salvador and Honduras shows that the more coercive state, El Salvador, more quickly and fully implemented capitalist relations throughout its population, even though it began the process with a much more divided population. El Salvador's elites did not then invite the masses into history, but slaughtered those who resisted, thus eliminating its Indian problem. In only one of the Central American states, Guatemala, was nation-building ever attempted in the context of inter-state competition among relatively equivalent entities, as Tilly (1975) suggests is the normal state of affairs. And that attempt (in 1831–1838) was very brief—and futile. In none of the Central American states do we see nation-building becoming a major effort of the state, once the state established itself securely, as Smith suggests we should expect. Nor does the elimination of noncapitalist relations of production bring on the effort. The only serious impetus toward nation-building in Central America (and in Mexico) has been brought on by revolutionary/reformist governments in the context of a major external threat to state autonomy.[22] This factor, though underplayed in European analyses of the national question, obviously applies to the process of nation-building in Europe as well.

Though no Central American state achieved national unity before World War II, Guatemala is unique in still having a markedly divided ethnic population, that is, in having an "Indian" problem.[23] The source of this problem can be found in the 19th century, and is both internal to Guatemala and external to it. The internal problem was sheer numbers, as they came to be *perceived* in the post-Carrera period. Insofar as Guatemala's non-white population remained politically unified, its white elite could not wield power. It could only wield power by dividing the masses. The external factor that helped create Guatemala's ethnic division was the world order of the late 19th century. In that period the elites of peripheral states had far more to gain from pursuing capitalist development (even though it be dependent development), than from building states legitimated by popular support. Certainly in Guatemala's case, the coercive state that came into being after Carrera rewarded its *creole* elites much more highly than the populist state under Carrera. The post-Carrera state, moreover, was stronger, wealthier, and more stable than any other state in 19th-century Central America, even though it was based on a polarized ethnic situation. And though coercive, the post-Carrera state was not incapable of building its own kind of legitimating myths (of racial difference), which were wholeheartedly endorsed by all but the Indians of Guatemala. Obviously, we cannot see the social relations and nationalist myths required to build this state as being "functional" for Guatemala in the long run. But we can see from the Guatemalan case that state-building in former colonies has requirements quite different from those of the colonizing nations.

Based on the nonfunctional fit between Guatemala's path of state- and nation-building, we might well begin to question the functional fit between state- and nation-building in the rest of the world. For the nation-building of the West created popular divisions, much like those between Guatemala's Indians and Ladinos, though on a world rather than national scale. These popular divisions were based on a new form of racism, much like Guatemala's new kind of racism, but again on a world rather than national scale. The creation in the 19th century of two unequal "nations" in Guatemala has led in the 20th century to total war between one of the world's most ruthless military dictatorships and one of the world's most brutalized native populations. The creation of nations on a world scale, based on similar divisions and processes, has the potential to play itself out in a similar way on a world scale.

Notes

Acknowledgments. What was once a single paper is now two: Smith (1990) takes off from the same historical materials to discuss the relationship between class and ethnicity in modern Guatemala. I would like to thank the following people for helpful comments on both papers: Howie Machtinger, Steve Palmer, Robert Carmack, Ralph Lee Woodward, Chris Lutz, Robert Williams, David McCreery, Brackette Williams, Katherine Verdery, Les Field, and Richard Fox.

1. While I believe my case, Guatemala, is generally relevant to the Third World, both nation- and state-building in Guatemala are distinctive in the way that all of Latin America is distinctive. That is, statehood was achieved with independence from Spain throughout Latin America in the 1820s, but in most cases, including Guatemala, modern state apparatuses were not fully established until the last decades of the 19th century. States were consolidated only as they undertook major economic transformations (Woodward 1987). I should note that theories about the relationship between state-building and nation-building apply rather poorly to the experiences of Latin America in general. In particular, they cannot explain the long gap between the rise of states (late 19th century) and the construction of national identities. No Latin American state constructed a convincing sense of national identity until well into the 20th century (Burns 1980) and some states, like Guatemala, have yet to do so.

2. Guatemala achieved independence from Spain in 1821. But from that point until the 1850s Guatemala was also a republic within the United Republics of Central America.

3. Its social relations most resemble those in neighboring Chiapas, Mexico (cf. Wasserstrom 1983), for similar political reasons.

4. In the latter part of the colonial period Guatemala did have a few major aristocratic families associated with indigo production and trade. But even these individuals owed their position to state protection through the merchant Consulado, a state-directed monopoly on export trade (Woodward 1966). Apart from these few families, most members of the *creole* elite in Guatemala, apart from the very powerful Church, did not have major economic enterprises that afforded them independence from the state like *creoles* in other Spain colonies, such as Mexico and Peru (Wortman 1982).

5. According to the usage of the period, *castas* were people of mixed descent, each particular "mixture" having its own label. By the end of the colonial period, most people of mixed descent were considered *mestizos*, a generalized category that excluded only Spaniards, Indians, and blacks (Mörner 1967).

6. MacLeod (1983) describes the different circumstances that led Indians to join the *castas* (as Ladinos) in the colonial period. He notes that few Indians north and west of the capital city did so, but that those Indians located near major cities, major sugar plantations (the southern region) or the indigo plantations (the eastern region) often did so, it seems in part because the Crown forbad Indian workers in these enterprises, so the owners often relabeled those Indians they forced to work on their enterprises. Lutz (1982) observes that Indians located in or around the capital city were more heavily exploited than Indians located elsewhere, yet could do relatively well as "free" Indians.

7. It is interesting to note in travel accounts of the 19th century that people from many different places used the term Indian in a primarily "racial" rather than cultural sense (cf. the various sources compiled in Parker [1970]). By that point the legal distinction between Indians and non-Indians had been abolished, the major distinction between the two having been that Indians could hold communal property and paid tribute, whereas *castas* did not. Thus it seems that the cultural difference between Indians and non-Indians in the

19th century was not so obvious to the casual observer. It is also clear that in the 19th century the system of nomenclature distinguishing different groups was in flux. Thus an English traveler, Henry Dunn, observed in 1829 that "The offspring of Negroes and Indians, of Whites and Indians, as well as the descendants of African Negroes, are included under the term Mulattoes, by which they are generally known; sometimes, however, they are called Mestizos, or Ladinos" (Parker 1970:114).

8. Both Conservative and Liberal ideologies in 19th-century Latin America were *creole* ideologies and differed mainly with respect to positions on "free" trade and democracy among *creoles*, not with respect to rights for the colored masses. Thus both Conservatives and Liberals opposed Carrera, though each group also tried to woo him to their side, failing to dominate him largely because of their own lack of unity. In most respects Carrera followed a "conservative" course, in that he reestablished many of the special protections and privileges of different interest groups (for example, the Church, merchants, and Indians) as they had been established in the colonial period. At the same time, however, he sometimes delimited the privileges of these groups in a fairly radical manner.

9. This part of this story is documented in C. Smith (1990). The most useful discussion of the current position of Ladinos in Guatemala can be found in Colby and van den Berghe (1969) and Pansini (1977); Brintnall (1979) describes current beliefs about the differences between Indians and Ladinos; C. Smith (1987) describes ethnicity in relation to class and race; and Lutz (1988) describes the particular development of the category "Ladino" in Guatemala in the colonial period.

10. Mariano Gálvez (1831–1838) was the first Guatemalan to pursue the strategy of attempting to lure European immigrants to Guatemala (Braiterman 1986), but in this he was only following a general trend in 19th-century Latin America (Mörner 1985). According to Mörner, Guatemala was less successful than most Latin American countries in this strategy. But the attempt continued throughout the 19th and early 20th centuries. Rufino Barrios (1873–1885) even tried to bribe white workers to come to Guatemala with offers of high wages (McCreery 1976), with notable lack of success, thinking that white workers would be much more productive than native workers. It may not be necessary to point out the racist assumptions in these strategies.

11. Indicative of the fluctuating loyalties of the period, del Valle had been closely associated with the Conservative forces. Charles Hale (1968) has observed that Conservatives accepted much in liberal thought, differing from liberals mainly on governmental form and the role of the Church.

12. The constitution of 1824 was that of the Central American Federal Republic, which included Guatemala, El Salvador, Honduras, Nicaragua, and Costa Rica. While much of its rhetoric resembles that of the U.S. constitution, historians point out that it is also modeled after the Cadiz Constitution of 1812 (Ingersoll 1972; Woodward 1985).

13. J. Daniel Contreras (1951) has argued that the major Indian revolt, which occurred in Totonicapán in 1820 and quickly spread to several neighboring townships, and which concerned the reimposition of the tributes, was the spark in Guatemala that led to the Independence movement. He also sug-

gests that Indians were not acting solely because of local grievances, but as early "nationalists." This argument may be somewhat far-fetched, but it is clear that Indians were less estranged from the Guatemalan nation in the 19th century than they were in the 20th century.

14. The Church, of course, held most of the privately titled land in the colonial period and was almost fully expropriated. The main assault on Indian lands occurred after 1871.

15. Observers of the time believed that an outbreak of cholera, which priests described as divine retribution against attacks on the Church, was the main factor behind the rebellion. Ingersoll (1972) carefully undermines this view and argues that the main factor was the Liberal attempt to privately title land. Yet if we are to take the rebels' own voice into account, their main concern seemed to be the Livingston codes and the head tax—as well as some, but far from all, attacks on religion (see Woodward 1971:56).

16. During the entire period that Carrera was in power, there was considerable concern about his racial background. His family historian concluded that he was 72% Spanish, 17 + % black, and 10 + % Indian (Ingersoll 1972:105). He was widely called "the Indian" because he "looked like one." It was widely rumored that he was adopted and that his antecedents were of either higher or lower racial status than his family background indicated, depending on whether the rumor originated with someone who admired or despised him.

17. Some grounds for this belief, as well as some notion of Carrera's basic populist philosophy can be gleaned from a series of articles written in 1840 by his supporters in Carrera's newspaper, *El procurador de los pueblos* (The Protector of the People) (Ingersoll 1972:272).

18. The Mita district was later broken into three departments by Carrera (when fighting the Lucíos revolt). The population in two of these departments (Jutiapa and Santa Rosa) is now more than 90% Ladino, and the other (Jalapa) is two-thirds Ladino. As described by Ingersoll, the Mita district was an area of farmers, merchants, and weavers that had been relatively prosperous in the colonial period, but had been in decline since the beginning of the 19th century. As Ingersoll describes the district, on the basis of local sources, it was predominantly Indian at the time of the revolt (Ingersoll 1972:47–49).

19. I use the terms infrastructural and despotic powers as Michael Mann (1986) has defined them: despotic power being the ability of the state to take a particular range of actions without negotiating with various entities in civil society; and infrastructural power being measured by the organization, information, efficiency, and technology at the command of the state.

20. The case of Paraguay gives some clues as to why these alternative possibilities never survived into the 20th century. According to Burns "from 1810 to 1870, a native alternative took form, influenced in almost equal parts by the American and European past" (1980:128). This native form was populist, pluralistic (respecting Hispanic and native cultures equally), economically autonomous (in the sense of eschewing foreign enterprise and loans), and nationalist. It was based on state ownership of most land made freely available to the people together with indigenous industry or artisanry. The experiment was ended by the War of the Triple Alliance, in which Brazil, Argentina and Uruguay "joined forces . . . to bring 'civilization' to 'barbarian' Paraguay

(1980:130). It took five years and the death of nearly 90% of Paraguay's adult male population to end the experiment, but it was ended by external intervention. Why did other nations intervene in Paraguay's fate? Burns explains it this way: "The rapid and genuine development of Paraguay under its own form of 'inorganic democracy' alarmed the elitist governments in neighboring states, whose own export-oriented economies had grown but failed to develop. They accused Paraguay of upsetting the balance of power in the Rio de la Plata. More realistically, they feared the appealing example Paraguay offered to wider segments of their own population" (1980:129). Such concerns are virtually a prophecy of concerns that have shaped events in Central America in our own decade.

21. Indian culture was in decline in El Salvador since 1880, with the implementation of a coffee economy similar to that of Guatemala's with the exception that coffee workers were fully displaced from their lands and thus more fully proletarianized from the beginning (Cardoso 1975). Indian culture was essentially eradicated as such when the remaining Indians participated in a massive revolt against the coffee oligarchy in 1932. The government retaliated by killing more than 50,000 peasants, most of whom were Indians—apparently taking indication of Indian culture (dress, language) as evidence of complicity in the uprising (T. Anderson 1971).

22. Among the six states in question, only three (Mexico, Nicaragua, and Costa Rica) can be said to have achieved a sense of national unity. In two cases (Mexico, Nicaragua) that sense of unity was achieved by revolutionary governments facing the threat of intervention by the United States. In the case of Costa Rica, national unity has been achieved by distinctive means, involving major governmental reform and a concerted effort to build a myth of Costa Rican "uniqueness" within the context of Central America, based partly on its distinctive racial composition. The myth, in short, is a racist one (cf. Gudmondson 1986).

23. One might argue that Nicaragua, too, has an "Indian" problem. That problem, however, has to be put in the context of a revolutionary transformation in which the handful of Nicaraguan Indians were used by counterrevolutionary forces as a potential means of establishing a strategic entry point for the violent overthrow of the revolutionary government (see Smith, Boyer, and Diskin 1988).

References Cited

Anderson, Benedict
   1980   Imagined Communities: Reflections on the Origin and Spread of Nationalism. London: New Left Books.
Anderson, Thomas P.
   1971   Matanza: El Salvador's Communist Revolt of 1932. Lincoln: University of Nebraska Press.
Braiterman, Jared I.
   1986   A Conflict Between Modernity and Peasant Society in 1830's Guatemala. Honor's thesis, Harvard College.

Brintnall, Douglas E.
　1979　Race Relations in the Southeastern Highlands of Mesoamerica. American Ethnologist 6:638–652.
Burns, E. Bradford
　1980　The Poverty of Progress: Latin America in the Nineteenth Century. Berkeley: University of California Press.
Cardoso, C. F. S.
　1975　Historia económica del café en Centroamérica (siglo XIX). Estudios Sociales Centroamericanos 10:3–57.
Carmack, Robert M.
　1979　Historia social de los Quichés. Guatemala City: Seminario de Integración Social.
Colby, Benjamin, N., and Pierre van den Berghe
　1969　Ixil Country: A Plural Society in Highland Guatemala. Berkeley: University of California Press.
Contreras, J. Daniel
　1951　Una rebelión indígena en el partido de Totonicapán en 1820. Guatemala: Imprenta Universitaria.
Gellner, Ernest
　1983　Nations and Nationalism. Oxford: Basil Blackwell.
Gudmondson, Lowell
　1986　Costa Rica Before Coffee. Baton Rouge: Louisiana State University Press.
Hale, Charles Adams
　1968　Mexican Liberalism in the Age of Mora, 1821–1853. New Haven: Yale University Press.
Ingersoll, Hazel
　1972　The War of the Mountain: A Study of Reactionary Peasant Insurgency in Guatemala, 1837–1873. Ph.D. dissertation, George Washington University.
Lanning, John Tate
　1956　The Eighteenth Century Enlightenment in the University of San Carlos de Guatemala. Ithaca: Cornell University Press.
Lutz, Christopher H.
　1982　Historia sociodemográfica de Santiago de Guatemala, 1541–1773. Antigua, Guatemala: CIRMA Serie Monográfica, no. 2.
　1988　Guatemala's non-Spanish and non-Indian Population: Its Spread and Demographic Evolution, 1700–1821. Unpublished ms.
MacLeod, Murdo J.
　1973　Spanish Central America: A Socioeconomic History, 1520–1720. Berkeley: University of California Press.
　1983　Ethnic Relations and Indian Society in the Province of Guatemala, ca. 1620–1800. *In* Spaniards and Indians in Southeastern Mesoamerica. M. J. MacLeod and R. Wasserstrom, eds. Pp. 189–214. Lincoln: University of Nebraska Press.
Mann, Michael
　1986　The Sources of Social Power. Volume 1. London: Cambridge University Press.
Martínez Peláez, Severo
　1971　La patria del criollo. Guatemala City: Editorial Universitario.

1973 Los motines de Indios en el período colonial guatemalteco. Estudios Sociales Guatemaltecos 5:201–228.
McCreery, David
　1976　Coffee and Class: The Structure of Development in Liberal Guatemala. Hispanic American Historical Review 56:438–460.
　1990　State Power, Indigenous Communities, and Land in Nineteenth Century Guatemala, 1820–1920. In Guatemalan Indians and the State, 1540–1988. C. A. Smith, ed. Austin: University of Texas Press.
Miceli, Keith
　1974　Rafael Carrera: Defender and Promoter of Peasant Interests in Guatemala, 1837–1848. The Americas 31:72–95.
Mörner, Magnus
　1967　Race Mixture in the History of Latin America. Boston: Little, Brown and Co.
　1985　Adventurers and Proletarians. Pittsburgh: University of Pittsburgh Press.
Nairn, Tom
　1977　The Break-up of Britain. London: New Left Books.
Newson, Linda A.
　1986　The Cost of Conquest: Indian Decline in Honduras Under Spanish Rule. Boulder: Westview Press.
　1987　Indian Survival in Colonial Nicaragua. Norman: University of Oklahoma Press.
Pansini, Joseph J.
　1977　"El Pilar," a Plantation Microcosm of Guatemalan Ethnicity. Ph.D. dissertation, University of Rochester.
Parker, Franklin D.
　1970　Travels in Central America, 1821–1840. Gainesville: University of Florida Press.
Smith, Anthony D.
　1983　State and Nation in the Third World. New York: St. Martin's Press.
Smith, Carol A.
　1984　Local History in Global Context: Social and Economic Transitions in Western Guatemala. Comparative Studies in Society and History 26:193–228.
　1987　Culture and Community: The Language of Class in Guatemala. In The Year Left 2: An American Socialist Yearbook. Pp. 197–217. London: Verso.
　1990　The Origins of the National Question in Guatemala: An Hypothesis. In Guatemalan Indians and the State, 1540–1988. C. A. Smith, ed. Austin: University of Texas Press.
Smith, Carol A., Jefferson Boyer, and Martin Diskin
　1988　Central America Since 1979, Part II. Annual Reviews in Anthropology 17:331–364.
Stephens, John L.
　1969[1841]　Incidents of Travel in Central America, Chiapas and Yucatan. New York: Dover Publications.
Tilly, Charles
　1975　The Formation of National States in Western Europe. Princeton: Princeton University Press.

van Oss, Adriaan C.
   1986   Catholic Colonialism: A Parish History of Guatemala, 1541–1821. London: Cambridge University Press.
Wasserstrom, Robert
   1983   Class and Society in Central Chiapas. Berkeley: University of California Press.
Woodward, Ralph Lee
   1966   Class Privilege and Economic Development: The Consulado Comercial de Guatemala, 1793–1871. Chapel Hill: University of North Carolina Press.
   1971   Social Revolution in Guatemala: The Carrera Revolt. *In* Applied Enlightenment: Nineteenth Century Liberalism. R. L. Woodward, ed. Pp. 45–70. Middle American Research Publication No. 23. New Orleans: Tulane University.
   1987   Central America: A Nation Divided. (2nd ed.) New York: Oxford University Press.
Wortman, Miles L.
   1982   Government and Society in Central America, 1680–1840. New York: Columbia University Press.